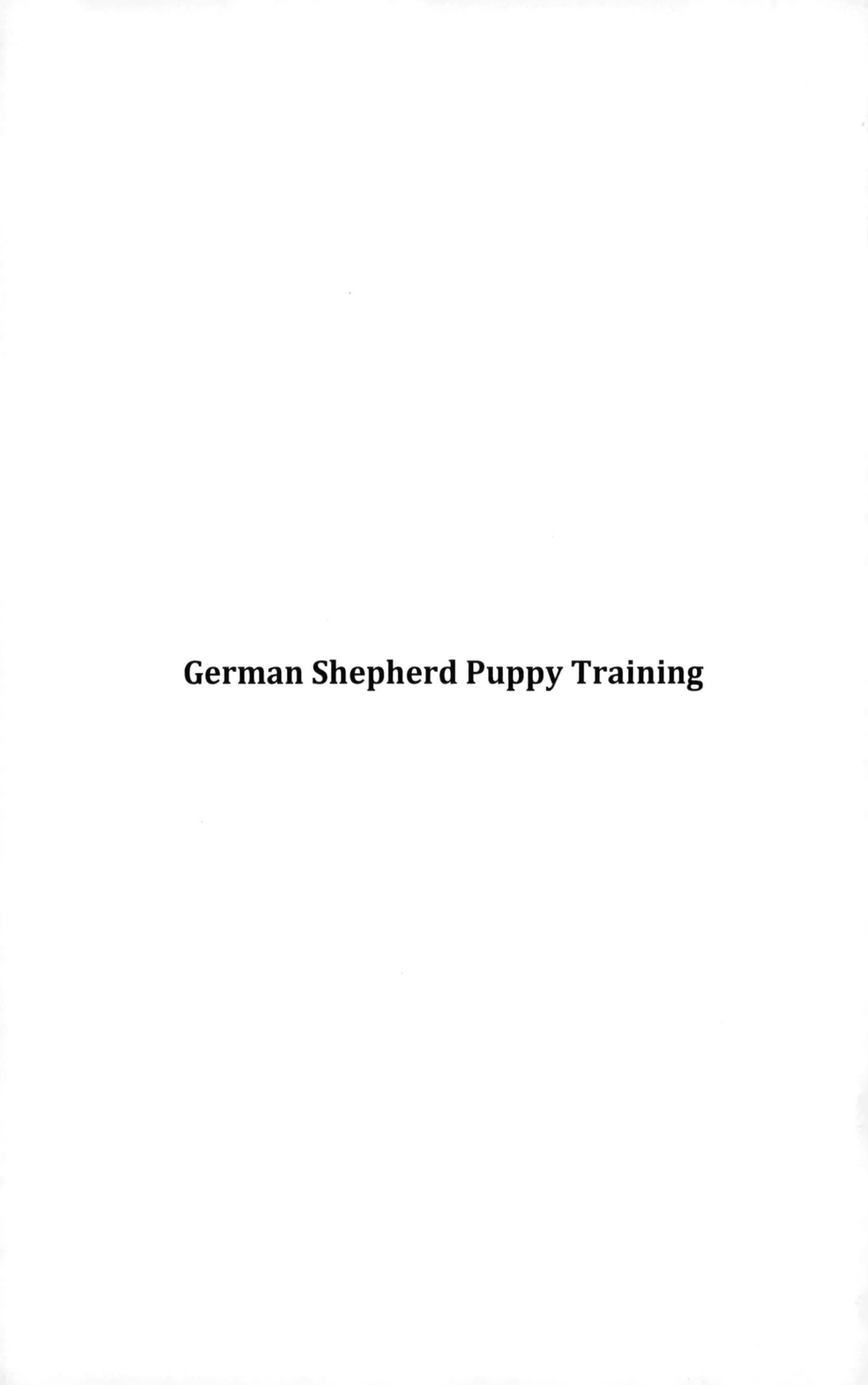

German Shepherd Puppy Training

German Shepherd Puppy Training

The Complete German Shepherd Puppy Training Guide for Caring, Raising, and Training German Shepherd Puppies

Copyright © 2015 Daniel Vega

Rank Roo Co. Publishing

Acknowledgment

Thank you to my family, friends, and cohorts that never waiver in their support towards me.

Table of Contents

INTRODUCTION 1
THE GERMAN SHEPHERD DOG 3
SELECTING A BREEDER 8
HOW TO USE THIS TRAINING GUIDE 19
COMMON FIRST TIMER MISTAKES 21
PUPPY PROOF HOME 27
BRINGING YOUR PUPPY HOME 30
COMMON PUPPY HEALTH ISSUES 35
PUPPY TRAINING PREP 39
SOCIALIZATION 57
SEPARATION ANXIETY 66
HANDLING YOUR GERMAN SHEPHERD 77
CLICKER TRAINING 85
SOLUTIONS FOR UNWANTED BEHAVIORS 92
REWARD VS. PUNISHMENT 96
ALPHA DOG'S 98
DOG LANGUAGE 102
ABOUT TREATS 115
TEETHING & CHEW-TOYS 120
CRATE TRAINING 129
HOUSETRAINING YOUR GSD 141
CLICKER RESPONSE 145
NAMING YOUR PUPPY 147
THE JUMPER 150
BARKING 154

NIPPING	162
DIGGERS	167
COMMANDS	171
"SIT"	171
"COME"	174
"LEAVE IT"	182
"DROP IT"	185
"DOWN"	190
"STAY"	193
"GO"	197
LEASH TRAINING	200
GROOMING	211
DOG NUTRITION	219
CONCLUSION	237
ABOUT THE AUTHOR	239

Introduction

PRICELESS MINDSET Dog Training

The ABC's of dog training is the PRICELESS acronym for dog training. To succeed in dog training requires the PRICELESS method that translates into **P**atience **R**esolve **I**mpartiality **C**onsistency **E**xcitement **L**earning **E**volution **S**implicity and **S**urrender. Using these priceless qualities in your mindset, in conjunction with my methods inside this training guide, you will be able to successfully train, shape behaviors, and better understand dogs.

When you accommodate these attributes into dog training, then you are already on your way to becoming an excellent dog trainer. Inside this guide, I will teach you how to train your new dog while having fun, and enjoying the entire process. I am sure that you cannot wait to begin learning, and I cannot wait to teach you the knowledge you deserve to know before and after you bring your new puppy or adult dog home.

Are you ready to start training and understanding your German Shepherd Dog? Purchase this book today and be on your way to using the PRICELESS mindset while training your dog. Additionally you will be learning about socialization, dog language, treating, nutrition, and many more crucial training and behavioral things that you need to learn before your puppy's first car ride to his or her new home.

Inside This Puppy Training Guide

- Selecting a breeder
- What you need to know before you bring your puppy home.
- Puppy proofing your home.
- Puppy training preparation.
- Socialization
- How to avoid and solve Separation Anxiety.
- *What an Alpha dog* is and how to be one.

- Clicker training – what it is and how to use it.
- Crate training
- Housetraining
- Leash Training
- Understanding dog communication.
- All of the commands a dog should know, such as his Come, *Sit*, S*tay*, *Down*, *Leave it*, *Drop it*, and Go.
- How to combat *Barking*, *Digging*, and *Nipping*.
- Treating – When, how, and what they are.
- Nutrition
- Basic Care and Grooming.

What does the PRICELESS Mindset consist? You probably already have the priceless qualities, but now you need to utilize them consistently and concurrently during obedience training and shaping your dog's behavior. You can find their definitions in the chapter "Puppy Training Prep" along with why you need to use each of them.

If you have yet to choose a breeder, go now to "Selecting a Breeder" and begin reading. If you have already brought your puppy home, begin reading the chapter "How to Use This Training Guide" then continues reading and discovering all of the information contained inside this PRICELESS training guide.

I wish you well in your new dog endeavor and a healthy, happy, long-lasting relationship between the two of you.

The German Shepherd Dog

The German Shepherd Dog is one of the few dogs that contain the word "dog" in its official name. The reason is to differentiate the dog from actual German shepherds that tend livestock. GSD's are regularly ranked within the top five most popular dogs in America. Additionally, they enjoy worldwide popularity.

The breed standard for the GSD (German Shepherd Dog) has eleven colors that are permitted for the breed; they are solid black, blue, gray, liver, sable, white, black and tan/silver/red/cream and bi-color.

German Shepherd Dogs are a large agile breed that require regular physical and mental exercise, but can live in apartments or large expanses. The key is daily vigorous exercise. They are relatively calm and relaxed when indoors. If properly socialized and trained they make fantastic family dogs, because they adore children, are naturally protective and in most cases tolerate other pets. They are best suited to active families that can commit to the daily exercise requirements.

You are responsible for the welfare of your new puppy or dog. Please treat him or her with respect and love, and this will be reciprocated tenfold. Dogs have been human companions for thousands of years, and they are living beings complete with feelings, emotions and the need for attachment. Before bringing home a new dog or puppy, please determine if you are capable and willing to provide all the needs that your new family member requires.

Naturally brave and courageous they will give their lives for their masters. Many a German Shepherd has been decorated for its valor in service and for competitive excellence in rally, tracking, show, and obedience. It is no wonder that this large versatile dog is such a popular breed. They are used as assistance, police, herding, army, rescue dogs for all types of disasters, drug and explosive sniffer dogs, guard, tracker, gas leak sniffer, protector, and of course the family dog.

German Shepherds love being close to their families and being included in their daily activities, so keep this in mind because they are not mentally healthy when isolated. They are protective and loyal to their handler, master, and family. Be aware when your GSD is issuing a warning bark, because they only bark when needed.

These dogs make a great family member that expects to sleep indoors with their families. When seeking a puppy for your family, find a breeder that temper tests their dogs and has a history of producing stable non-aggressive dogs.

For proper family and societal integration, begin socializing from the moment you procure your puppy. Problems occur when German Shepherds believe that they are the pack leader. These dogs must have daily physical and mental exercise; they need to be kept engaged. Owners must be calm, possess natural authority, firmness, confidence, and remain consistent. If properly trained and socialized they are normally good with children and other pets.

Their obedience training must be firm and begin early in puppyhood.

If they do not have a strong handler, they can become shy, edgy, and possibly prone to fear biting or guarding issues. As mentioned above, before purchasing a German Shepherd puppy you need to discern that you can be the strong trainer and owner this breed deserves. If you are, and train them well, you will have yourself one amazing dog.

Exercise

Besides two thirty minute long, brisk daily walks, German Shepherds require at least an hour per day of varied types of exercise, whether this is achieved through play, games or sport. After each walk, a rigorous session of fetch, tracking games or other sport will deplete their energy reserves, mentally stimulate, and calm them.

GSD's are not lazy dogs that are suited to lying idly around. German Shepherds love cardio based intense activity. A long run, sport, hiking, or bicycling must be included in their daily routine. Additionally, regularly challenging their intellect with games that require problem solving will add to the vigor of your dog. Remember that loneliness and boredom are enemies of the GSD.

Health

Like humans, dogs have the potential to develop ailments and diseases. Many of these ailments and diseases vary in type and prevalence, from breed to breed. Consider this fact when picking out your new puppy, and beware of any breeder that makes a claim that the puppies of their particular breed are *"100% healthy."* A reputable and honest breeder should know and share any health related issues that the breed you are purchasing or inquiring about might have, or that could potentially surface.

For the German Shepherd Dog the following are some of the inherited diseases that can potentially surface. *Hip and elbow dysplasia*, digestive problems, blood disorders, epilepsy, chronic eczema, keratitis, and flea allergies. Other possible problems are tumors on the spleen, DM (degenerative myelitis spinal cord disease), EPI (pancreatic insufficiency), and perianal fistulas, and Von Willebrand's disease. Please consult the German Shepherd Club of America website and the CHIC site for more health and testing information.

Bloat and possible gastric torsion is a potentially fatal condition that can occur in GSD's and owners should learn and thoroughly understand how to identify the signs and symptoms so that lifesaving help can be quickly administered to the affected dog.

History

The German Shepherd only dates back a little over a The origin of the German Shepherd begins in 1899 when Max Von Stephanitz saw the realization of his dream. His dream was to make a standardized herding dog from the existing pool of many German farm dogs. He standardized an assemblage of German farm dogs into one strong, sturdy, smart, amicable working dog, which has become known as the German Shepherd. This dog became known worldwide for its ability to serve man in a variety of vocations, conditions, climates, and has done this through world wars and natural disasters.

During WWI, reports were received about a German wonder dog that was used as a courier, silent patrol dog, and to locate and recover wounded. After the war ended, other militaries adopted the German Shepherd for similar duties and more. Then in 1923, Rin Tin Tin, a German Shepherd brought back form WWI became a film star in American cinema and the GSD popularity skyrocketed.

When WWII broke out, Duncan, the founder and owner of Rin Tin Tin, began the American military's K-9 division. Eventually, he and

Rin Tin Tin III over saw the deployment of over five thousand dogs and handlers into military service.

After WWII, the German Shepherd population of Germany had been severely depleted and it took some time and diligence for the German breed to recover, but by nineteen forty-nine, quality dogs began to reappear in Germany. However, in America breeding thrived and produced many fine specimens.

In the 20th century, German Shepherds became one of the world's most popular working breeds. The downside to its popularity was that it drove over-breeding that muddled the gene pool and caused some issues inherent to the breed that would otherwise not exist. Demand drove the market to produce masses of puppies for the awaiting new owners.

Lack of proper over-sight in breeding selection has led to health issues such as hip and eye problems. This had previously happened in America following the years after WWI and experts from Germany had to be brought in to rectify the problem. Many kennel clubs and breeders work hard to continue furthering the health of the GSD breed and producing quality healthy puppies.

The German Shepherd was officially recognized by the American Kennel Club in nineteen hundred and eight. As of 2015, GSD popularity is holding steady and they are ranked as the second most popular breed registered with the American Kennel Club.

Selecting a Breeder

*Before Rin-Tin-Tin, there was **Strongheart**. He was one of the earliest canine stars and from 1922-1927 he starred in six movies. Before his premature death, he was adored by moviegoers that greeted him everywhere that he visited. He has his own star on the Hollywood Walk of Fame.*

When it is time to locate a breeder for the German Shepherd Dog breed that you have chosen, you will want to find an ethical and responsible breeder of German Shepherd Dogs. A new dog owner should want to do this for his own peace of mind, but also so that they do not support unethical breeders. As a new puppy owner, you should have already read about many breeds to find that the German Shepherd Dog fits your family's lifestyle. It is strongly suggested to read further so that you can jot down questions of your own to ask potential breeders. Make a list of the pros and cons of the German Shepherd Dog so that you are not surprised when a negative attribute might surface, and furthermore a list of anything that requires explanation or clarification.

Some words to know as you read. *Sire* refers to the male dog used to mate with the female that is named *dam*. *Pedigree* refers to a dog's ancestry. *Bitch* refers to a female dog. *Kennel clubs* are organizations that exist to provide dog owners with quality registration services and record keeping. They promote the activity of breeding purebred dogs for type and function, as well as providing breed information, education, many other services, and access to a wide range of dog competitions.

1. In general, quality breeders do not advertise in newspapers or on wholesale puppy sites. A reputable breeder will have high standards and is not in the business for quick money, but instead is in the trade to produce high-quality animals that will further the German Shepherd Dog breed and benefit its owners. My statement does not infer that good breeders cannot be found on those sites. I am stating that wholesale breeders are generally not as concerned with genetic testing, limited litters, and many other quality control items that contribute to breeding exceptional animals. Quality breeders tend to participate in breeding because of their love of the species.

2. Inferior breeders are not known for their involvement in clubs, showing, and organizations that promote responsible ownership and breeding. A quality breeder should be active in their dog community and upon request easily supply you with a lengthy list of referrals from elated customers, and other respected breeders. These referrals should assure that the breeder of interest is producing quality dogs. If referrals are not readily available, then future puppy buyers should look elsewhere.

Other items to beware are fancy wording in ads about a puppy's pedigree. Statements such as "champion bloodlines" can refer to champions in the pedigree, and not the *actual* sire or dam that produced your puppy. A statement such as champion bloodlines does not guarantee that the dogs used to produce your puppy have been properly tested, evaluated, and approved to be breeding quality dogs.

3. When seeking to purchase a new puppy for yourself or family a person should look for breeders that participate in OFA, CHIC, (defined below) and have registered their dogs with the AKC or other kennel club registries for purebred dogs. Globally, there are registries in many countries, and some countries have more than one national registry. Kennel clubs promote good breeding practices that further the breeding of healthy, well-adjusted puppies. Furthermore, kennel clubs have an agreed upon breed standard for all purebred dogs. Beware of breeders that do not disclose the full registered names of the dogs they have registered. However, kennel clubs do not always have a comprehensive breed welfare program. Many of the national breed clubs delve deep into diagnosing, solving, and testing for German Shepherd Dog breed specific illnesses, and work in conjunction with kennel clubs, so those clubs should always be added to the list of sources of investigative information.

Ask your breeder to provide the test results so that you can verify the tests have been done, and what the scores are. If the breeder participates then you can confirm health clearances by checking the OFA web site. You should expect to see health clearances from the Orthopedic Foundation for Animals (OFA), as well as a clearance from the Canine Eye Registry Foundation (CERF), certifying that the eyes are healthy.

Official OFA, Pennhip, CERF, or other recognized organizations evaluation scores should be the only acceptable proof that the sire and dam are certified healthy breeding stock. Beginning at four months, preliminary hip evaluations are available for dogs under the age of two, and the final official evaluations are available from two years forward.

If a breeder cannot provide these test scores stating that the parents of your litter are healthy, then it is suggested to look for a different breeder. Other warning signs are if a breeder states a version of "I am only breeding dogs to be pets, not to compete or show." This type of statement should be a warning that your breeder is not breeding to the standards adopted by clubs and other breeders. There is no reason that you should settle for a lesser puppy that does not come from tested and sanctioned breeding stock.

4. A conscientious breeder should be able to answer or explain to you the strengths and weaknesses of the sire and dam, and have thorough knowledge of their pedigree. The breeder should be forthright about the temperament, and any health issues the sire and dam might have. Breeding stock should be, or near the age of two years, so that official hip and elbow clearances can be obtained from a recognized testing body. They should apply the same strict standards to outside bitches that come to their stud dogs, which they apply to their own breeding stock.

5. Avoid litters born to dogs under the age of one, and breeders that continue to breed the same two dogs year after year. The goal should be to improve the breed and therefore breeders should be finding stud dogs that complement the dam. Breeding the same two dogs year after year only produces more puppies, and does not contribute to the betterment of the breed. In most cases, there is no reason to breed the same pairing more than twice, but the breeder could have a reason to share with you why they produced further litters.

6. A good rule used to gauge the quality of a breeder is the number of litters they produce annually and the number of breeds that they are breeding. Breeders that only breed two to three breeds and produce one to two litters per year are conscientious and limit themselves to this yearly number so that they can properly care for their puppies and dogs, provide lifetime support for behavioral and health issues, and keep proper records of their puppies.

Responsible breeders do not sell puppies to pet stores because they insist on screening their potential clients to ensure that their puppies are a good fit for their future owners, and often times have prearranged customers before breeding their dogs. Remember, matching the owner to the puppy is important to the breeder so that the new owners do not return or abandon their puppies. In general, responsible breeders will take the time to ask you many questions so that they can qualify you and your living conditions as a good fit for the puppy and then adult dog. Most reputable breeders assume lifetime responsibility for the dogs that they produce and want their puppies to go to the best of homes and owners.

7. After the puppy goes to their new home, a quality breeder will follow up and be available for questions regarding feeding, grooming, training, and anything else that can potentially surface. Another item that requires discussion is an education on spay/neutering, and the suggestions to have your puppy spay or neutered unless the new owner plans to become a breeder. If the new owner does plan to breed their dog, they might offer to mentor the new owner/breeder to insure that everything proceeds properly, including pedigree research, health, temperament, structure, and movement for the German Shepherd Dog.

Questions to Ask a Breeder

These questions are not in any particular order, but are quality questions that should be answered by your prospective breeder.

1. What is the duration that you have been involved with knowledge of the German Shepherd Dog breed?

2. Which activities and organizations are you a member that promote responsible dog breeding and ownership?

3. How old are the sire and dam for this litter?

4. How many total litters per year do you produce, including other breeds?

5. Can I see the official OFA test results for the sire and dam?

6. Can you provide me documentation that these evaluations were done outside of your personal veterinarian and completed by an official registry?

7. What other tests, if any do you perform yearly on your sire and dam?

8. Can you tell me why you chose these particular sire and dam to breed? What were the characteristics that made these two a desirable match?

9. Have you bred these two before, and if so why are you repeating?

10. What is your protocol regarding support after the puppy has left your care?

11. Will you let me return the puppy if I am unable to continue providing a home? Is there an age limit?

Proactive Measures for GSD Puppy Selection

If you want to buy a German Shepherd puppy, be sure to find a reputable German Shepherd breeder who will provide proof of health clearances for both of the puppy's parents. Health clearances are official documents that prove a dog has been tested for, and cleared of any, or all breed specific conditions, however a clearance does not guarantee against acquired diseases or congenital abnormalities. Remember, even under the best breeding practices and proactive care measures, puppies can still develop diseases.

Any breeder that does not have knowledge, will not provide genetic testing or states that testing is unnecessary, should be considered an inappropriate provider of German Shepherds. Beware of any breeder that refuses or does not know the answers to questions about their breeding practices and health of their dogs. Avoid Puppy Mill breeders that are only breeding dogs to make money and are unconcerned with the health of their dogs and the puppies they produce. Unfortunately, many of these dogs end up in pet stores, so be diligent when searching for your new puppy. The best practice is to deal directly with breeders, find referrals, and if possible visit their establishment.

A breeder that takes pride in producing healthy and attractive dogs will perform genetic testing and additional testing on its dogs. Any breeder performing these tests is potentially a conscientious breeder worth considering as a provider of your new puppy. Furthermore, good breeders will remove aggressive animals from their breeding program. Breeders should welcome questions and be able to answer easily all questions that you have about their breeding stock, housing, genetics, German Shepherd specific ailments, breed standard, and number of litters per year that they produce.

Explain to the breeder the type of dog that you are seeking so that they can match the appropriate type of GSD to your family. Tell them whether you are seeking a companion, competitive, or show type of dog. Working lines are more energetic and expect to have daily tasks to perform, where as a breeder producing show dogs will generally have more docile GSD's. Avoid shy or nervous puppies; look for an alert outgoing happy puppy. Quality breeders take pride in matching their dogs to appropriate families. It is of great importance to them because they are responsible for returns, the health issues of their puppies, and must keep records of where they are.

If German Shepherd popularity wanes, it will turn out to be good news for the breed, because less puppy demand can allow the purebred dog line to be more selective. Sub-par breeders that only concentrate on profit and not producing quality dogs that further the breed will switch to breeds that are more profitable. If this happens, it will allow the breed to remedy some of the health issues. Because of their popularity, it is very important to find a reputable breeder with a history of producing high-quality puppies.

For the German Shepherd breed, you should expect to see health clearances for the parents from the Orthopedic Foundation for Animals (OFA) for hip and elbow dysplasia, and a temperament test, as well as a clearance from the Canine Eye Registry Foundation (CERF), certifying that the eyes are healthy. Other optional tests are cardiac, autoimmune thyroiditis, and a degenerative myelopathy DNA based test performed by the UFL or University of Missouri. You can also confirm health clearances by checking the OFA web site. For more information, refer to the club website, breeder, or veterinarian. Consult the CHIC database for all tests and their schedules.

Additionally do not hesitate to consult your breeder regarding the temperament of the dogs that they are producing. The American Temperament Test Society and German Shepherd Dog Club of America can test the temperaments of dogs and provide a certificate of the test results. GSD's are strong agile dogs that can be difficult to control if aggressive or unstable. Any breeder performing these tests is usually a conscientious breeder that takes pride in producing fine specimens.

What Are Puppy Mills?

Beware of puppy mills. *Puppy mill* is a term used for large-scale commercial operations that place profits above the well-being of its dogs. Dogs are often severely neglected, and the operation is usually run without regard to responsible breeding practices. The outcome is generations of dogs with unchecked hereditary defects. Puppies being produced in this manner can carry a long list of problematic health conditions, which is why it is suggested not to purchase puppies from these operations.

Puppy mills range in size from ten to one-thousand breeding dogs. Some are licensed and inspected while others are not. However, just because a mill is registered or inspected does not imply that the living conditions and puppies are appropriate or under any scrutiny that would force them to improve both. Unfortunately, federal laws are inadequate when it comes to humane treatment of animals. When seeking a quality puppy it is suggested to evade these types of operations and their wholesalers. The more persons educate themselves and quit buying from these low standard cruel operations, the better off all dogs, breeds, and puppies will become.

The primary concern of this type of breeder is only profit, thus you often read about dogs living in horrific conditions being rescued from these mills. Many times a broker will sell these dogs to pet shops who unbeknownst purchase dogs with falsified lineage papers. Other avenues for these puppy mills to sell their dogs are via the internet, newspaper ads, and swap meets. Not every pet store sells puppies from a puppy mill; some have legitimate, shelter, or rescue dogs available, but it will take some research to verify.

Backyard Breeder is a term that labels small versions of for profit breeding and many or all of the same problems exist in these smaller for profit operations. This term is a blanket term that has negative implications. However, backyard breeder can also refer to non-commercial or unplanned breeding that occurs.

Further information on puppy mills and backyard breeders is readily available at the ASPCA, Humane Society, and other places.

Testing Organizations and Databases for Health Issues

For more information on testing and health issues for your breed, refer to your countries regional or national German Shepherd Dog club website. Consult the CHIC database for other tests and their recommended schedules. When seeking a breeder for your new puppy, search for breeders that are testing for the items listed in the CHIC database for your breed, and if your breed is not listed, then consult the national German Shepherd Dog club for suggested testing that should be performed.

The Orthopedic Foundation for Animals (OFA offa.org) maintains an open registry with evaluations of hips, elbows, eyes, thyroid, cardio, and many additional canine health issues. They also provide clear definitions of the test categories to help you understand the grading system. PennHIP (pennhip.org) is another registry that tests and evaluates dog's hips. Instructions explaining how to read the test results are available on the websites.

The American Kennel Club (AKC) conducts large canine research studies on diseases that affect purebred dogs. Their health program is under the direction of the Canine Health Foundation (CHF), and is in partnership with OFA, and additionally does breed testing and provides a centralized canine health database called, the Canine Health Information Center (CHIC). The results of these tests are maintained in a registry, and dogs that have completed all of the required exams, including testing of the hips, elbows, and eyes, receive a CHIC number.

Along with the breed-testing program, there is the CHIC DNA Repository. CHIC is trying to gather and store breed DNA samples for canine disease research. The goal is to facilitate future research aimed at reducing the incidence of inherited diseases in dogs. You can search the database to find out if a specific dog has information listed about it. More information about CHIC is available here: caninehealthinfo.org

To be accepted into the CHIC database, breeders must agree to have all test results published. This enables the reader to see both good and bad results of the testing. Obtaining a CHIC number does not imply that the dog received good or passing evaluation scores. The CHIC registration also does not signify as proof of the absence of disease. All information must be read and evaluated. CHIC allows the information collected to be readily available to anyone with an inquiry.

Like humans, dogs have the potential to develop ailments and diseases. Many of these ailments and diseases vary in type and prevalence, and from breed to breed. Consider this fact when picking out your new puppy, and beware of any breeder that makes a claim that the puppies of their particular breed are *"100% healthy."* A reputable and honest breeder should know and share any health related issues that the breed you are purchasing or inquiring about might have, or that could potentially surface.

Prior to acquiring your dog of choice, I recommend reading about canine health related issues and common breed specific ailments. By familiarizing yourself with the signs and symptoms of a potential disease or sickness, you will be empowered to be the first line of defense in support of your dog's health and wellbeing. After bringing your new dog home, completing routine physical examinations of your dog, frequent fecal inspections, as well as recognizing any gastrointestinal problems, all helps to assure optimal health of your companion. By observing and understanding your dog's healthy behaviors and regular patterns, you will easily be able to identify when your dog is not feeling well, and to deduce if medical attention is needed.

How to Use This Training Guide

Learning - *From here forward, the trainer learns information about GSDs and dog training.*

I am glad you are here. First, take the time to read the entire guide, so that you can familiarize yourself in a general manner with the information, methods, and instruction contained within. To avoid feeling overwhelmed from the density of information contained within this guide, pace yourself during your first reading.

After your initial read, keep it nearby so that you can *easily reference it as needed*. Having the guide handy at all times, will help to keep the information and instruction fresh in your mind. Just as your dog requires ongoing training practice, you as the owner and trainer need to remain sharp on the training points, processes and methods. It is important for you, as the commander and chief, to maintain a focus on the goals and outcomes of the training.

• While following the training steps let your dog learn and proceed at his own pace, as there is no set timeline to advance to subsequent steps contained inside each training section. Do not rush to the next step because *you* are ready; make the decision to move forward based on your dog's obedience of the commands, or compliance to the requested actions.

• If you are on a training step and you realize your dog is not ready to have advanced, back up a step and repeat practicing over a few training sessions. Then proceed to the next after your dog is performing the current step successfully at a proficient level.

• Always remain alert to the possibility of your dog feeling weary or having a low concentration day. If you are, stop the session and return to it at another time. Try to end it on a high note.

• Always remain attentive to the possibility that *YOU* may be feeling weary, having a low concentration day, or are in a bad mood. If you are experiencing any of these signs, do not start the training session, and simply wait until your status improves.

• If your puppy is not progressing, or appears not to be hearing your commands, you should consider a visit to your veterinarian. It's possible that a problem with your dog's hearing, sight, or a medical condition is impeding his training.

• If you are using treats in your training, and your dog has recently eaten, *do not train*. His full stomach will reduce the effectiveness of the intended reinforcement of the food rewards. Wait at least two hours after feeding to improve the effectiveness of the treats.

• Because training can sometimes be very taxing on you and your dog, and at times your dog will push your buttons, never let him know that you are angry, or at your limits. Remember, it is always of great importance to maintain a light heartedness, and use plenty of laughter, during training

• Keep the PRICELESS mindset active throughout training and living with your dog.

Note: Throughout this training guide, *Click and Treat is sometimes written as C/T.* In addition, for ease of writing, even though I know many people have female dogs I refer to the gender of your dog in the male form. Please take no offense to this.

Common First Timer Mistakes

If you have previously owned dogs, then you probably recognize some of these potential mistakes. If this is your first time bringing a dog into your family, then being aware and prepared of the most common mistakes made by first time dog owners is your best means of identifying and preventing these issues *before* they surface. Below is a short overview of some things to watch out. This is not a complete list, but meant for awareness of some potential major issues that you can thwart by becoming self-aware that you are not accidentally falling into any of these negative thought processes. This training guide will delve deeper into these topics with further explanation and detail on how to tackle them.

"It's a lot more work than I expected. Owning a dog isn't what I thought it would be. "

Many first time dog owners will confess that they were unprepared for the burden of responsibility that comes with dog ownership. Most people who acquire a dog are often uninformed and frequently ill prepared to have a dog under their care. There is a romantic notion that comes with the idea of keeping a dog; it's all playful romps on the beach, delightful trots down sidewalks and trails, games of throw and fetch in the park, automatic obedience, all effortless, simple, intuitive, and low-maintenance relationship with man's best friend. While some of these things can become a reality, this idealistic, romantic notion has certainly caused many dogs, and their humans, unnecessary misery and heartache.

The reality of dog ownership is it consists of great responsibility and commitment. When you have chosen to adopt a puppy, you have signed an unseen contract obliging you to a lifetime of care for an animal that looks to you for leadership. You will assume the role as the *alpha*, and for the wellbeing of your new companion, you must follow through with all of the responsibilities that comes with this important position.

"There is definitely a communication problem between my dog and I."

This is a common issue frequently reported by first time dog owners. Identifying the signals within the behavioral displays of your dog will help clue you into his needs. By reading your dog's body language and other subtle cues in his manners, you will be empowered to resolve what appear to be issues of miscommunication. This miscommunication often manifests during housetraining. If your dog continues to relieve himself indoors, then maybe you are not identifying the signals that he displays which indicates his need to relieve himself. First, you need to pay close attention to your puppy, so keep him within view, observing for signals that should cue you to his needs. Sniffing the floor, revisiting a previous relief spot, circling, looking at, or walking towards the door is certain indicators he is in need of a potty break. Eventually, you will begin to recognize your dog's signals of communication. With a proactive attitude, combined with sensitivity to the unspoken needs of your companion, your response time to his needs will certainly improve over time.

A couple of things to ask yourself is, *"Have I taught my dog what I am trying to communicate?"*, or *"Has he learned the command or rule yet?"* Just because you completed a couple of training sessions does not necessarily mean that your dog has retained the command you are issuing, or even understood what you were attempting to teach. Make sure to follow through with your training, and remember not to demand something from your dog that he has not been given a chance to learn yet.

"My dog is a wilding and he is riddled with behavioral issues."

It is common for first time dog owners to find themselves with a juvenile dog afflicted with a multitude of behavioral problems. Negative behavioral issues manifest themselves in various ways, such as jumping up on people, aggression, possessiveness, excessive barking, playing rough, biting, and growling or snapping when commands are issued. Each of these behaviors stems from a historic lack of rule enforcement and incomplete training during the puppy's developmental years. Lenient owners who frequently gave in to their dogs when challenged, or owners who were permissive, letting their dogs run amuck, are common causes of poor behaviors in adulthood.

Often, because early in life these dogs are poorly supervised and trained, they appear seemingly uncontrollable. The poor beasts that have the misfortune to grow up without structure are regularly given away, put into shelters, or even sometimes euthanized. This can be avoided by remaining proactive in your dog's development through implementing proper methods of training, becoming well versed in canine behaviors, and becoming intimately familiar with your dog's various patterns of communication. Early, consistent rule establishment and enforcement is imperative. The time you invest in observation of your dog will have high returns. In addition, your willingness and diligence in understanding and cataloguing his various expressions, is value added. The most important question to ask yourself, prior to dog ownership, is *do you have enough time and patience to train and properly care for a puppy?* If yes, then it is up to you to provide unconditional love, patience, guidance, and structure immediately upon the arrival of your new addition to the family. These are the basic essentials any new dog owner should have available in their toolbox in order to assure that the puppy can grow into an obedient, well adjusted, and *wanted* dog. Whether this is your first or tenth dog, if the proper commitment is made, owners and their canine companions can live a life of harmony with a mutual understanding that the human retains the power as commander and chief.

"My dog is untrainable; he will not listen or obey anything that I say."

Dogs thrive under clear, well-defined rules, issued under confident, unwavering leadership. Guidelines and directions need to be well structured and consistent. By establishing a distinct set of rules for your dog to learn and follow, paired with consistent obedience enforcement, you will turn out an easier to train, well behaved, and relaxed dog. By following a regular daily schedule for walking, feeding, training, and play, your dog will surely flourish. Being in charge does not mean that you have to be overtly physical, hostile, or excessively vocal. Remain firm but reasonable in your administration and enforcement of the rules established. As pack leader, your dog will look to you for cues and direction. To be an effective superior you must always project yourself with steadfast confidence, and it is essential that you maintain continuity in your guidance. Within the processes of training your dog, the consistency of your teaching and the uniformity of your rule enforcement will firmly establish *you as the alpha.*

"I will treat my dog like a human child."

That is not going to work, and you and your dog are doomed to failure if you begin your relationship with this approach. Yes, your dog is a living, feeling creature that certainly deserves all of the love and respect that we humans can offer them, but remember that your dog is a completely different species, and his care should reflect this fact. Dogs have instinctual behaviors, including barking, digging, marking, chewing and more. All of these attributes serve them well in the wild, but as a domesticated pet, these things certainly need shaping and curbing. As everyone is well aware, dogs can be aggressive and will bite if provoked. This often inflicts injury on those in harm's way. Biting is a behavior, that if not nipped in the bud early in life, can cause dangerous problems in the future.

The behavioral modifications to shape and steer a dog will be much different from that utilized in the training and upbringing of a human child. Even though it might be tempting to personify your cute little pup, it is a serious mistake to treat dogs as humans. A dog's body language and vocalizations are quite different from a human, and if you try to interpret their actions from a human perspective, then there will likely be a lot of misinterpretation, resulting in frustration and mishandling. Approaching your dog as a human can lead to all sorts of problematic communication issues, and create fertile grounds for negative behaviors to grow from. For you and your dog's sake, you should make a concerted effort to learn about dog communication and behavior, maintaining a species-specific sensitivity, thereby assuring continuity in communication. With this respected, you will be empowered to form a healthier and happier relationship, that you will continue throughout the lifetime of your dog.

"I will train my puppy when I have time."

That statement reveals an undesirable recipe to have an unruly, out of control puppy who knows no rules or boundaries, and I poorly equipped to act appropriately in various situations. Owning and training a puppy requires an ongoing and consistent commitment of your time and energy. Immediately after bringing your puppy home, you have to begin investing time into establishment and enforcement of rules, thereby giving your puppy a chance to gain your trust. A daily, weekly, and monthly schedule for puppy activity and training, paired with effectual socialization requires regular time spent with your puppy. None of this is optional. If you neglect investing time in your new companion, you will likely end up with an uncontrollable puppy that in order to train in obedience, and train out unwanted, negative behaviors will likely require some serious hands-on-work from a professional.

"I will choose a dog based upon their looks."

Although looks are to be considered, it should not be the singular factor in making the decision. There are many factors to consider when choosing a dog for you and your family. Breed traits, personality, grooming, health, trainability, indoor or outdoor, and much more. New dog owners first need to know that they have the time necessary to train and care for a new dog or there is no reason to continue. It is unfair to bring a dog into an uncaring environment. Afterward they must diagram their schedules and choose a breed that best fits the family's lifestyle, likes, and dislikes. Armed with that information you can begin reviewing breeds that fit well with your family lifestyle and research further. Then after narrowing your search begin to find a reputable breeder. Selecting a dog breed that fits correctly with your lifestyle will begin the process of having a successful, prolonged, dog-human relationship. Start today by acquiring more free information about puppies.

Puppy Proof Home

You have selected your German Shepherd puppy, and you are excited that finally the day has come that you are bringing your new puppy home. A second of panic occurs as you wonder, "Do I have everything my new puppy needs?" I do not want you to have those thoughts. I have put together a small list of items that everyone needs to have in their home and car before bringing a new furry creature into their home.

Puppy proofing your home entails removing all harmful items that a puppy might chew or swallow, unfortunately, that means everything. Puppies love to put anything into their mouths. After all, they are kids learning about the world.

It will be necessary to elevate electrical cords, remove floor debris, and all other random objects that a puppy can chew, eat, or swallow. Thoroughly inspect your entire house that is accessible to your puppy. Apply bitter spray to appropriate furniture and fixed objects that require protection. Take extra caution removing all chemicals, pharmaceuticals, and other toxic liquids from puppy reach.

Baby gates can be used to quarantine areas away from your puppy. Not Bill Gates baby, but gates that keep babies out of trouble. Avoid any accordion type gating system because they can cause harm to your puppy. Make sure the gates fasten securely and are structurally sound. Stairs and workrooms should be blocked in addition to any other rooms that your new puppy should not be allowed.

BEWARE! Puppies will investigate anything new and easily accessible. It is *time to change habits.* From the time your puppy is coming home you can no longer walk in and carelessly place anything onto the floor. This includes your backpacks, groceries, clothes, briefcases, containers, handbags, leashes, collars, plastic or paper bags, and all other objects or clothing that you normally toss carefree onto the floor.

Your home is a landscape that needs to remain puppy proof. *Train your mind* to be puppy proof. Anything accidently dropped or spilled must be immediately retrieved or cleaned from the floor.

"What do I need to do to make my home ready for a new puppy?"

1. A correct sized *crate.* Your puppy will be spending quite a bit of time in its crate and it should be comfortable and sized appropriately for your puppy. Your puppy should be able to stand up, lie down, and turn around in the crate but not much more, because it will make it more likely that your puppy will have an accident inside the crate. Add something soft and washable for him or her to sleep on. Thoroughly clean any messes that occur inside the crate. Try diligently to avoid crate accidents. Your puppy's crate will be used for sleeping and resting and the sooner he is used to it, the better.

2. Playpen made from wire or wood. Wire pens can be configured into varying sizes and shape, but wood are limited to four sides and a fixed sized wall. Avoid accordion style walls.

3. Chew toys of varying kinds. Be aware of the size and durability. You need durable toys because most puppies will try to tear them apart. Beware that puppies are able to swallow balls larger than their jaws. Nylabones™, rubber balls, tough squeaky toys, and rawhide are desirable.

4. Collar and *leash.* Choose an appropriate sized collar and style for your puppy. A good idea is a wide, flat, buckle type collar that can be expanded as they grow. Your puppy will be growing astonishingly fast for the first few months. Your puppy is small, so select a lightweight leash that is about six feet (2meters) in length.

Begin introducing your puppy to wearing their collar and introducing the leash before venturing outdoors. Your puppy can sport the expensive designer collar after they are grown.

5. ID tags. Regular tag with contact information, or one that is electronically chipped.

6. Puppy food that is recommended by your breeder or veterinarian. Use only high quality foods without bi-products and artificial additives. If you are interested, research and consult experts about raw foods diets. Raw food diets or combinations provide a healthy alternative or addition to puppy foods.

7. Food bowls. Stainless steel bowls retain fewer bacteria than glass or plastic.

8. Puppy proof spray to apply to items that you do not want your puppy chewing. Sprays that humans cannot smell but are bitter to puppies and keep their mouths off furniture and other items. Bitter apple is a common spray.

9. Relief accident cleaner. *Enzyme cleaners* are recommended for eliminating odors.

10. Pee pads. If necessary due to your living arrangement.

Bringing Your Puppy Home

Consistency - *Begins from day one forward. This is one of the foundation blocks for building the human-dog relationship and it will bond your puppy to you.*

Now it is time to bring your puppy home. There are a couple of things to keep in mind on this day. First, that you are a stranger to him; he has probably never been in a car or away from his mom or littermates. As you can imagine this will be a stressful moment for your puppy, so try to make the ride to your home as stress free as possible.

Before departure, allow your puppy to relieve itself, and during the ride provide a soft comfortable place in a crate or nestled in a humans arms. He may cry or bark during the ride, but that is normal behavior and you must handle it calmly. This will begin to establish that you are there to help. By speaking calmly and evenly, and not speaking harshly, you will show your puppy that you care and are not to be feared. If possible, bring along the entire family and begin the bonding process on the car ride home. Many times the person that brings the puppy to the home is the person that the puppy will begin forming the tightest bond. Drive straight home to keep the drive short. Avoid over handling from family members during the ride home.

If you have to stop for a pee/poop stop, be sure to carry your puppy to an unused area and properly clean up afterward. Your puppy is not yet vaccinated and could have worms or parasites in his feces as well needs to avoid exposure to other dogs.

Ride home checklist

- Cleaning supplies, just in case.
- Soft towel or blanket.

- Collar – if you use a collar be sure it is tight. If you can fit one finger between the collar and your puppy's neck then it is correctly tightened.

- Leash

- Newspapers, paper towels, and plastic bags.

- Smile, good mood, and cheerful tone of voice.

- Crate (optional).

- Pet odor neutralizer (optional).

First couple of Days and Nights

Upon arriving home, take him to the predesignated outdoor relief spot.

- Clear the indoor area of other pets and place your puppy down to explore. Do not crowd the puppy and if children are present have them provide the puppy plenty of space. Allow him to come to them on his own terms. Have everyone remain calm and gentle when interacting.

- All puppies act differently. Some take off exploring the house, others just curl up and voyeur the surroundings and might doze off.

- Keep in mind that if your puppy was flown in, or from a shelter that they may have brought stress with them and be extremely tired from the previous day/night. Expect that the following day they will be rested and livelier.

- Separation anxiety is natural and you might hear your puppy whine, squeal, or howl. They might have difficulty sleeping the first few days or weeks. Your puppy has to get used to being away from his sisters, brothers, and mom that he used to snuggle.

- Move slowly with introducing your other pets to your new puppy. The crate, baby gate, or exercise pen puts a barrier between them and allows both to adjust to one another without direct physical contact.

• After about three or four days, take your puppy to the veterinarian for a complete check-up.

• It is very important to show your puppy that they are wanted and cared for. This is of the utmost importance during the first few days.

"Where does my puppy sleep?"

• The first night will most likely be the most difficult for your puppy, but do not isolate him because he is vocalizing his loneliness. Try not to keep him far from where you are sleeping. He is alone in a strange place, and you want him to feel comfortable and welcomed. For example, do not put him in the garage or basement.

• Options for not isolating your puppy are a dog bed or blanket on the floor near your bed, or in his crate near your bed or just outside the opened bedroom door. For a variety of reasons, it is advised *not* to have your puppy in your bed.

• Even though your puppy is whimpering, do not go to him and pay too much attention every time he is vocalizing distress. This can become a negative behavior used to get you to come to him. Persevere throughout the first few nights.

Relief Time

• Take him out for relief every half hour. Soiling accidents are common the first couple of days so clean them thoroughly and use pet deodorizers so that there is no trace. Gradually over the coming days and weeks, you will increase the duration between relief times.

• Always take them to relieve themselves in the designated outdoor relief spot.

• Do not become angry about relief accidents. If you see him going, if possible, pick him up and let him finish outdoors and afterward praise him while still outdoors.

• Escort your puppy outside and begin praising him for taking care of his relief business.

• To prevent frequent accidents take notice if you need to shorten the time between taking him outside.

• Track your puppies schedule for eating and pees/poops, this can help you eliminate accidents and begins housebreaking. Tracking will help you to learn your puppy's pattern.

• After feeding, always take your puppy outdoors.

• Pick up the water bowl around 8pm each night.

• Continuously praise your puppy when he or she eliminates waste outdoors and not indoors. This will strengthen your bond and begin building trust.

• Before bedtime, always take your puppy out to relieve his bodily functions. Often a short walk assists them in falling asleep.

• Take your puppy out first thing in the morning.

• Allow him to relieve himself in full. Most puppies will take several small amounts to finish relieving.

Things to Know and Consider

- Constantly show patience during training and daily interaction.

- Handle your puppy gently.

- Do not strike or yell at your dog.

- Teach good manners from the moment you bring your puppy home.

- Learn about socialization and put it immediately into practice.

- Learn about nutrition and optional diets to implement. Knowing the diet that you will be providing your new puppy will make your life more relaxed because it eliminates second-guessing.

- Check in with yourself to see if you are being consistent in rule establishment and enforcement. Are you employing the *alpha role* properly?

- Be prepared for your training sessions. Before the session consult your notes to remind yourself of what, where, when you did the last training session.

- From the time you bring your pup home, positive training is a great start to introducing your new pack member to your household. You should be aware and sensitive to the fact that dogs have an amazing capacity for memory and recollection of those experiences. With this in mind, please refrain from harsh training tactics that may intimidate your puppy and that potentially can negatively affect personality or demeanor.

- When you train your new puppy, give him the respect deserved, and utilize all available positive reinforcements. The result of your positive, proactive training methods and behavior modifications will be that your dog's abilities, traits, and characteristics that are buried within the genetic profile of the GSD will shine.

- I am an advocate for beginning with rewards based clicker training, followed by vocal and physical cues for your young dog to learn and obey.

Common Puppy Health Issues

We all want our pets to be healthy and enjoy vibrant lifestyles. It takes proper nutrition, healthy foods, exercise and diligence to keep our dogs healthy. Whether you have a new puppy, middle-aged, or elderly dog, there are certain diseases and ailments that tend to be prevalent during those three periods of a dog's lifetime.

Below is a short-list of *common ailments* that puppies are stricken. Observing your puppy when they are healthy will aid you in diagnosing symptoms of an ailment that requires treatment.

Mild Diarrhea and Vomiting - Short periods of diarrhea and vomiting can be caused by dietary problems or less severe infections. If your puppy *has not* received a full course of initial vaccinations and it has an upset stomach, then you should contact your veterinarian for advice.

Gastrointestinal Foreign Bodies - Puppies love chewing! It is common for them to eat inappropriate objects, which then become lodged within the stomach or intestine. If diagnosed promptly, these obstructions have a high success rate for being completely resolved with surgery. Look for low appetite, vomiting after eating, lethargy and abdominal pain. Consult a veterinarian if you are concerned.

Parvovirus – This very severe disease suppresses the maturation of fast dividing cells. As such, it is particularly deadly to puppies as they have rapidly expanding immune tissue and gastrointestinal tissue. It causes severe diarrhea and vomiting, fever, as well as suppression of the immune system. With prompt, appropriate veterinary care, most puppies will survive. The best protection is appropriate vaccination administered by a veterinarian, combined with ensuring that your puppy visits only "trustworthy" environments until fully vaccinated.

Distemper - This is less common than parvovirus, but still diagnosed in many areas in the world. This viral disease causes a high fever, neurological problems, gastrointestinal problems (vomiting and diarrhea), discharge from the eyes and nose, and hardening of the pads of the feet and the nose. Dogs that develop disease due to distemper virus usually cannot be treated successfully. However, vaccination against distemper is highly effective.

Coughs / Sneezing – Puppies are more susceptible to respiratory infections than adult dogs. Often these are not particularly serious, however if you are concerned you should consult a veterinarian.

Parasites - Puppies are generally more prone to parasitism than adult dogs. This includes both internal parasites (roundworms, tapeworms) and external parasites like fleas and ticks. Puppies should be given an intestinal worm treatment regularly (every two weeks from 2 weeks old to 10-12 weeks old, then every month until six months of age, then every three months for life). Appropriate controls for external parasites should also be used - the appropriate parasite control methods vary greatly based upon where you are geographically located on earth.

Growth Abnormalities - Many puppies end up underweight due to insufficient feeding (particularly stray puppies, or puppies from pet stores and poor quality breeders). Some puppies develop growth abnormalities in their bones due to mineral imbalances in their food, genetics or a combination of both.

Injuries - Common in dogs of all ages! Puppies are more susceptible to injuries due to their naivety, curiosity and high activity levels. Fortunately, they are light and tend to have flexible joints and bones, meaning that injuries that might cause severe damage in older dogs can be less damaging in puppies.

Ocular (eye) Abnormalities – These are often caused by foreign material (particularly grass seed heads). However, there are many possible causes of weepy, sore eyes. Almost all are either completely treatable or can be easily managed with prompt veterinary care.

Vomiting and Diarrhea – Both are often caused by dietary changes, "dietary indiscretion" (garbage guts enteritis). However, vomiting and diarrhea are also caused by other serious conditions, such as pancreatitis or gastrointestinal obstructions.

Itchy skin / other skin diseases - Common in young and old dogs. There are many possible causes. The most common cause is flea allergy dermatitis - ensure your dog receives a high quality flea prevention product such as imidacloprid (Advantage) or selamectin (Revolution), and that the environment in which your dog lives is as clean as possible (wash bedding in hot water, if appropriate, use " flea bombs" carefully).

Heartworms – Spread by mosquitos. They are common in some areas (tropical climates), uncommon or not a problem at all in others. Heartworms can be easily prevented with a variety of routine treatments, but if untreated can cause severe disease.

Tick-borne illnesses - Blood parasites like Ehrlichia, Babesia and Theileria can cause very severe anemia. Paralysis ticks in many areas in Australia (cause very severe paralysis), paralysis ticks in North America (less severe but can still be life threatening). Ticks may also spread a Lyme disease like illness to dogs (this is a controversial topic) - can generally be managed with appropriate topical agents (Fipronil, Pyrethroids, Amitraz) and some newer oral drugs. However regardless of treatments it is important to search your dog's coat thoroughly every day and promptly remove any ticks that are found.

Arthritis – Is very common in old dogs of all breeds, but particularly a concern for purebred dogs and large dogs. However, early pro-active measures can lessen the symptoms of age. Maintaining a healthy (lean) body weight, regular exercise (particularly swimming) and a healthy diet containing ample high quality proteins and Omega 3 fatty acids will help support joints throughout life. When arthritis becomes a problem many pain relief and other management options are available.

Dental Disease - Very common, particularly in smaller designer breed dogs, dogs with malformed jaws/mandibles, dogs with crowded teeth. Chewing somewhat regularly on appropriate toys or raw, fresh, large bones (not more than once a week) can be very helpful. Tooth brushing is also helpful, but can be hard to start at an older age, so begin early. Special dental diets are also available to help keep teeth clean. Once the dental disease has progressed to the point that gingivitis exists and there is a layer of tartar present, the teeth will need cleaning under general anesthetic.

Coughs / Colds / Sneezing - Often caused by "infectious canine cough" agents (*Bordetella bronchoseptica, Parainfluenza virus*). In many cases self-limiting, however veterinary care is warranted any time that you are concerned by coughing/sneezing from your dog.

Ocular (eye) Abnormalities – Are often caused by foreign material (particularly grass seed heads). However, there are many possible causes of weepy, sore eyes. Almost all are either completely treatable or can be easily managed with prompt veterinary care.

Puppy Training Prep

As promised, here are the definitions and reasons behind using the PRICELESS MINDSET. Bring these personality traits into your training and dog relationship.

Patience **R**esolve **I**mpartiality **C**onsistency **E**xcitement **L**earning **E**volution **S**implicity and **S**urrender

Patience – It is a necessity to incorporate patience while dog training. Things move at the dogs pace not yours, there will be difficulties, forward progress and setbacks, and you have to be able to remain patient and unflustered through it all. You will inevitably discover that some training sessions will not go well, but know that others will be highly efficient and successful.

Resolve – You have to remain *firm* but fair, and your dog has to respect you as the alpha and understand that you make the rules and enforce them. No matter how cute, cuddly or sad eyed that they look to you, you must display resolve and remain steadfast in your leadership decisions.

Impartiality – Be *fair* with rule enforcement, avoid harsh vocal tones and never use physical aggression towards your dog.

Consistency – From the day you bring your dog home, establish a schedule for feeding, walks, play, training, elimination breaks, and stick to that schedule. It reinforces your alpha stature and helps to support your dog's confidence that he or she is well looked after. Dogs crave structure, so this will have a calming effect on your dog.

Excitement – Bring your pep, smile, and fun to all training and play sessions. It assists training when your dog thinks of it as a game and fun instead of a chore with little reward. Above all, remain positive.

Learning – The human factor. It is up to you to study and absorb as much information about dogs as you can while learning about your dog. Study your dog's posture, vocal tones, and their different meanings. What is he or she trying to tell you?

Evolution – Training your dog is a lifelong process for them and you. The two of you must learn and grow together. As the two of you continue to practice commands and shape behaviors, the successes will grow and lock in confidence between the two of you.

Simplicity – Keep command words to one or two syllables. Do not overload your dog with more training than one command per training session. Avoid over repetition; keep training sessions short, mix up your rewards, and commands.

Surrender – Not everything is going to go as plan or at the pace that you desire. You have to surrender to the fact that there will be setbacks along with forward progress. Laugh it off and recognize when to end a session, and take notice whether you or your dog are tired. Recognize the times that are good times for training sessions. Humor will help you greatly.

Before Training Reminders

I will assume that you have already read in depth about GSDs and you understand the journey that you will be embarking upon, but your puppy is there, frightened in a new home and you have been making him or her feel comfortable and loved beginning with the car ride home. Now you wish to teach your puppy its name and other commands.

- Read this German Shepherd dog-training guide.

- If you have not yet done so, purchase a clicker, leashes, treat pouch, harness, and collar.

- Establish a consistent schedule for feeding, exercise, relief breaks, and playtimes. This should be started as soon as you bring your puppy home.

- Notice if your puppy begins following your around the house. This is a good sign that you are bonding.

- Remember that besides breed traits, all dogs have their own personalities.

- Always be patient, gentle, and kind towards your puppy.

- Implement the PRICELESS Mindset in training, rule enforcement, and daily living.

- Begin to observe and get to know your puppy's behaviors including what physical actions they make when they do or do not like something. Observe them during play, exercise, relaxing times, and so forth. Write notes about their actions. This will help you to understand your puppy's personality, but additionally assists in identifying possible health issues throughout their lifetime. Observation and understanding will be an ongoing lifelong process.

- Practice your alpha posture, keeping an even temperament, and clicker timing.

- Read all of the information contained inside the guide before beginning to train. Research and further read anything that needs clarification.

- As a dog owner in training, always keep laughter and light heartedness in mind, because it is of the greatest importance. This is because sometimes training is very difficult on you and your dog. Sometimes your dog will push your patience to the limits. Remember to try and never let your dog know that you are at your limits.

- Keep humor at the forefront; it will get you through the challenging moments.

Training Landmarks

A. Avoid future problems by early correction of issues. Stop bad behaviors before they escalate.

B. Begin training on the first day that your puppy arrives home. Do not force anything, but as the trainer keep all of this in mind.

- Immediately begin establishing the household rules.

- Begin house-training.

- Begin chew-toy training.

- Begin minimal socialization.

C. Common achievement timelines that should be set up for completion. Footnote on your training calendar and keep track of your puppy's progress. These general milestones and your training progress will let you know if you need to solicit help in any of the following.

- Socialization to humans by 12 weeks.

- Biting & Nipping training successful by 18 weeks.

- *Well socialized* by 5 months of age. At this stage your dog can meet and greet other humans and animals in a calm friendly manner. Your dog handles transportation well and is understanding all basic etiquette for strange encounters. Meeting this goal will set the precedence for your adult dog to have good manners and be *trustworthy* as an adult. Keep in mind that socialization is a lifetime endeavor.

- *Housetraining* completion ranges from six months to twelve months. By four months most puppies often know to wait, but might still have issues. Many puppies are completely housetrained by six to eight months, or mostly trained by six months with occasional accidents.

Beginner Trainers

Dogs are genetically programmed to hunt, beg, dig, chew, bite, growl, jump, whine, howl, and scavenge. The labels of scavenger or opportunist are appropriate, but they are simply beneficial survival instincts, and dare I say, that we humans share similar. Dogs have a deep, innate hunting instinct that includes digging as a key instrument in their toolbox of survival. Digging is not simply an action that is utilized during the pursuit of prey, but is also an effective survival attribute that assists them in search of roots and other underground foods. Additionally it can create a cool place to lie down.

All of these behaviors are built into your dog for the benefit and success of living away from their human companions, and your dog should never be considered at fault for expressing them.

Fortunately, these behaviors can be shaped, or curbed to conform to a more desirable and manageable life together. Digging dogs love to dig, and this is a tough one to train out of them, so your best intervention is to allow them a place to dig.

Early recognition of your dog's propensity towards a certain behavior will allow you to integrate specific action into your training that target and shape the behavior to your liking, while allowing your dog to express what comes naturally. Negative behaviors, such as biting, chewing, begging, and jumping are conquerable with training and focused behavioral modification, so breathe deep and relax knowing that these challenges have solutions.

Dog obedience vs. Dog Behavior

The difference between dog obedience and dog behavior is commonly defined as this. Obedience involves teaching your dog to do something, and behavior is teaching your dog not to do something. The differences lie in the goal, reward structure, and outcome. The two are of equal importance so it is necessary to understand the difference.

Dog Obedience

Obedience is the commands we teach to our dogs when we want them to quickly comply with our verbal or hand cues. Examples include the basics, of *come*, *sit*, and *stay*. Usually these are begun teaching at the time that your puppy arrives at your home, and if you enroll your puppy in classes, will continue there.

Teaching obedience sets the base for both you and your puppy to move forward. Using his name to get his attention and focus on you during training sessions establishes the first steps in human to dog communication. Training sessions are when humans begin the learning process of how to communicate using the dog's language. The dog is also simultaneously learning to speak the human language and this creates a strong lasting bond.

Dog Behavior

The difference between dog obedience and dog behavior is that behavior modification addresses and alters the psychological (mind) and physiological (bodily processes) state of the dog. In dog behavior, the goal is to identify the primary cause of an unwanted behavior. When you identify this root cause for the dog's unwanted behavior, you can begin shaping the unwanted behavior so that they do not ever engage in that behavior.

An example might be that your dog immediately takes off running when you open the car door. It does not matter if he *comes* when called, because this action can be dangerous for your dog. The issue that needs to be addressed is why he is bolting the minute the car door opens.

No matter the scale of severity, the cause needs to be identified so that the behavior can be modified. Remember it is important to identify the root causes of your dog's behavior. Knowing the root cause of behaviors will help make you a better trainer because you understand the motivation, not just the dog's action. The result is a better relationship between the two of you. Using obedience and behavior modification in tandem, results in having a well-balanced dog.

Keep in mind that this is a learning process and requires awareness of yours and your dog's actions. Study is required for the human to learn the skills and knowledge to speak canine language proficiently. Often dogs will duplicate your behavior, so using body language along with calm even energy, is crucial in your dog's success for obedience and behavioral modification.

If there are unwanted behavioral issues present that you cannot seem to find a solution, then investigate your GSDs inherent traits and identify any possible medical or environmental issues that might be present and causing these unwanted behaviors. If they are found to be present, you may need to hire a behavioral specialist to help change the emotions causing the challenging behaviors. For example, most herding breeds naturally herd children and some nip heels. In this case, the root cause is most likely their herding heritage.

I hope that you are excited to learn more about dog language and training, because it plays a large role in your dog's successful obedience training and behavioral modification. Simultaneously addressing both obedience and behavior is powerful training. Be flexible in attitude and prepare for some challenges, but enjoy the process of bonding with your dog and growing together in knowledge and understanding. The end-result will be a well-balanced dog living inside a joyful family environment.

Training Outline

Establishing yourself as the alpha immediately begins with the creation of your puppy's schedule for playtime, food, exercise, and controlling his toys along with providing love and affection. This begins on the first day that you bring your puppy home.

Simultaneously you will be doing the following, housetraining, establishing your alpha position, and socializing your puppy. After your puppy has been home for a couple of days, you can begin clicker response and training your puppy *name recognition.*

- You should have already read this guide. Begin by gradual socialization to all household members. Be patient, kind, firm, *consistent*, fair, gentle, and have fun. Allow your puppy to engage with the household members at his or her own pace.

- Always end training sessions with a win for your puppy while using cheerful upbeat tones when praising.

- *Do not forget always to use eye contact when addressing your puppy.*

- Remember that training is a lifetime commitment. After your puppy has learned a command, he will need occasional reinforcement to stay sharp and obedient.

- After your puppy knows its name, then you can move onto *sit, come, leave it, drop it* and other important commands. This training will be concurrently happening while housetraining, chew-toy training, and nipping/biting training are occurring.

- Although you will be training more than one command during your puppy's life, always train only one command per training session. Depending upon how you and your puppy are feeling you can instruct one to three short training sessions per day.

- When your dog is progressing and learning commands you can begin phasing out the treats and substituting praise, toys, and play as rewards, and then phasing out the clicker as well. The end goal is that you have an obedient dog that does not require regular praise for obeying, but every so often reward your dog so that he understands you appreciate his obedience.

• Training a puppy does not mean they are supposed to only obey one master, or alpha, they must learn to obey all commands given to them by the entire family and friend circle. In essence, when you are training, and learning to be a trainer, you also need to teach other family members and friends the correct way to issue these commands and consistently enforce the same rules that you have established.

To begin training, establish your *alpha position* from the moment you bring your new dog or puppy home. Leading as the alpha means that you are always consistent, calm, cool, and collected while consistently enforcing rules and making corrections using a firm but fair attitude. The alpha always acts as though he or she knows that they are in charge.

The best time to begin training your puppy the basics is at around six weeks to eight weeks of age. Once your puppy realizes that you control schedules, toys, mealtimes and all the things he or she cherishes, he or she will respect you as the alpha in the family hierarchy. Remember that all family members and humans are above your dog in ranking, and it should remain that way. Importantly, all family members must be consistent in enforcing the decided rules for dog behaviors, thus backing up the alpha's precedence.

Leading as the alpha assists you both in working together towards the goal of understanding the rules of conduct and obedience. Your dog will be at ease when the rules are understood. Remain in control of toys and play time so that your puppy understands that you control all good things. This is important, because if your puppy doesn't have this structure early in life, he or she will grow up thinking that they can do as they wish. No matter how wonderful and easygoing your little puppy seems now, most likely that will change with age.

Begin training all new commands indoors in the lowest distraction area. This includes silencing all of your audio-visual devices that act as distractions to dog's sensitive ears. Your puppies focus should be aimed directly upon you alone.

Gradually begin socializing your puppy from the time you bring him or her home. Proper early socialization that continues throughout your puppy's lifetime will provide you with a well-adjusted dog that is able to handle almost any situation in a calm manner. Early, thorough, and continual socialization is important for your German Shepherd. You do not want your dog being territorial and wary of strangers, so it is important to expose them early to a variety of situations, animals, people, and places. Socialization benefits you and your dog by providing you both with peace of mind. With good socialization, you can expose your German Shepherd to different situations with the assurance that he or she will look to you for guidance in rules of etiquette for the indoor and outdoor world. Socialization is the foundation for all well-adjusted dogs throughout their lifetimes.

An effective incentive is to make everything you do seem fun. Always refrain from forcing your puppy to do anything they do not want to do. Highly prized treats are usually a great incentive to do something, and you will find that a fun, pleasant, friendly, happy, vocal tone combined with the treats will be ample reward for good behaviors and command compliance. Begin training all new commands indoors. This includes silencing all of your audio-visual devices that act as distractions to dog's sensitive ears.

Training should always be an enjoyable bonding time between you and your dog. Remember that all dogs are different, and that there is no set time limit for when your dog should learn, understand,

and properly obey commands. Always have fun during training, remembering to keep your training sessions short, and stop if either of you are tired or distracted. I always suggest beginning training new tricks or commands in an area of least distraction. I promote starting with rewards based clicker training and ending with vocal and or physical cues for your dog to follow.

There exists many different ways to train puppies. Using clicker and rewards based training is an effective and humane way to train dogs. Lying ahead of you will be the task of navigating your dog's unique personality, which will affect your training and relationship. Although, you have no doubt read and watched much about training, spoken with friends and breeders, *your dog's personality is why it is imperative to keep an open mind and use your intuition to guide you while training.*

Your consent as the owner is the one thing that will allow your dog to become disobedient, out of control, and possibly a danger to your family and the outside world. Arming yourself with knowledge about dog behaviors, and understanding your own dog's personality will greatly assist you throughout the process of training and companionship alongside your dog. It is your responsibility to guide and train your dog to be a socially adjusted obedient dog so that the two of you have a fruitful trusting relationship.

Below is a list of items that you will need when training your puppy.

Tools of the Trade
- **Dog treats**
- **Dog crate**
- **Clicker**
- **Dog collar and harness**
- **Dog leash 6-foot (2meters) & Long-line 20-30 feet (6-9 meters)**
- **Treat pouch**
- **Chew-toys**
- **Treat dispensing toys**

- **Books and videos**
- **Confident mindset**
- **Sense of humor**

Please read forward and pay special attention to the chapters on *socialization and clicker-training* while you begin the adventure of dog training.

Further Training Help

Knowing what you want to train your dog to do is as important as training your dog. A puppy is a blank slate and does not know any rules, therefore it is a wise idea to make a list and have an understanding of how you would like your puppy act and be capable of performing. What are the household rules and proper dog etiquette?

As he grows, the same principle applies and you may adjust training from the basics to more specialized behaviors, such as making your dog a good travel, hiking, agility, hunting, or simply a companion dog. Know what conditions and circumstances you plan to expose your dog or puppy to outside of the household and strategize to be prepared for those encounters by slowly introducing your dog to those situations.

Training should be an enjoyable bonding time between you and your dog. Remember that there is no set time limit defining when your dog should learn, understand, and then obey commands. Use short training sessions and be aware that if either of you are tired, it is recommended that you stop and try again later. If something does not seem quite right with your dog, in any way, have him checked out by a veterinarian.

Timing is crucial when rewarding for good behaviors and making corrections for bad. *Patience and Consistency* are your allies in the training game. An easy way to avoid the onset of many different behavioral problems is to give your dog or puppy ample daily exercise to keep them fit, healthy, and destructive behavioral problems away. Always provide consistent structure, firm but fair authority, rule enforcement, and importantly, love and affection. By maintaining these things, you will help to create a loyal companion and friend. Reward good behaviors, but not just for being cute, sweet, loveable, and huggable. If you wish to reward your dog, always reward after you issue a command and your dog obeys appropriately.

Only train one command per session. Puppies only have the attention span to go about 10 minutes per session, but never exceed 15 minutes. Training a command once per day is enough for your dog to begin to learn and retain, but whenever the opportunity presents itself you should reinforce the training sessions throughout the day. For example, first command, "stay" before opening a door and be sure not to reward your dog unless your dog obeys. The most important thing to remember is to remain relaxed, keep it fun, and enjoy this time of bonding and training your dog or puppy.

We all love treats, and so does your dog. Giving your dog a treat is the best way to reinforce good behavior, and to help change his behavior. Make the treats small enough for him to get a taste, but not a meal, kernel sized. Remember, you do not want him filling up on treats as it might spoil his dinner and interfere with his attention span.

- Keep a container of treats handy with you at all times. You do not want to miss a chance to reward a good behavior or reinforce a changed behavior. Always carry treats when you go on a walk. Remember the treats your dog likes most and save those for special times.

- Ask for something before you give the treat. Tell your dog to sit, stay, or lie down, print two copies of your resume, anything, before you reward your dog with treats, petting, or play. By asking for good behavior, before you give your dog a reward, you demonstrate you are in charge, in an easy manner.

There is a common misconception that dogs are selfless and wanting to behave only to please out of respect for you. This is not the case. This line of thinking is incorrect and detrimental to your success with the training. You have to make sure that your dog knows exactly why he should be listening to you. You are the alpha, the keeper of the treats, the provider of the scratching and the purveyor of toys. Keep this balance of power and the results will be your reward.

- Be positive. Think about what you want your dog to do, instead of what you do not want him to do. Do not send mixed messages. Simply, ignore the bad behavior and reward your dog when he does the action you request to be done. Teach your dog some simple commands such as sit and *stay* to communicate the action you desire.

- Keep the training sessions short at 15 minutes maximum per session. You will be continuously training your companion, but use the formal training sessions to focus on one objective. Any session longer than 15 minutes will make it difficult for your dog to stay focused. During training, this is the attention span of most canines. Ten minutes per session is a good time limit for young puppies. Use a variety and an abundance of different treats and rewards. Rewards are play, toys, praise, affection, treats, and anything that you know that your dog enjoys.

- It is understood that your dog will be much happier if you run your dog every day. Run your dog until his tongue is hanging out. If he is still full of energy, run him again and he will love you for this. Before a training session begins, use a little exercise to release some of your dog's energy, this can increase his ability to focus during the session.

- It is very important that you make sure your dog is comfortable in all sorts of situations. All dogs, even your sweet tempered GSD, have the potential to bite. Making sure, he is comfortable in various situations and teaching your dog to be gentle with his mouth will reduce the risk of unwanted bites. Mouthing should not be acceptable behavior because it leads to worse actions.

- The notion that kids and dogs are as natural a pairing as chocolate and peanut butter is simply not true. Kids are often bitten by dogs because they unintentionally do things that frighten dogs. Sometimes a child's behavior appears like prey to a dog. Never leave a dog and a child together unsupervised, even if the dog is *good* with children. Teach children not to approach a dog that is unfamiliar to them. The way a child behaves with the familiar family dog, may not be appropriate with another dog that they meet for the first time. Instruct children that tail pulling, hugging their necks tightly, leg pulling, and hard head pats are not acceptable.

Training Your GSD

You will find that German Shepherds are intelligent quick learners highly capable of performing many tasks and commands. The keystone to training your German Shepherd will be to begin training and socialization from the moment that you acquire and bring your new dog home. Follow the steps for socialization by regularly and thoroughly performing the ongoing task of socialization and consistent training, schedules, and rule enforcement.

If you do not possess a strong will and establish yourself as the pack leader, they will not listen and comply, however they also do not respond well to harshness. Yelling and scolding will get you nowhere with your GSD, so find a firm but fair place to lead from. A natural authoritative demeanor gets the most respect from German Shepherds. They are one of the smartest dogs and must be treated with respect and natural authority; therefore, it is suggested to study canine instincts and body language. This will help you in all aspects of dog ownership.

Because of their intellect and work ethic, they are highly trainable dogs that enjoy learning and keeping busy, so the more you engage your dog the happier you will both be. You will be amazed how trainable and capable these dogs are!

GSD's are large powerful dogs, thus you will want to spend extra time on leash training, and the commands *leave it*, *come*, and *stay*, so that you have complete control of your dog; furthermore that they regularly look to you for guidance on how they should act. You must be committed to training and shaping your dog into an upstanding member of society that thoroughly understands his place in the family and society.

If you notice any negative behavioral issues, and are not quite sure if you are offering your dog proper socialization and necessary training, do not hesitate to enter your puppy into a puppy kindergarten class to assist you with training and socialization. Behavioral issues do not have to be present to enroll your dog into a puppy kindergarten; this assistance will benefit the both of you. Properly research the available classes so that their approach matches your own. The time to enroll your puppy is usually around eight to ten weeks of age, and after their first round of shots, although some kindergarten classes will not accept puppies until they are three to four months of age.

If you wish to reward your dog, always reward after you issue a command and your dog obeys the command. During your training sessions, be sure to mix it up, add a variety of toys and treats, and do not forget to have fun.

Remember to provide them with ample daily exercise to keep them fit, healthy, and to keep behavioral problems away. Provide consistent structure, firm authority, rule enforcement, love and affection, and you will have one heck of a dog for you and your family.

Socialization

To understand the importance of socialization, and why it is regularly mentioned by dog trainers, let us begin by looking at how a puppy's social development process is played out from puppy to adulthood.

Dog socialization is learning and maintaining acceptable behavior in any situation, especially when the dog or puppy does not want too. The goal is learning to handle any normal experience that occurs in life without becoming overly stimulated, fearful, reactive, or aggressive. The goal is that no matter what the circumstance; your dog is able to go with the flow, keep centered, and calm. Proper socialization of your German Shepherd is a crucial part of preparing them for the rest of their life.

Exposure to the many things we take as normal, our little puppies and adult dogs do not. Mechanical noises such as appliances, lawnmowers, car horns, blenders, coffee machines, dishwashers, stereos, televisions, and other similar items are all noises that dogs have to adjust too. Beyond mechanical noises are living creatures, which represents other household pets, neighbor's dogs, and critters in the yard such as gophers, rabbits, squirrels, birds, family members, friends, neighbors, and of course the imposing stranger.

All of these are new to most eight-week-old puppies arriving at your house. Immediate gradual introduction to these machines, noises, and living creatures begins from day one. Always be alert to your puppy's reactions and willingness to either dive forward or withdrawal, and never force him or her to interact with things they do not wish too. Proceed at their pace by presenting the interaction and then observing their willingness of participation. When strangers approach your dog do not allow them to automatically reach out and touch, leave a little space and time for your puppy's reaction to be observed, and then you can grant or deny permission based upon you and your puppy's intuition.

Socialization Summary Goals

- Learning to remain calm when the world is buzzing around them.

- Exposure in a safe manner to the environment that will encompass his or her world, including the rules and guidelines that accompany it.

- Learning to respond to signals when they do not want too. For example, in the midst of a chasing session with another puppy, or an irresistible squirrel.

The first phase of socialization begins as early as 3 weeks and lasts to approximately 12 weeks old, during this time puppies discover that they are dogs and begin to play with their littermates. Survival techniques that they will use throughout their lives, such as biting, barking, chasing, and fighting, begin to be acted out. Concurrently during this time-period, puppies experience big changes socially and physically. Learning submissive postures and taking corrections from their mother, interaction with their littermates begin to teach them about hierarchies. Keeping mother and puppies together for at least 7-8 weeks tends to increase their ability to get along well with other dogs and learn more about themselves and their actions, such as the force of a bite on their brothers and sisters.

Keep your puppy out of harm's way when he is little. During this time, he can easily pick up diseases from sniffing other dog's feces and urine. When you are first exposing your puppy to new living creatures and places, it is good practice to carry him to and from the car. Follow this practice when near any dog clinics, both inside and outside. Keeping your pup protected from contaminated ground surfaces will help keep him healthy. Until he has had his vaccines, and is a bit older, avoid areas where you suspect other dogs might have eliminated.

Between the ages of 7-12 weeks, a period of rapid learning occurs and they learn what humans are, and whether to accept them as safe. This is a crucial period, and has the *greatest impact* on *all future social behavior*.

This is the time we begin teaching puppies the acceptable rules of conduct. Take note that they have a short attention span, and physical limitations. This is the easiest period to get your puppy comfortable with new things, and the chance to thwart later behavioral issues that stem from improper or incomplete socialization. Puppies are not out of harm's way from all diseases at this time, but the risk is relatively low because of primary vaccines, good care, and mother's milk immunity. Behavioral problems are the greatest threat to the owner-dog bond and the number one cause of death to dogs under 3 years of age.

Enrolling your puppy in classes before 3 months of age is an outstanding avenue to improving socialization, training, and strengthens the bond between you and your puppy. You can begin socialization classes as early as 7-8 weeks. The recommendation is to have your puppy receive at least *one* set of vaccines, and a de-worming *seven* days prior to starting the first class.

From birth, puppies should be exposed to handling and manipulation of body parts, and exposure to different people, places, situations, well socialized animals, and more. Encourage your puppies exploring, curiosity, and investigation of different environments. Games, toys, and a variety of surfaces such as, tile, concrete, tunnels, and steps are all things to expose your puppy too and should continue into adulthood to keep your dog sociable and not shy.

It is important for your puppy to be comfortable playing, sleeping, or exploring alone. Schedule alone play with toys, and solo naps in their crate or another safe area. This teaches them to entertain themselves and not become overly attached, or have separation issues with their owners. Getting them comfortable with their crate is also beneficial for travel and to use as a safe area for your puppy to relax.

Two phases of fear imprinting occur in your growing puppy's life. *A fear period is a stage during which your puppy or dog may be more apt to perceive certain stimuli as threatening.*

During these two periods, any event your puppy thinks is traumatic can leave a lasting effect, possibly forever. The first period is from 8-11 weeks and the second is between 6-14 months of age. During these periods, you will want to keep your puppy clear of any frightening situations, but that is not always easy to determine. A chrome balloon on the floor could possibly severely frighten your little pup. There is no one size fits all in knowing what is fearful for your puppy. Becoming familiar with canine body language can help you diagnose your pups fear factor. The second period often reflects the dog becoming more reactive or apprehensive about new things. Larger breeds sometimes have an extended second period.

Keep a few things in mind when seeking play dates for socialization of your puppy. A stellar puppy class will have a safe, mature dog for the puppies to learn boundaries and other behaviors. When making play dates, puppies should be matched by personality and play styles. Games, such as retrieve or drop, help to curb possessive behaviors, as well as to help them learn to give up unsafe or off limits items, so that the item can be taken out of harm's way. Another important lesson during play is for puppies to learn to break away from playing and come back to their human. *Your dog should be willingly dependent upon you and look to you for guidance.*

Teach mature easily stimulated dogs to relax before they are permitted to socialize with others. If you have an adult dog that enjoys flying solo, do not force them into situations. Teach your dogs and puppies less aroused play and encourage passive play.

This includes play that does not encompass dominance, mouthing, or biting other puppies. If you have rough play happening between multiple dogs or puppies, then interrupt the rough housing by frequently calling them to you and rewarding their attention. The attention then is turned to you. As a distraction to dissuade mouthing contact, try to interject toys into the play. Elevated play can lead to aggression as they grow, especially breeds that can easily get to full arousal in seconds.

Proper socialization requires patience, kindness, and consistency while teaching. You and your dog should both be having fun during this process. Allow your dog to proceed into new situations at his or her own pace, never force them into a situation that they are not comfortable. If you think that your dog may have a socialization issue, seek professional advice from a qualified behavioral person.

Socializing your puppy, especially before the age of six months, is a very important step in preventing future behavioral problems. Socializing can and should continue throughout the lifetime of your dog. Socializing in a gentle and kind manner prevents aggressive, fearful, and potential behaviors that affect humans. A lack of socializing may lead to *fear*, *aggression*, *barking*, shyness, *destruction*, territorialism, or *hyperactivity*.

The earlier you begin socializing, the better. However, all puppies and dogs can gradually be brought into new and initially frightening situations, eventually learning to enjoy them. Canines can adapt to various and sometimes extreme situations, they just need your calm, guiding hand.

Expect that the socializing of your dog will be a lifelong endeavor. If your puppy does not engage with other dogs for months or years at a time, you can expect his behavior to be different when he encounters them again.

Methods that can be used when exposing your dog to something new, or something he has previously been distrustful contacting.

- Remain calm, upbeat and if he has a leash on, keep it loose.

- Gradually expose him to the new stimulus and if he is wary or fearful never use force. Let him retreat if he needs to.

- Reward your dog using treats; give him a good scratch or an energetic run for being calm and exploring new situations.

Try on a regular basis to expose your dog to the things that you would like him to be capable to cope. His gained familiarity will allow him to calmly deal with such situations in the future. Be careful of the same old-same old. Though dogs love routine, periodically expose your dog to new things. This allows you to assess his need for further socialization. You certainly wouldn't want to go on vacation to the same place every single year, so why would he.

Examples of situations that benefit the social temperament of your GSD:

- Meeting new kinds of people, including but not limited to, children, crowds, people wearing hats, disabled folks, and people in local services such as postal carriers, fire and police officers, and more. *"Introducing your puppy to a circus clown is saved for another chapter."*

- Meeting new dogs is encouraged. Because of canine diseases, be aware that you should wait at least 4 months before introducing your puppy to dog parks or places where there are groups of adult dogs. You can begin puppy socialization classes at around 7 weeks, just be sure your puppy has a round of vaccines at least a week prior. Slowly expose your dog to other pets, such as cats, horses, birds, llamas, pigs, gerbils, and monitor lizards.

- Your dog's crate is not a jail. Be sure and take the time to teach your puppy to enjoy the comfort and privacy of his own crate. You want your dog's crate to be a place that he or she feels safe.

Socialization Checklist

- To avoid doggy boredom, make sure you have plenty of toys for your dog to choose from out of the toy bin. A Nylabone®, a Kong®, dog chews, ropes, balls, and tugs are many of the popular things your dog can enjoy.

Be sure your dog is comfortable with the following:

- Human male and female adults.

- Human male and female children.

- Other household pets and dogs.

- Meeting strange dogs.

- Your house and neighborhood.

- Mechanical noises, such as lawn mowers and vehicles.

- Special circumstance people, for example, those in wheel chairs, with crutches, braces, or even strange family members.

To assure that your dog is not selfish, make sure that he or she is comfortable sharing the following:

- His food bowl, toys or bed being touched by you or others.

- The immediate space with strangers, especially with children. This is necessary for your puppy's socialization so that he does not get paranoid or freak out in small places. For example, elevators in Hollywood filled with celebrities or at the next-door neighbor's house.

- His best friend, YOU, and all family members and friends and is NOT overprotective or territorial.

For road tripping with your dog, make sure he or she is:

- Comfortable in all vehicles, such as a car, truck, minivan, or in a form of public transportation.

- Always properly restrained.

- You stop for elimination breaks and hydration.

- *Knows how to operate a stick shift as well as an automatic.*

In general, a happy puppy should have the following:

- You should provide at least 10 hours of sleep per night for your dog. This should occur in one of the household's adult bedrooms, but not in your bed. He or she should have their own bed or mat available to them.

- Regular health checks at the veterinarian are essential. He or she should receive at least the basic vaccinations, which includes rabies and distemper. Read up before agreeing on extra vaccinations and avoid unnecessary vaccinations or parasite treatments.

- Unless you are going to breed your dog, it is necessary that they be neutered or spayed.

- Maintain a proper weight for your dog. You should be able to feel his ribs but they do not stick out. He or she will have their weight checked at the vet and this will inform you on your dog's optimal weight.

- Plenty of playtimes outside with proper supervision.

- It is essential that your dog have daily long walks, play, sport, or games.

The Importance of Play

When observing dogs in a pack or family, one will notice that dogs and puppies often enjoy playing with one another. During play puppies learn proper play etiquette, such as how hard to bite or mouth, and how rough to play. His mother and littermates provide feedback for him to assist in this learning. Play is instinctual, and as an innate dog behavior, it is something that needs to be satisfied. Humans and dogs both play throughout their lifetime and many studies show that this social interaction is important for the mental and physical health of the individual.

Providing your dog with ample amounts of play through games, such as fetch, tug, or chase helps to satisfy their need for play, and assists in strengthening the bond between dog and owner. When guided in play, your dog will not only acquire the rules of play, but his physical and mental needs will be met during the activity.

One terrific bi-product of play is that it burns off dog's excess energy, and as a result, it helps keep negative behaviors from surfacing. Dogs are naturally full of energy, and they need an outlet to avoid these potential negative behaviors, which includes chewing, digging, and barking. While these behaviors serve them well in the wild, when living with humans they can be a detriment to the harmony and success of the relationship.

Separation Anxiety

What is it all about?

Separation anxiety (SA) in dogs is defined as a condition in which a dog exhibits distress and behavioral problems whenever it is separated from its handler. Generally, this behavior will surface within thirty minutes of the separation from the dog's handler.

Separation anxiety can occur not only within puppies, but it can also manifest in adult dogs. With puppies, anxiety related behaviors usually begin when they are first removed from their littermates and mother. The reasons for anxiety behaviors in adult dogs can vary, though they can also be related to the original separation from its family when they were a puppy. Other events that can be responsible for the presence of anxiety in an animal can be related to a traumatic event, such as some type of previous physical injury, mistreatment, and abandonment, all of which can be causes for anxiety related behaviors when separated from its owner.

It must be taken into consideration that some of the normal processes of aging in an animal, such as hearing and sight loss can also contribute to, or exacerbate the potential for higher levels of anxiety. It is important to be able to recognize healthy and abnormal behaviors. By recognizing the signs and symptoms of abnormal behaviors, then you can be prepared to intervene with proactive measures to reduce the negative effects.

Several of the normal behaviors that may occur for those puppies who have recently arrived into a new home can manifest in many ways. Ongoing whining, a constant want for touch or affection, and their need to shadow you wherever you go are some of the most common signs of separation anxiety. Since the puppy is experiencing a variety of new sensations in an unfamiliar environment these behaviors are normal.

The instinct to survive, will motivate a puppy to remain near to their caretaker, thus sticking close to their new provider should be a normal and expected behavior. Often, if a puppy is left alone, he or she will whine, bark, or even howl to express their discomfort from being alone. Your dog's individual personality will dictate how long these behaviors last during your absence.

It is common that your dog will find something to pacify itself in this alone time, such as gnawing upon one of his chewy toys. It is usual for these behaviors to cease after a short time, and should not be an ongoing, day and night occurrence that last regularly over thirty minutes. Yes, these sounds can be distressing to listen to, but remember that they are normal expressions while they learn to adapt to their new environment. Do not be alarmed because this is just a phase in their development, and it will soon pass.

Allowing your new puppy to remain alone for periods of time, is a necessary component of his socialization training which allows him to experience time alone and gradual exposure to mechanical noises, other humans, animals, and the exciting world of his new environment. As said prior, it is important to keep in mind that sometimes the upsetting behaviors he displays are normal but they will subside over time. Positive training in combination with consistent socialization will empower your puppy to overcome these anxieties and gain the self-confidence to develop into a well-adjusted adult dog. Training sessions work as an important component for building self-confidence and a puppy's character, but in itself is not a cure for separation anxiety.

Deeper Separation Anxiety

Identifying a puppy or adult dog that is experiencing a deeper, chronic anxiety can be detected by awareness that his separation behaviors are heightened and frequently displayed. Clinically, this would be diagnosed by a veterinarian as a chronic, pathological form of separation anxiety, and may need psychological or medical intervention. For example, extended durations of whining, barking, or crying lasting thirty minutes to an hour or more is an indication of a greater problem. In extreme cases, this heightened behavior might be intermixed with a more frantic barking, and perhaps howling or whining that may continue until your puppy becomes completely exhausted from his expressions of stress.

Other signs of anxiety can appear in an inability to remain calm or still, acting out by pacing rapidly, spinning in place, or jumping up and down sometimes in a hysterical and frantic manner. While being contained in his crate or gated area, he might tear excessively at the interior, his blankets, flooring, toys, or anything else he can get his little razor teeth, or tiny paws into. This behavior should be recognized not as a regular chewing behavior that well-adjusted dogs' display, but instead intentional destructive behavior, physically acting out his anxiety and deep-rooted distress.

Signs of *stress* also can manifest in the form of drooling, continuous panting, and frequent yawning. Loss of bladder and bowel control can lead to frequent accidents, and diarrhea and loose stools are common when an animal is stressed. Obsessive-compulsive behaviors such as excessive gnawing, licking or chewing upon his own body, including the feet need to be treated by a veterinarian.

If your dog is displaying signs of depression, anxiety, or excessive excitement each time you prepare to leave, or if his greetings are hysterical and unrestrained, and he is following you from room to room, these are indicators of separation anxiety, and need immediate attention.

If you have determined that your puppy is suffering from Separation Anxiety by his signs and symptoms, then you have to begin the important journey of teaching your puppy that not everything is bad or has a potential for lasting trauma. Instead, teach him that his new environment and the world is a nurturing place, not something to be feared, and that if you are not around, his world will not end. Treating your puppy's issues will take some time and patience and perhaps some assistance from professionals who are trained in these animal behaviors.

Preventing Separation Anxiety from developing is the best plan to undertake, first beginning in puppyhood, and then following up with your adult dog who perhaps exhibits the symptoms. Following these simple steps below should keep your puppy or full-grown dog from developing or displaying any severe behaviors and reduce the symptoms of separation anxiety.

Prevention of Separation Anxiety

• Your new pup is the cutest fur-ball of joy that you have ever seen, *right*. Heck, you picked him out of the litter and brought him home to become a member of your family. Although the desire to hold, coddle, cuddle, and fondle our pets whenever possible, may be a deep part of our human nature, it is during these times of innate urges to display a little restraint.

As difficult as I know it can be, refrain from carrying him around with you wherever you go and limit your compulsion to shower him with constant, syrupy affection. These actions, though pleasing to the both of you, can serve as the catalyst for the onset of separation anxiety. These actions create a dependency for that loving warmth that you lavish on him. If not nipped in the bud early on, this will be more difficult to curb in the future.

• Whether awake or asleep, give your little pup some space of his own. A little distance and autonomy goes a long way to help create healthy independence. Remember as you are doing this, it is neither cruel nor neglect, but in actuality this distance constitutes an essential element of the proactive measures that will help him feel secure when he is on his own.

What you want to avoid is creating a puppy that never wants to leave your side, and is in constant fear of being away from the safety, comfort and attention that you may continually bestow upon him. Although well intended, the attention that you may continually shower on him will result in having a "shadow" dog, which will neither benefit you, nor will it be healthy for him. Give him some space throughout your days together, and resist the craving to keep him with you everywhere you go.

• Begin leaving your puppy alone from the first day that you bring him home. Whether contained in his crate or restricted to his gated area, I advise that keep you keep him out of eyesight. Start the periods of separation with short durations of about 2-4 minutes each. As he begins to cope with this initial interval without freaking out and becoming agitated, then gradually, increase the extent of time that he is left alone. Leaving your pup alone should be done at least two or three times per day. During this time, it is essential to *ignore* any of his whimpering, whining, or any other form of agitation he may express. Do not confuse this exercise with neglect.

• *How to act when leaving your puppy alone.* Don't make a big deal of it when you are leaving, especially by showing exaggerated or disproportionate emotions that may in fact display your own *human separation anxiety.* This is dangerously contagious to our canine friends. Before you depart, simply make sure he is confined in an area that is of a comfortable temperature, that he has plenty of chew-toys, and fresh water. Oh! In addition, please don't forget to let the little guy relieve himself before you take off.

In the moment of your departure, use a positive tone of voice and a brief expression of farewell, using a simple phrase, such as "Goodbye, be back soon," will suffice. Stay clear of sappy, long and drawn out emotional partings. If you make a dramatic sendoff, this may become the creation of fear and concern, setting into motion a situation that may promote an elevation in the level of anxiety he will experience as you leave, thus resulting in all of the negative behaviors associated with SA.

• *Act similar upon returning.* Upon returning home, do not immediately make eye contact with your pup, or run to him as though it has been days since you have seen each other. If you have been gone for over an hour, then it is fine to go pick him up and say hello, immediately followed by a relief break. When he is finished with his business, place him back into his puppy area and return to your business. If you have only been away for a few minutes, a casual hello or quick pet will suffice, and it is not necessary to immediately make eye contact with him, or even acknowledge his existence.

• As I have covered in prior material, as part of supporting good puppy health and maintaining your alpha dominance, it is important to set a consistent schedule for feeding, playing, training, and relieving times by creating a routine of the activities for daily living.

• *Human advice.* Control your temper; he cannot help crying out for attention. If your puppy is getting upset and simply driving you crazy with his whimpering, crying, barking, or howling, remember to keep your alpha composure by being even-tempered, firm, fair, and consistent in your actions. Keep in mind that *you* are in charge and it is *you* that dictates the rules and schedules, *not your darling, adorable little sidekick.*

Troubleshooting Separation Anxiety

If you have a puppy or an adult dog that is displaying what appears to be clinical symptoms of moderate to severe separation anxiety, it is likely that professional interventions need to be sought out, followed by more advanced and focused training methods. Even though S.A. occurs in a very small percentage of domestic dogs, a dog with separation anxiety will nonetheless make life difficult for you and your family. If left untreated, this can lead to health complications and ongoing behavioral problems.

If your puppy or adult dog has a range of negative behaviors ranging from excessive destruction of property, fearfulness, barking, whimpering, whining, or anxiousness, then below are some techniques that can be used to relieve some of the symptoms. If your dog is suffering from some these behaviors, it is possible that with your proactive measures and concerted efforts your dog will be capable of displaying calmer mannerisms and an improved mental health. Reducing the effects SA is having upon your puppy will also greatly improve your mental health status.

Minor symptoms of nervousness can be handled with some simple dog training techniques.

- Remove *boredom* from your puppy's life. Supply plenty of chew-toys, at least 30- minutes of daily vigorous exercise (age appropriate), one to two daily training sessions of obedience commands, and socialization sessions.

- Exercise in the form of a brisk walk or short game of fetch before your planned absence can burn away any surplus energy reserves that if not expended can serve to trigger further anxiousness during your absence.

- While you are gone, it can be soothing to leave a low volume radio or television on to distract or comfort him. *Prior to doing this*, test it out to see if it is actually soothing rather than agitating your puppy.

- Occupy alone time with stuffed chew-toys. These toys can be stuffed in such a way that make it a time consuming project for him to extract the food, thus keeping him distracted for long periods of time. The nice thing about these chew toys is that it is impossible to bark, whine, or cry while chewing them.

Moderate symptoms will appear as more severe than the features of minor nervousness, and needs to be tackled with more intensive behavioral modification techniques that will require daily practice through focused dog training that can take weeks or months to solve the issue.

- First, increase the daily exercise routine keeping within the recommended limits of your Koolie puppy. Take care to make sure your little pup does not over-heat, and if he is an extra-large breed be careful that he is not jumping or doing anything that may injure his growing bones.

Begin multiple daily rigorous exercise regimens that utilize games, brisk walks, and if possible, fit in 2-3 outings of fetch games. If your dog refuses to play fetch, then substitute some other type of play or exercise that will increase his heart rate and use up some of his energy reserves. Try for a minimum of two 30-minute activity based periods per day.

- Two daily short 10-minute training sessions of the basic commands, followed by teaching down-stay or sit-stay is advised. The commands of sit-stay and down-stay are great in creating confidence in your dog so that he can be left alone by teaching him to accept distance between the two of you in different places, and at different times.

- Another great option is that when your puppy is old enough, and had at least his first round of shots, is to enroll him into a puppy kindergarten class. This will increase his socialization skills, and build confidence under the guidance of a trained professional. These classes also instruct humans on how to train and interact with their puppies.

• If you have a dog that we refer to as a "Shadow dog," which means a dog that refuses to leave your side, then it is essential that you work on gradually increasing the space between the two of you. This is easy to do by using his crate or gated area as his isolation areas, and progressively increasing the duration that you are separated.

Beginning with short durations of time apart or when you notice a pause in his fretting is the time you should free him from his confines. When you free him from his confines, be sure not to make a big deal about it, act as if it is just a normal daily routine. Take special care and make appropriate adjustments if your dog is still displaying destructive behaviors or becoming extremely agitated in his isolation areas, especially in his crate. If this is the case, do not use his crate for this particular training. We want our puppies to love their crates and find them a safe haven.

Desensitizing your puppy to your absence is another way to help him through the miseries of his separation anxiety. Sometimes the simplest action, such as grabbing your jacket, bag or the sounds of keys clanging can be a stimulus for your puppy to begin feeling anxious in anticipation of your absence.

• To begin to desensitize your puppy to your departures, start by acting out the preparations to leave, but not actually leaving the house. Go through the motions, such as grabbing your house keys, or briefcase, but instead of leaving, just walk around the house for a couple of minutes carrying your things, afterward put your things away.

Practice this three to five times a day until your dog ceases showing signs of agitation or nervousness during your *faux departure* preparations. The success of this training varies in duration from dog to dog. Depending upon your dog and his predisposition, this training could take a day, a couple of days, a week, or even longer.

- The next step is to repeat the step above, but now leave the premises. Begin by leaving for only a few seconds and then returning indoors. During this training, gradually increase the time that you wait outside of your house before returning inside. The key here is never to make a big deal of leaving or coming home, just act as if it is an event not worthy of attention or emotion. Simply grab your things and leave. Continue this training until your dog becomes less and less disturbed by this whole affair of you coming and going.

- Upon returning home after a lengthy leave, walk inside and immediately tend to your normal life, ignoring your dog for at least five to ten minutes. After this duration, or when you are ready to show attention and affection, then go to your dog and give him the love he deserves.

How to lessen your dog's symptoms when you are going to leave

1. Take your pup for a quick fast-paced walk or vigorous exercise session.

2. If this has proved to be soothing and not agitating, turn on the radio or television to lessen the loneliness.

3. Leave plenty of toys to keep him busy.

4. When you leave, leave quickly without emotional outpourings towards your dog.

Extra Helpings for Separation Anxiety Training

1. Hire a pet sitter or dog walker to visit at least once during the day.

2. Ask your neighbors how your dog is acting while you are away.

3. Once or twice a week, drop your dog at a doggie day-care facility.

4. If the dog training tips within this guide do not seem to work for you, solicit outside help from a professional trainer and speak with your veterinarian.

5. As a last resort, after trying all of the suggestions above, there are medications available to help calm your dog. I recommend that this is a temporary solution, as a part of a holistic therapy, *while you continue* to shape and change your dog's behavior using the methods and techniques described. If choose to use medication, research for the safest natural product on the market, or rely on the advice of your dog's vet.

6. Avoid leaving your dog crated for long periods.

7. Avoid punishments for SA related accidents or incidents. Remember that because of the deep-seated nature of his problem, a dog with SA is not in control of himself. For example, as demonstrated by soiling issues related to his anxieties.

The goal and final outcome of this training is to have a healthy, happy, well-adjusted dog that can handle any situation that comes his way. As previously mentioned, prevention of Separation Anxiety can afford you the peace of mind knowing that you will not have to go through this rigorous training, as well as never having to deal with the aggravation of incessant whimpering, barking, gnawing, tearing, and other doggie anxiety actions that will negatively affect you, your family, visiting friends and your neighbors. Some statistics indicate that only about 10-15% of the population of domestic dogs become afflicted with some degree of separation anxiety.

Handling Your German Shepherd

Teaching your GSD to be still, calm, and patient while he is being handled is a very important step in your relationship. When you master this one, it will make life easier for both of you when at home, and at the groomer or vet. Handling also helps when there is unwanted or accidental touching and especially when dealing with small children who love to handle dogs in all sorts of unusual and not so regular ways. This one will take patience and a few tricks to get started. Remember, that it is important to begin handling your new puppy immediately after you find each other and are living together.

The sooner your puppy accepts your touches and manipulations the easier life will be for the both of you. Handling is needed for grooming, bathing, lifting, affection, inspecting for ticks, fleas, and injuries.

Recognize that muzzles are not bad and do not hurt dogs. They can be an effective device and a great safety feature when your dog is learning to be handled. Easy cheese or peanut butter spread on the floor or on the refrigerator door can keep your puppy in place while he learns to be handled. If your puppy does not like to be handled, he will slowly learn to accept it.

You must practice this with your puppy for at least one to three minutes each day so that he becomes comfortable with being touched. All dogs are unique and therefore some will accept this easier and quicker than others will. Handling training will be a life-long process.

With all of the following exercises, follow these steps:

- Begin with short, non-intrusive gentle touching. *If your puppy is calm* and he is not trying to squirm away, use a word such as "good," "nice," or "yes," and give your pup a treat.

- If your puppy squirms, keep touching him but do not fight his movements, keeping your hand lightly on him while moving your hand with his squirms. Use your hand as though it were a suction cup and stuck to the place that you are touching. When he settles, treat him and remove your hand.

- Work from one second to ten seconds or more, gradually working your way up to touching for longer durations, such as 2,4,6,8 to 10 seconds.

- Do not go forward to another step until your puppy adapts, and enjoys the current step.

- *Do not* work these exercises more than a couple of minutes at a time. Overstimulation can cause your puppy stress. Continue slowly at your puppy's comfortable speed.

Handling the Body Parts

Paws

It is a fact that most puppies do not like to have their paws touched. Proceed slowly with this exercise. The eventual goal is for your puppy to adore his paws being fondled. In the following exercises, any time your puppy does not squirm and try to get away, *click and treat* your pup. If he does squirm, stay with him using gentle contact, when your pup ceases wiggling, then *click and treat*, and release when he calms down. Each one of these steps will take a few days to complete and will require at least a dozen repetitions.

Confirm that you successfully complete each step and your puppy is at least tolerant of the contact before you go on to the next one.

- *Do each step with all four paws, and remember to pause a minute between paws, allowing your pup to regain his composure.*

- Pick up your puppy's paw and immediately click and treat. Repeat this five times and then continue forward by adding an additional one second each time you pick up his paw until ten seconds is reached.

Hold the paw for ten to twelve seconds with no struggling from your dog. Begin with two seconds then in different sessions work your way to twelve.

During holding the paw, begin adding the following.

- Hold the paw and move it around.

- Massage the paw.

- Pretend to trim the nails.

Side Note: Do not trim your dog's nails unless you are positively sure you know what you are doing. It is not easy and if you are not properly trained can cause extreme pain to your dog.

The Collar

Find a quiet, low distraction place to practice, grab treats, and put your puppy's collar on him.

- While gently restrained, touch your dog's collar underneath his chin, and then release him right away simultaneously clicking and treating him. Do this about ten times or until your puppy seems comfortable and relaxed with the process.

- Grab and hold the collar where it is under his chin and hold it for about 2 seconds, C/T, and repeat. Increase the amount of time until you have achieved about ten seconds of holding and your puppy remains calm. Click and treat after each elapsed amount of time. By increasing the hold time by 2 seconds, gradually work your way up to ten seconds of holding. This may take several days and sessions.

- Hold the collar under his chin and now give it a little tug. If he accepts this and does not resist, click and treat, and repeat. If he squirms, keep a gentle hold on the collar until he calms down, and then C/T and release him. Repeat this step until he is content with the procedure.

Now, switch to the top of the collar and repeat the whole progression again. Remember slowly increase the time held and the intensity of the tug.

You can pull or tug, but *do not jerk* your puppy's neck or head because this can cause injury and interfere with your outcome objectives of the training exercise. You can practice touching the collar while you are treating during training other tricks. Gently hold the bottom or top of the collar when you are giving your dog a treat reward for successfully completing a commanded behavior.

Mouth

- Gently touch your puppy's mouth, *click and treat*, and repeat ten times.

- Touch the side of your puppy's mouth and lift a lip to expose a tooth, *click and treat*, then release only after he stops resisting.

- Gently and slowly, lift the lip to expose more and more teeth on both sides of the mouth, and then open the mouth. Then release when he does not resist, *click and treat*. Be cautious with this one.

- Touch a tooth with a toothbrush, then work up to brushing your puppy's teeth for one to ten-seconds, and then later increase the time. Brushing your puppy's teeth is something you will be doing a few times weekly for the lifetime of your dog.

Ears

- Reach around the side of your puppy's head, and then briefly and gently touch his ear. Click and treat, repeat ten times.

- When your puppy is comfortable with this, continue and practice holding the ear for one-second. If he is calm, click and treat. If he squirms, stay with him until he is calm. When your puppy calms down, click and treat, then release the ear. Do this until ten seconds is completed with no wiggling.

- Maneuver your pup's ear and pretend that you are cleaning it. Do this gently and slowly so that your puppy learns to enjoy it. It will take a few days of practice until your puppy is calm enough for the real ear cleaning. If your puppy is already sensitive about his ears being touched, it will take longer. See ear cleaning in the Basic Care section.

Proceed slowly at your puppy's comfortable pace. There is no rush just the end goal of your pup enjoying being handled in all sorts of ways that are beneficial to him.

Tail

Many puppies are sensitive about having their tails handled, and rightly so. Think about if someone grabs you by the arm and you are not fully ready. That is similar to the reaction a puppy feels when grabbed, especially when their tails are handled.

- Start by briefly touching his tail. When moving to touch your puppy's tail move slowly and let your hand be seen moving towards his tail. This keeps your puppy from being startled. Repeat this ten times with clicking and treating, until you notice your puppy is comfortable with his tail being touched.

- Increase the duration of time you hold his tail until you achieve the ten-second mark.

- Tenderly and cautiously, pull the tail up, brush the tail, and then tenderly pull on it until your dog allows you to do this without reacting by jerking, wiggling, or whimpering.

Children

You must prepare your poor puppy to deal with the strange, unwelcome touching that is often exacted on them by children. Alternatively, you could just put a sign around his neck that says;

"You must be at least 16 to touch this puppy." However, it is very likely that your puppy will encounter children that are touchy, grabby, or pokey.

- Prepare your puppy for the strange touches that children may perpetrate by practicing while clicking and treating him for accepting these odd bits of contact such as ear tugs, tail tugs, and perhaps a little harder than usual head pats, kisses, and hugs. Keep in mind, as previously mentioned, puppies and kids are not a natural pairing, *but cheese and wine are*. Even a puppy that is *good with kids* can be pushed to a breaking point and then things can get ugly, and nobody wants that.

Always supervise children around your dog. ALWAYS! – It is a dog ownership law.

Lifting Dogs

An emergency may arise that requires you to pick up your dog. As you do these maneuvers, move and proceed slowly and cautiously. First, briefly put your arms around your dog and then give him a click and treat if he stays still. Increase the time duration with successive repetitions. Your dog should be comfortable for ten to fifteen seconds with your arms around him. Next, slowly proceed lifting your dog off the ground just a few inches or centimeters, and then back down. Each time he does not wriggle, click and treat. Increase the time and the distance that you lift him from the ground and then move your dog from one place to another. Calculate the time it might take to lift and carry your dog from the house and place him into your vehicle. This is a good time goal to set for carrying your dog.

Eventually, by lifting your dog up and placing him on a table, you will be able to prepare your dog for trips to the groomer, open spaces, or the vet. If you own an extra-large dog, or dog that is too heavy for you to lift, solicit help for this training from family or a friend. *Giant dogs* may take two to lift safely and properly, or use one of the methods below.

Once up on the table you can practice handling in ways a groomer or veterinarian might handle your dog. This is good preparation for a day at the dog spa or veterinary procedures.

How to lift a dog

To lift a large dog properly, always start by approaching the dog from the side. Place one of your hands upon the dog's rear end with the tail in the down position, unless it is a curly tailed Spitz type dog that will not enjoy having its tail forced down. This protects the dog's tail from being forced painfully upwards should your arm slip.

You should be holding your dog directly underneath the dog's rear hips. Your other hand should be in the front of the dog around his front legs with your arm across his chest. Now your arms should be on your dog's chest and butt area. Then gently press your arms together as in a cradling position and lift using your legs. The human's body position should be that of having bent legs and crouching down so that the power in the legs is used to lift you and your dog upright. To prevent injury to yourself, keep your back as straight as possible.

Small dogs are simpler to lift and require much less effort, but still take great care not to inadvertently injure them. Place your hand in between the back and front legs underneath the dog's underbelly. Supporting the rear with your forearm, additionally placing a hand on the dog's chest is a good idea for safety in the event that your dog squirms when being lifted.

For extra-large or dogs that are too heavy for you to lift, purchase and utilize a ramp so that your dog can walk itself into your vehicle. This saves you and your dog from possible or inevitable injury. It is always best to use caution instead of risking a painful, costly, or permanent injury. Of course, you can also teach your dog to jump into the vehicle. Later when your dog becomes aged, you can then utilize the ramp.

Some large dogs can be taught to put their front paws up onto the vehicle floorboard or tailgate, thus allowing you to help push them from their buttocks and assist them jumping in your vehicle.

Never grab, pull, or lift a dog by its fore or rear legs. This can cause serious pain and injury to a dog.

Brushing

- Get your puppy's brush and lightly touch him with it all over his body. If he remains unmoving, give him a click and treat, then repeat. Repeat this until you can brush every part of his body without him moving.

Your puppy will become comfortable with all varieties of touching and handling if you work slowly, patiently, and with plenty of good treats. Handling training is a very important step in your dog's socialization.

Clicker Training

Why and How Clicker Training Works

The important reason I put this information together is that it is essential to understand why timing and consistency is important, and why clicker training works. If any of this is confusing, do not worry, because I walk you through the training process, step-by-step.

Clicker training started over seventy years ago and has become a tried and true method for training dogs and other animals. The outcome of using a clicker is an example of conditioned reinforcement. Rewarding the animal in combination with clicker use has proven highly effective as a positive reinforcement training method. It is a humane and effective way of training dogs without instilling fear for non-compliance. I know that my mother wished she would have known about clicker training when my brother and I were growing up. I am sure she would have put the clicker into action so my brother would place his dirty clothes inside the bin, rather than on the floor.

In the 1950s, Keller Breland, a pioneer in animal training, used a clicker while training many different species of animals, including marine mammals. He met great success using this method of training on these animals. His system developed for clicker training marine mammals is still in use today. Keller also trained dogs using the clicker. Because of its effectiveness, it was brought into use by others in the dog training community. Gradually, clicker training for dogs gained more and more popularity and by the early 1980's its use became widespread. The success of the clicker spans 7 decades and now is a widely accepted standard for dog training.

A trainer will use the clicker to mark desired actions as they occur. At the exact instant, the animal performs the desired action, the trainer clicks and promptly delivers a food reward or other reinforcements. One key to clicker training is the trainer's timing, as *timing is crucial.* For example, clicking and rewarding slightly too early or too late will reinforce the action that is occurring at that very instant rather than the action you were targeting the reward for. The saying goes, "you get what you click for."

Clicker trainers often use the process of *shaping*. Shaping is the process of gradual transformation of a specific action into the desired action by rewarding each successive progression towards the desired action. This is done by gradually molding or training the dog to perform a specific response by first, reinforcing the small, successive responses that are similar to the desired response, instead of waiting for the perfect completion to occur. The trainer looks for small progressions that are heading in the direction towards the total completion of the desired action and then clicks and treats. It is important to recognize and reward those tiny steps made in the target direction. During training, the objective is to create opportunities for your dog to earn frequent rewards. In the beginning, it is acceptable to increase the frequency of a C/T to every 3-4 seconds, or less. By gauging the dog's abilities and improvements, the trainer can gradually increase the length of time between C/T. It is necessary to assess the dog's progress from moment to moment, adjusting C/T to achieve the desired actionable outcome.

During training, and in conjunction with clicker use, the introduction of a cue word or hand signal can be applied. Eventually, the clicker can be phased out in favor of a cue or cues that have been reinforced during the training sessions. As a result, your dog will immediately respond by reacting, obeying, and performing actions to your hand gestures or verbal commands. Watching this unfold is a highly satisfying process, which empowers your friend to be the best he can, and while you have fulfilled your role as *alpha* and pack leader.

Why is clicking effective over using a word cue first?

The clicking sound is a unique sound that is not found in nature, and it is more precise than a verbal command. Verbal commands can be confusing because the human voice has many tonal variations, whereas the clicker consistently makes a sound that your dog will not confuse with any other noise. It is also effective because it is directed at him and followed by good things. Therefore, your dog completely understands which action is desired and your dog will quickly understand that the click is followed by a reward.

The clicker sound is produced in a quick and accurate way that is in response to the slightest actions that your dog makes. This clarity of function of this tool increases the bond between you and your dog, as a result making your dog more interested in the training sessions, and ultimately your relationship more engaging and entertaining. Dare I say fun? On that note, do not forget to always have fun and add variety to your training sessions. Variety is the spice of life, mix up those treats, rewards, and commands.

Clicker training works this way

At the *exact* instant the action occurs, the trainer clicks. If a dog begins to *sit*, the trainer recognizes that, and *at the exact moment the dog's buttocks hits the ground the trainer clicks and offers the dog a reward*. Usually the reward is a small kernel sized food treat, but a reward can be a toy, play, or affection. Whatever the dog enjoys is a reward worth giving.

In as soon as 2-3 clicks have been issued a dog will associate the sound of the click with something it enjoys. Once the association is made, it will repeat the action it did when hearing the click. Click = Reward. When this goes off in the dog's head, repeating the action makes sense.

The three steps are as follows:

1. *Get the action* you request

2. *Mark the action* with your clicker

3. *Reinforce the action* with a reward

How do you ask for actions when clicker training your dog?

During clicker training before adding a cue command such as "stay," you wait until your dog completely understands the action. A cue is the name of the action or it can be a hand signal that you are using when you ask your dog to perform a specific action. Your dog should know the action *stay* from the click and reward before you verbally name it. *He or she has connected being still to receiving a click and reward.*

When training you do not want to add the *cue* until your dog has been clicked 5-10 times for the action, and is accurately responding in a manner that clearly shows he understands which action earns the click and reward. This is called introducing the cue.

Teaching your dog the name of the cue or action requires saying or signaling before your dog repeats the action. After several repetitions, begin to click and reward when your dog performs the action, be sure the cue is given before the reward. Your dog will learn to listen and watch for the cue, knowing that if he does the action a reward will follow.

Clicker Training Help

If your dog is not obeying the cue, answer the following questions and then revise your training process so that your dog knows the meaning of the clicker sound cue during all situations. Importantly, be sure that your dog is and feels rewarded for doing the correct action.

Trainers never assume the dog is intentionally disobeying without asking the questions below.

1. Does your dog understand the meaning of the cue?

2. Does your dog understand the meaning of the cue in the situation first taught, but *not* in the different situations that you gave the cue?

3. Is the *reward* for doing the action you want, satisfying your dog's needs? Is the treat or toy worth the effort?

Once you have answered these questions, change your training process to be certain that your dog understands the clicker/cue in all situations, including high distraction situations such as at a busy park. Then be sure your dog is adequately rewarded and that it is clear your dog feels that he or she has been properly rewarded. This will help put you two back on the path of mutual understanding during your training sessions.

When starting to train a new command ease into it by practicing a couple of repetitions of a command that your dog already knows. This establishes a training session and gains your dog's attention. Try to end all training sessions with success, either by ending with a previously learned command or a successful action of the current command being taught. Ending training sessions on high notes keeps your dog's mind positive. Play or free time after each training session further enforces that training is something they should look forward too.

Clicker Training Questions

A clicker is a small device that makes a sound that is easily distinguished and not common as a sound in nature, or one that humans normally produce. This unique sound keeps the dog that is being trained from becoming confused by accidently hearing a word used in conversation or another environmental noise. You click at the exact time when your dog does the correct action then immediately follow the click with a treat or reward.

The clicker is used to inform your dog that he did the right thing and that a treat is coming. When your dog does the right thing after you command, like drop your Chanel purse that is dangling from his mouth, you click and reward him with a nice treat. Using the clicker system allows you to set your puppy up to succeed while you ignore or make efforts to prevent bad behavior. It is a very positive, humane system, and punishment is *not* part of the process.

Here are some questions often asked about the clicker training:

- "Do you need to have the clicker on your person at all times?" *No*. The clicker is a teaching device. Once your dog understands what you want your dog to do, you can then utilize a verbal or hand cue, and if inclined verbal praise or affection.

- "Can rewards be other things besides treats?" *Sure*. Actually, you should mix it up. Use the clicker and a treat when you first start teaching. When your puppy has learned the behavior you want, then switch to other rewards, such as, petting, play, toys, or lottery tickets. Remember always to ask for the wanted target behavior, such as, *sit*, *stay*, or *come*, before you reward your dog. These verbal reinforcements can augment the clicker training and reward giving.

- "With all these treats, isn't my dog going to get fat?" *No*. If you figure treats into your dog's daily intake and subtract from meals accordingly, your dog will be fine. The treats should be as small as a corn kernel, just a taste. Use food from his regular meals when you are training indoors, but when outdoors, use fresh treats like meat or cheese. There are many distractions outside and a tasty fresh treat will help keep your puppy's attention. Dog's finally honed senses will smell even the smallest of treat, and this keeps them attentive. -"What do I do if my dog doesn't act out the command?" *Simpl*e, if your dog disobeys you, it is because he has not been properly trained yet. Do not C/T (Click and Treat), or verbally praise for any wrong actions, ignore the wrong action. Continue training because your dog has not yet learned the command and action you are teaching him to perform. He, after all, is just a dog. If he is

90

disobeying, he has been improperly or incompletely trained, maybe the treats are not tasty enough. Try simplifying the task and attempt to make the reward equal to, or better than what is distracting your dog. Eventually your dog will understand what action should be performed when the command word is spoken.

Help

- *Conceal the treat! Do NOT* show your dog the treat before pressing the clicker and making the clicking sound. If you do this, he will be responding to the treat and not the click and this will *undermine* your training strategy.

Solutions for Unwanted Behaviors

Proactive Measures

Everyone likes his or her own space to feel comfortable, familiar, and safe. Your dog is no different. A proper living area is a key factor to avoiding all kinds of potential problems. Think of all the things your puppy will encounter in his life with humans, such as appliances and mechanical noises that are not common in nature, and can be frightening to your dog. It is essential to use treats, toys, and praise to assist you and your dog while in the midst of training and socializing.

Dogs are social creatures and it is essential to communicate with them. Communication is always the key to behavior reinforcement. Showing your dog that calm behavior is frequently rewarded, and that you have control over his favorite things, acts as a pathway to solving problems that may arise down the road.

Keep your dog's world happy. Make sure he is getting a proper amount of exercise and that he is being challenged mentally. Make sure he is getting enough time in the company of other dogs and other people. Keep a close eye on his diet, offering him good, healthy, dog-appropriate foods. Avoid excessive helpings when treating.

It is important that you be a strong leader. Dogs are pack animals and your dog needs to know that you are the *alpha*. Do not let situations fall into questionable scenarios that your dog is uncertain about who is in charge. Your puppy will feel confident and strong if he works for his rewards and knows that he or she has a strong, confident leader to follow. Let your dog show you good behavior before you provide rewards. With a little work from him, he will appreciate it more.

Your dog's first step towards overcoming the challenges in life is in understanding what motivates his own behavior. Some behaviors your dog will exhibit are instinctual. Chewing, barking, digging, jumping, chasing, digging, and leash pulling are things that all dogs do because it is in their genetic make-up. These natural behaviors differ from the ones we have inadvertently trained into the domestic canine. Behaviors such as nudging our hands asking to be petted, or barking for attention, are actually accidently reinforced by us humans and not innate.

What motivates your dog to do what he does or does not do? You may wonder why he does not come when you call him while he is playing with other dogs. Simply, this may be because coming to you is far less exciting than scrapping with the same species. When calling your dog you can change this behavior by offering him a highly coveted treat and after treating, allow him to continue playing for a while. Start this training aspect slowly, and in short distances from where he is playing. Gradually increase the distances and distractions when you beckon your dog. After he is coming regularly to you then begin to diminish the frequency of treating, and supplement verbal or physical praise.

Here are some helpful tips to use when trying to help your GSD through challenging behavior.

- Are you accidentally rewarding bad behavior? Remember that your dog may see any response from you as a reward. You can ignore the misbehavior if you are patient enough, or you can give your puppy the equivalent of a human *time out* for a few minutes. Make sure the time out environment is in a calm, quiet and safe, but very dull place that is not his crate.

- Think about the quality of his diet and health. Is your dog getting enough playtime, mental and physical exercise, and sleep? Is this a medical problem? Do not ignore the range of possibilities that could be eliciting your dog's challenging behavior.

- Be sure and practice replacement behavior. Reward him with something that is much more appealing than the perceived reward that he is getting when he is acting in an undesirable manner. It is important to reward his good behavior before he misbehaves. If done consistently and correctly, this will reinforce good behaviors, and reduce poor behaviors.

For example, in the hopes of receiving love, your dog is repeatedly nudging your hand; teach him to *sit* instead by only giving him love after he sits, and never if he nudges you. If you command, "sit" and he complies, and then you pat him on the head or speak nicely to him, or both, your dog will associate the sitting compliance with nice things. If he nudges and you turn away and never acknowledge him he will understand that behavior is not associated with nice things. In a scenario where your dog is continually nudging you for attention, catch him before he comes running into your room and begins nudging. When you see him approaching, immediately say, "sit" to stop him in his tracks.

- While practicing the replacement behavior, be sure you reward the right response and ignore the mistakes. Remember, any response to the wrong action could be mistaken as a reward by your dog, so try to remain neutral in a state of ignoring, this includes, sight, touch and verbal acknowledgement. Be sure to offer your dog a greater reward for the correct action than the joy he is getting from doing the wrong action.

- Your dog's bad behavior may be caused by something that causes him fear. If you decipher this as the problem, then change his mind about what he perceives frightening. Pair the scary thing with something he loves. For example, your dog has a problem with the mail carrier. Pair the carrier's visit with a delicious treat and lots of attention. He will soon look forward to the daily arrival of the mail carrier.

- Always, remain patient with your dog and do not force changes. Work gradually and slowly. Forcing behavioral changes on your dog may lead to making the behaviors worse. Training requires that you work as hard as your dog, and maybe harder, because you have to hone your observational skills, intuition, timing, patience, laughter, and the understanding of your dog's body language and demeanor.

Reward vs. Punishment

Impartiality - *Be fair with rule enforcement, avoid harsh vocal tones and never use physical aggression towards your dog.*

It is always better to reward your GSD instead of punishing him or her. Here are a few reasons why.

- If you punish your dog, it can make him distrust, or cause fear, aggression, and avoidance of you. If you rub your dog's nose his feces or pee, he may avoid going to the bathroom in front of you.

- Physical punishment has the tendency to escalate in severity. If you get your dog's attention by a light tap on the nose, he will soon get used to that and ignore it. Shortly the contact will become more and more violent. As we know, violence is *not* the answer.

- Punishing your dog has bad side effects. For example, if you are using a pinch collar, it may tighten when he encounters other dogs. Dogs are very smart, but they are not always logical. When your dog encounters another dog, the pinching of the collar may lead him to think that the other dog is the reason for the pinch. *Pinch collars have been linked to the reinforcement of aggressive behaviors between dogs.*

- Electric fences will make him avoid the yard.

- Choke collars can cause injuries to a dog's throat as well as cause back and neck misalignment.

- You may inadvertently develop and adversarial relationship with your dog if you punish your dog instead of working through a reward system and correctly leading. If you only look for the mistakes within your dog, this is all you will begin to see. In your mind, you will see a problem dog. In your dog's mind, he will see anger and distrust.

- You ultimately want to shape your dog's incorrect actions into acceptable actions. By punishing your dog, he will learn only to *avoid* punishment. He is not learning to change the behavior you want changed, instead he learns to be sneaky or to do the very minimum to avoid being punished. Your dog can become withdrawn and seemingly inactive. Permanent psychological damage can be done if a dog lives in fear of punishment.

- If you punish rather than reward neither you nor your dog will be having a very good time. It will be a constant, sometimes painful struggle. If you have children, they will not be able to participate in a punishment based training process because it is too difficult, and truly no fun.

- If you train your dog using rewards, you and your dog will have a healthier time and relationship. Rely on rewards to change his behavior by using treats, toys, playing, petting, affection, or anything else you know your dog likes. If your dog is doing something that you do not like, replace the habit with another by teaching your dog to do something different, and then reward him or her for doing the replacement action, and then you can all enjoy the outcome.

For example, your dog is barking, and you command, "sit," he complies, you reward with his favorite tug. This successfully took his mind off the barking, and he was rewarded for sitting, thus you replaced barking with sitting.

Alpha Dog's

Resolve - *Becoming and remaining the alpha in the family is the time your determination will pay its first dividends. Your confidence and firmness in decision-making will impress your puppy. After establishing this coveted spot, then every rule enforcement and command must be made using resolve without aggression.*

Importance of Leading by Being the Alpha Dog

Having the respect from the entire pack and remaining unchallenged as to who is the leader of the pack, is the goal for all dog trainers and owners. Although evidence exists that today's dogs are far removed from wolves, wild dogs still respect an alpha leader to follow. The *alpha* wields absolute power. The facts are that dogs thrive under structure and understanding of rules. If they know that their needs are being met by their alpha leader, they are more relaxed and at ease.

Alpha dogs possess poise, confidence, bravery, intelligence, and self- control. Additionally they tend to be affectionate, making them very good pets. An alpha does not have to be overly strong, savage, or large to be in the power seat. To personify an alpha's attributes, they tend to hold a keen mental fortitude made up of a combination of wisdom, intelligence and charisma, or some combination thereof that makes them good leaders, and allows them to dominate.

Dogs are still the only species that have allowed humans to dominate them. Dogs willingly live with humans and assist them with their lives. We have all heard the saying, "man's best friend" since we were children, and of course they are also "women's best friend." This saying truly fits dogs, as they are intelligent enough to take our orders but can also discern if you deserve their respect as the alpha of the pack.

Many breeds will absolutely challenge humans as alpha. If you pay attention, you will notice that in every family there is one member above all others that the family dog respects. That person is the *alpha*.

Being the alpha keeps you in charge and respected. This allows living with your dog to be an easier and healthier arrangement. Knowing that your dog will listen when necessary, and obey your commands, makes life together less challenging and more rewarding.

Unfortunately, many dog owners abandon their dogs. Complaints are many and vary widely, but common complaints are that their dog is "untrainable" and that "My dog will not obey commands." What these dog owners do not realize is that you have to show dogs that you deserve the respect, loyalty, and obedience from them. For the entire population of those seemingly non-trainable, hyperactive, house destroying dogs, there is an owner who was unable to achieve the alpha position and be the leader of the pack.

Dogs need a leader to follow so they can be taught acceptable social behaviors. They are innocent to knowing what behaviors are acceptable until they are taught. Without a leader, they have no direction and act out their own desires. If they do this and are not disciplined they end up with anti-social behavior. Dogs that will be living alongside humans must have an owner capable to be the pack-leading alpha they want to follow.

Being the Alpha

Inside your family unit, an *alpha* needs to be chosen to lead your dog and the entire family needs to support this family member in his or her alpha role. In order for your dog to obey and become social, a family member needs to be the alpha your dog admires. An alpha needs to be confident, intelligent, and charismatic for commanding respect. For this reason, the other family members must never undermine the alpha rules for acceptable dog behavior.

In a sense, the rest of the family needs to act as though they are in your pack and follow your lead in any dog related activities. *This will establish all humans above your dog in the pecking order.* The other members of the family (think pack), as well as visiting friends and family, will help to reinforce and establish acceptable dog protocol.

The alpha is the top dog and his word needs to be the final word. This essential concept cannot be emphasized enough. The alpha needs to be above all others in the house. He or she should still show affection towards their dog. The leader *does not* need to be mean or physically abusive. The pack boss makes rules and is first in everything. It is understood that these rules are final.

It should be made clear that the alpha will eat first, drink first, walk through doors first, leads on walks, and so forth. These same rules should be adhered by the entire family and all visiting friends, therefore establishing all humans above dogs.

Human's private spaces, such as beds and sofas are not for dogs. Dogs should be taught what spaces and locations are off limits to them. Certainly, you do not want your dog inside your closet.

Start by being a loving alpha and always come from a place of love. Know yourself and your dog. Dogs are smart and you must prove that you are at a level above them and deserve their respect. Begin by learning the things that your dog does and does not like, their body language, fears, and what makes them happy. Be consistent with reprimands and love. *Good timing* will keep your dog from getting confused as to which behavior is being disciplined, or rewarded. Timing is crucial in dog training.

Being the alpha leader means that you are in control and you maintain this control through the power of your mental abilities, and *not from your physical responses*. You are there to gently, but firmly lead your dog into the correct direction by shaping his behavior. Whether it is in obedience training or socialization, vigilant and thoughtful leadership will eventually create a pleasant life together as your dog's leader and friend.

Essentially the alpha dog remains calm, consistent, even-tempered, fun loving, and firm but fair throughout training and rule enforcement, while always delivering commands and corrections with the energy of confident authority. Additionally he or she shows love, affection, and reliability towards their dog, all of these combined, gains and keeps the respect of the owner's dog, allowing for a lifetime of joyful harmonious living.

Dog Language

Those upright ears - *Sound frequency is measured in Hertz (Hz), the higher the Hz number, the higher the frequency. GSD's can hear noises at four times the distance that a human can. Humans hear best at around 20 Hz to 20,000 Hz, but GSD's hear best at 45,000 Hz to 65,000 Hz. Helping is the upright and natural curvature shape of their ears. This is why we can't hear dog whistles and why some mechanical noises scare the slobber out of our dogs.*

Training your dog seems like a daunting task, but it is a unique and rewarding experience. It is the foundation of a healthy and long relationship with your new dog or puppy. You must be the one in charge of the relationship and lead with the pack leader mentality, all the while showing patience and love.

Without a doubt, it is nice to have an obedient friend by your side through good times and bad. Owning a dog is a relationship that needs tending throughout the years. Once you begin training, it will continue throughout the life of your dog and friend. An obedient dog is easier to care for and causes less household problems and expense. You know what needs to be done, but what about your dog. How do you read his messages in regards to what you are attempting to accomplish? I am going to cover dog's body language and vocal language to provide insight into what it is your dog is trying to tell you. This should prove to be an asset while training your dog.

Remember that we cannot always read a dog's body language accurately. All dogs have their own unique personality; therefore will express themselves in their individual way. It is possible that a dog's happy wagging tail could be another dog's way of conveying that it is nervous or anxious. Keep in in your thoughts when reading a dog's body language that it is difficult to be 100% accurate in our interpretations and to use caution around strange dogs.

Body Language Basics:

What is body language? Body language is all of the non-verbal communication we exhibit when engaged into an exchange with another entity. Say what? All of those little tics, spasms, and movements that we act out comprise of non-verbal body language. Studies state that over 50% of how people judge us is based on our use of body language. Apparently, the visual interpretation of our message is equal to our verbal message. It is interesting how some studies have indicated that when the body language disagrees with the verbal, our verbal message accounts for as little as 7-10% of how the others judge us. With that kind of statistic, I would say that body language is extremely important.

Similar to humans, dogs use their bodies to communicate. Their hearing and seeing senses are especially acute. Observe how your dog tilts his head, moves his legs, and what is his tail doing while you are engaged. Is the tail up, down, or wagging? These body movements are all part of the message your dog is trying to convey. With this knowledge, I think it is safe to say that we should learn a little about human and dog body language. In this article, I will stick to a dog's body language and leave the human investigation up to you. What do you think my posture is right now?

The Tail:

The tail is a wagging and this means the dog is friendly, or maybe not. With most dogs that have tails it can convey many messages, some nice, some nasty. Specialists say a dog's wagging tail can mean the dog is scared, confused, preparing to fight, confident, concentrating, interested, or happy. Some dogs have curly Spitz type tails and therefore it will take a keen eye to see and denote what their tail position might be conveying so you will have to rely more on facial and body postures. Breeds with docked tails, flat faces, and that are black in color make it more difficult to read what they are trying express. From distance black colored dogs facial expressions can be difficult to see. Creating further difficulties are breeds that have puffy hair, long hair, or extensive hair that hides their physical features.

How do you tell the difference? Look at the speed and range of motion in the tail. The wide-fast tail wag is usually the message of "Hey, I am so happy to see you!" wag. The tail that is not tight between the hind legs, but instead is sticking straight back horizontally means the dog is curious but unsure, and probably not going to bite but remain in a place of neutral affection. This dog will probably not be confrontational, yet the verdict is not in. The slow tail wag means the same; the dog's friendly meter is gauging the other as friend or foe.

The tail held high and stiff, or bristling (hair raised) is a WATCH OUT! Red Flag warning for humans to be cautious. This dog may not only be aggressive, but dangerous and ready to rumble. If you come across this dog, it is time to calculate your retreat and escape plan.

 Not only should the speed and range of the wag be recognized while you are reading doggie body language, one must also take note of the tail position. A dog that is carrying its tail erect is a self-assured dog in control of itself. On the flip side of that, the dog with their tail between their legs, tucked in tight is the, "I surrender man, I surrender, please don't hurt me" posture.

The chill dog, a la Reggae special is the dog that has her tail lowered but not tucked in-between her legs. The tail that is down and relaxed in a neutral position states, the dog is relaxed.

While training your dog or simply playing, it is a good idea to take note of what his or her tail is doing and determine if your dog's tail posture is matching their moods. Your understanding of your dog's tail movements and body posture will be of great assistance throughout its lifetime.

Up Front:

On the front end of the dog is the head and ears with their special motions. A dog that cocks his head or twitches her ears is giving the signal of interest and awareness, but sometimes it can indicate fear. The forward or ear up movements can show a dog's awareness of seeing or hearing something new. Due to the amazingly acute canine sense of hearing, this can occur long before we are aware. These senses are two of the assets that make dogs so special and that make them fantastic guard and watchdogs.

"I give in, and will take my punishment" is conveyed with the head down and ears back. Take note of this submissive posture, observe the neck, and back fur for bristling. Sometimes this accompanies this posture. Even though a dog is giving off this submissive stance, it should be approached with caution because it may feel threatened and launch an offensive attack thinking he needs to defend himself.

"Smile, you are on camera." Yep, you got it, dogs smile too. It is usually a subtle corner pull back to show the teeth. Do not confuse this with the obvious snarl that entails a raised upper lip and bared teeth, sometimes accompanied by a deep growling sound. The snarl is something to be extremely cautious of when encountered. A snarling dog is not joking around--*the snarl is serious*. This dog is ready to be physically aggressive.

The Whole Kit and Caboodle:

Using the entire body, a dog that rolls over onto its back and exposes his belly, neck, and genitals is conveying the message that you are in charge. A dog that is overly submissive sometimes urinates a small amount to express his obedience towards a human or another dog.

Front paws down, rear end up, tail is a waggin.' This, "hut, hut, hut, C'mon Sparky hike the ball," posture is the ole K-9 position of choice for, "Hey! It is playtime, and I am ready to go!" This posture is sometimes accompanied with a playful bark and or pawing of the ground in an attempt to draw you into his playful state. I love it when a dog is in this mood, albeit they can be aloof to commands.

Whines, Growls, Howls, Barks and Yelps.

We just had a look at the silent communication of body language. Now, I will look into the doggie noises we cherish, but sometimes find annoying. Just what is our dog trying to tell us? Our canine friends often use vocal expressions to get their needs met. Whines and growls mean what they say, so when training your dog, listen carefully. As you become accustomed to the dogs vocal communication, and are able to begin understanding them, the happier you will both become. Some dog noises can be annoying and keep you awake, or wake you up. This may need your attention, to be trained out as inappropriate vocalizations.

Barking:

What does a dog bark say and why bark at all? Dogs bark to say "Hey, what's up dude," "I am hungry," or "Look at me!" A bark may warn of trouble, or to convey that a dog is bored or lonely. I think we all know that stimulated and excited dogs also bark. It is up to us to survey the surroundings and assess the reason. We need to educate ourselves about our dog's various barks so we can act appropriately.

Whining and Whimpering:

Almost from the time they are freshly made and feeding upon their mother's milk, our little puppies begin to make their first little furball noises. Whimpering or whining to get their mothers attention for feeding or comfort is innate, and as a result, they know mom will come to them. They also use these two W's on us to gain our attention. Other reasons for whimpering or whining are from fear produced by loud noises such as thunderstorms or fireworks. I think most of us have experienced the 4th of July phenomenon where the entire dog population is barking excessively until the wee hours of the morning when the last fireworks are ignited, and the final "BOOM!" dies off.

Growling:

Growling means, you had better watch out. Be acutely aware of what this dog is doing or might do. Usually a dog that is growling is seriously irritated and preparing to be further aggressive. However, this is not always true, sometimes a dog will issue a growl requesting for petting to continue.

Howling:

Picture the dark silhouette of a howling dog with a full moon backdrop. A dog's howl is a distinct vocalization that most dogs use, and every wolf makes. Howling can mean loneliness, desire, warning, or excitement. A lonely howl is a dog looking for a response. Dogs also howl after a long hunt when they have tracked and cornered their prey. Some Scenthounds use a distinct sound named a bay.

Natural Dog Behavior

The art of *understanding dog behavior* has been described as a partnership of species in which instinct and intuition are utilized over logical thought to enable work in collaboration. Humans need to be flexible and responsive, and able not only to lead, but also to follow. Humans need to open their sensory awareness and place high importance upon nonverbal communications. It is further defined as the understanding of how dogs communicate with one another in their own canine language and being able to communicate with dogs in their language. When you understand some or most of the techniques dogs use to communicate with each other, then you can apply it when communicating with dogs. To do this you have to be able to isolate your human emotions and put the needs of the dog at the forefront. When a dog is born into this world, environmental and genetic factors will affect that dog's behavior. Additionally they have behaviors coded into their DNA that dictates their inherent canine behaviors. In dog-to-dog communication, every movement, growl, and gesture has a meaning. This can be extremely subtle in action and difficult for humans to see and interpret.

Although dogs are intelligent and can learn human communication methods, it is not always the most efficient way to communicate with a dog. Dogs are simpler than humans are, and it is more challenging to teach a dog to understand human communication than it is to use dog communication methods to communicate with your dog. If a person is able to be open up to the idea, then they can learn the language dogs use to communicate with each other and incorporate that into their communication with dogs. Using this method, you begin to work in harmony with the dog and their natural instincts, instead of against them.

Commonly humans forget to address or never consider what a dog's natural instincts are. Embedded in their genetic code is the thirst for rules, boundaries, and structure. Dogs enjoy knowing what the rules of etiquette for all situations are, and having the structure of a daily schedule for walks, playtimes, exercises, and feedings. They also crave consistency in actions, and this is something that some humans will struggle with providing. Therefore, it is essential to provide your dog with the things that they need, such as physical and mental exercises, leadership, play, rule establishment and enforcement, and the essentials that are food, water, shelter, love, kindness, and all the other things that dogs need to live a fruitful life. The entire family should understand the rules of etiquette for your dog so that rule enforcement is always the same. An example of failed consistency is if your daughter is reprimanding your dog for an action that you let happen, there will be a conflict in your dog's brain. Your dog will not know which way to act and this will cause your dog distress and possibly anxiety.

Human behavior can have an entirely different meaning to a dog, and this is why commonly a dog-owner may be perplexed by his dog's behavior. The owner is thinking in human terms and not in dog terms. Negative dog behaviors are mostly a result from something missing from their life, and instead of blaming our dog for its behavior, we must figure out the root cause of this negative behavior and remedy it for our dogs, thus showing our leadership abilities and doing our job as their leader. A dog's temperament is shaped by the owner's ability to provide him with what he instinctually needs. Educating yourself about dog communication and behaviors is your first step to achieving *understanding of natural canine communications*. Owning and properly caring for a dog requires a knowledge base that has been diagramed and written about to help you learn through personal observation. Studying your dog's behaviors and allowing your intuition to guide you will enable you to learn dog communication techniques. I am including downloadable charts and links to assist you in getting started with the basics.

Using Human Body Language to Communicate

There is a pair of important things to keep in the forefront of your mind regarding human movements around dogs. The first is a tough one to master. *Stay calm even when you are not. Avoid fast erratic movements* such as jumping back, *making a loud noise* when surprised or frightened, and *flinging your arms* into the air. These types of movements mimic prey or the dog can mistake these movements for a type of game that they want to play. The dog's reaction might be that it attempts to put his mouth upon your fast moving limbs, jumps up, or gives chase. The difficult part when you are surprised or nervous is to freeze in place and to avoid eye contact while simultaneously slightly turning your head away. If you feel it is necessary, fold your arms to your chest. If you need to move away from a dog then use slow fluid movements while backing away from the dog. As a startled human we sometimes hold our breath, so do not forget to breathe and calm yourself. A dog may perceive your held breath as a sign that you are tense and going to react. This could escalate tensions.

Eye contact is very important to dogs and assists you in conveying to your dog that you are serious and in command. Always use direct eye contact when issuing commands or calling your dog by name.

If a dog jumps up on to you the best method of reaction is to *not* engage with your eyes, fold your arms across your chest, and freeze in place. In essence, you are to avoid to the best of your ability any physical or eye engagement with the dog. Jumping dogs usually want attention but when they continually do not get that attention, they begin to catch onto the fact that jumping is an unwanted and undesirable behavior. I realize that their claws might hurt you, and some dogs are large enough to move you, so do the best that you can to ignore the dog and not make any sudden movements.

Dogs can sense our inner feelings by the way we use our tone of voice, body language and facial expressions. They are able to read us humans much better than most people can read a dog's body language. Their keen abilities to observe us intensely are used by them to interpret and anticipate what we want from them. Using the correct body language helps you when meeting unfamiliar dogs, and in controlling your own dog. The following is an example of how a dog interprets human action. If you approach a *submissive dog* by leaning forward towards him and then move your hand towards his head, it will usually cause a negative reaction because you are acting out a dominate behavior and is therefore intimidated by you. Since the dog has already taken the submissive posture, the dog is not expecting a dominate action. Conversely, if you approach the same dog by first crouching down beside him and then bring your hand from his chest up to his head this should produce a much different reaction. Our instinct is to pet dogs on their head, but when interacting with a submissive dog it is better to pet their chest to avoid intimidating him.

"How do I identify a submissive dog?" That is a good question and the answer will help in many ways. A submissive dog will commonly lower its head and tail making its body smaller, while simultaneously avoiding eye contact. Sometimes owners mistake this for a dog feeling sad, when in fact he is submitting to that alpha owner, and stating that they are his leader. If your dog is showing this submissive posture, this means that you have achieved the alpha position and your dog is following your lead. Your dog is happy because he is comforted in knowing that he has a leader that is taking good care of him. A happy and secure submissive dog that lowers itself is not a dog that is recklessly jumping around vying for attention and trying to control its owner. Realizing what the submissive posture is and not confusing it with thinking that your dog is upset or sad will help you from sending your dog confusing signals. The fact that your dog is showing this posture instead of

jumping on you and trying to steer you is a good sign and does not mean that you need to cheer your dog up or act differently to address the posture.

Have you ever had trouble with your dog obeying your "come" command? Try this body movement. Instead of becoming angry, yelling, or begging, turn your back and crouch down. This position tells your dog that he is not in trouble and that you are not a threat to him. Do not repeatedly say the *come* command. This body position is an invitation instead of a demand. This position often works, and when your dog comes to join you, then reward him. As a last resort, you can try running away from your dog. This will commonly be perceived as play and often your dog will come running. If your dog is not obeying, continue to work on training your dog to obey the "come" command so that you do not have to resort to these physical cues. Maybe you have not been offering a good enough reason for your dog to come and need to improve your rewards, he has not retained the command, or you are still earning the dogs respect. Whichever the case, practice until your dog comes to you upon command. The *come* command is extremely important for the safety of your dog and your peace of mind.

In leash training, body language plays an important role. Every time your dog is pulling, you should change directions and walk the other way. Using this body language, you are teaching him that you are the one in control and decide the direction and speed of walking. In addition, when you are walking your dog on the leash, you want him to maintain a close distance but never impede your walking and direction changes. If your dog is not keeping the proper distance and moving with you, but instead crowding, slightly bumping him while changing directions will stop him from crowding or impeding your walk. This can be practiced during training sessions that include many direction changes and serpentine walking. Your dog must know that you are in charge and make the rules, and soon he will learn not to crowd or impede you so that the two of you can harmoniously walk with a loose leash.

Body language is equally important to communicating with dogs as it is with humans, but the difference is that communicating with humans usually comes more naturally to us. Standing upright, remaining calm, confident, and consistent is how all alphas should act when directing their dogs, and if you notice, many powerful people do the same when interacting with humans. Keep this in the forefront of your mind, and the more you practice, the more natural and easy it will become. It takes practice to be able to control our reactions, facial expressions, and tones. Having this type of control helps some people to be better trainers than others. Remember that you are under constant observation from your dog and they respect their confident leader. Whenever you act less confident, your dog will immediately *notice* it. Enjoying the process and having a good time with your dog is also important, so do not be afraid to laugh and smile. You don't have to be unemotional or act like a statue while learning about dogs and yourself.

Learning Natural Dog Behaviors

Remember that we cannot always read a dog's body language accurately. All dogs have their own unique personality; therefore will express themselves in their individual way. It is possible that a dog's happy wagging tail could be another dog's way of conveying that it is nervous or anxious. A dog's breed, size, or appearances are not proper indicators of whether a dog will bite, but his body language is. Keep in in your thoughts when reading a dog's body language that it is difficult to be 100% accurate interpreting and to use caution around strange dogs.

Observe your dog and verify if he is consistently using a body posture or movement that illustrates his mood. It is a good idea until you memorize your dog's movements to keep a journal, and log your observations so that you know what your dog is saying to you with his body movements.

Some dogs have curly Spitz type tails and therefore it will take a keen eye to see and denote what their tail position might be conveying so you will have to rely more on facial and body postures. Breeds with docked tails, flat faces, and that are black in color make it more difficult to read what they are trying express. From distance black colored dogs facial expressions can be difficult to see. Creating further difficulties are breeds that have puffy hair, long hair, or extensive hair that hides their physical features.

Observing your dog's ears, eyes, lips, mouth, body postures, and tail movements, then matching them to your dog's emotional state will take some time, but when you begin to easily identify and understand your dog's emotions and intentions from his body language, you are then on your way to a better long-lasting relationship. Additionally you will improve your training and communication skills with your dog and other person's dogs. This is your first step to mastering *the language of dogs*. This skill can only be learned through the observation of dogs, trusting in your intuition, and in tandem with studying about dog communication. Using daily focused observations, you will gradually become aware of your dog's communications and their meanings.

Some dogs body language is easy to see and define so do not feel overwhelmed or intimidated by the process that I have outlined. Previous dog owners will attest that the more time spent with dogs the more you glean from their behaviors. Gradually you will become more aware of dog behavior and then subtle changes will occur in the way that you interact with all dogs. The process is enjoyable because you are spending time with your German Shepherd. All dog trainers are continuously honing their dog language skills.

About Treats

You are training your puppy and he is doing well, *of course*, because he is the best dog in the world! *Oh yes he is.* Because of this fact, you want to make sure that you are giving your dog the right kind of treats. Treats are easy. As long as you stay away from the things that aren't good for dogs, such as; avocado, onions, garlic, coffee, tea, caffeinated drinks, grapes, raisins, macadamia nuts, peaches, plums, pits, seeds, persimmons, chocolate, whiskey & soda, Guinness Stout, just to name a few.

You can make treats from many different foods. First, treats should be small, kernel sized, and easy to grab from a pocket or concealable container (treat pouches are available). When you are outdoors and there are many distractions, treats should be of a higher quality and coveted by your pooch, we call it a higher value treat because it is worthy of your dog breaking away from the activity he is engaged. Perhaps cubes of cheese, dried meat, special kibble or the neighbor cat (just joking all you cat lovers). Make sure you mix it up and keep a variety of snacks available when you are out and about. Nothing is worse during treat training than your dog or puppy turning his nose up at a treat because he has grown bored of it or it holds a lesser value than something else does that currently interests him.

Here are some treat ideas:

- No sugar, whole grain cereals are good. Cheerios are good choice. There is no need for milk, bowl, or a spoon. You can just give your dog the goods, as is.

- Kibble (dry foods). Put some in a paper bag and boost the aroma factor by tossing in some bacon or another meat product. Dogs are all about those yummy smell sensations.

- Beef Jerky that preferably has no pepper or heavy seasoning.

- Carrot, apple pieces, and some dogs even enjoy melons.

- Baby food meat products. You know the ones, those strange little suspect pink sausage things.

- Commercial dog treats. Be careful, there as there are tons of them on the market. Look for those that do not have preservatives, by products, or artificial colors.

- Cubed meats that are preferably not highly processed or salted.

- Shredded cheese, string cheese or cubed cheese. Dogs love cheese!

- Cream cheese, peanut butter, or spray cheese. Give your dog a small dollop to lick for every proper behavior.

- Ice Cube, Not the rap star but the frozen water treats. Your dog will love crunching these up. . If your dog has dental problems, proceed cautiously.

Avoid feeding your hairy friend from the dining table; because you do not want to teach your dog to beg when people are sitting down to eat. When treating, give treats far from the dinner table or a good distance from where people normally gather to eat.

Providing the Treats

Treats, treats, *treats!* *"Come and get 'em."* How many times have you heard a friend or family member tell you about some crazy food that their dog loves? Dogs do love a massive variety of foods; unfortunately, not all of the foods that they think they want to eat are good for them. Dog treating is not rocket science but it does take a little research, common sense, and paying attention to how your dog reacts after wolfing down a treat.

I am going to throw out some ideas for treats for training as well as some regular ole "Good Dog" treats for your sidekick and friend in mischief. I will touch on the proper time to treat, the act of giving the treat, types of treats, and bribery vs. reward.

Types of Treats

Love and attention is considered a reward and is certainly a positive reinforcement that can be just as effective as an edible treat. Dog treating is comprised of edibles, praise, love, and attention. Engaging in play or allowing some quality time with their favorite piece of rawhide is also effectual. At times, these treats are crucial to dog training.

Human foods that are safe for dogs, include most fruits and veggies, cut up meats that are raw or cooked, yogurt, peanut butter, kibble, and whatever else you discover that your dog likes, but be sure that it is good for him, in particular his digestive system. Remember, not all human foods are good for dogs. Please read up on the dos and don'ts regarding human foods and dogs. A "treat" is considered something about the size of a kernel of corn. All a dog needs is a little taste to keep him interested. The *kernel size* is something that is swiftly eaten and swallowed, making it non-distracting from training. Remember, a treat is just quick tasted, used for enticement and reinforcement.

Giving the Treat

Try to avoid treating your dog when he is over stimulated and running amuck in an unfocused state of mind. This can be counterproductive and might reinforce a negative behavior resulting in you not being able to get your dog's attention.

When giving the treat, allow your dog to get a big doggie whiff of that nibble of tasty food treat, but keep it up and away from a possible attempt at a quick snatch and grab. Due to their keen sense of smell, they will know long before you would that there is a tasty snack nearby. Issue your command and wait for him to obey before presenting the doggie reward. Remember when dog treating, it is important to be patient and loving, but it is equally important not to give the treat until he obeys. Try to use treating to reward the kickback mellow dog, not the out of control or over-excited dog.

Some dogs have a natural gentleness to them and always take from your hand gently, while other dogs need some guidance to achieve this. If your dog is a bit rough during treat grabbing, go ahead and train the command "gentle!" when giving treats. Be firm from this point forward. Give up no treats unless taken gently. Remain steadfast with your decision to implement this, and soon your pup or dog will comply, if he wants the tasty treat.

Time to Treat

The best time to be issuing dog treats is in between his or her meals. During training, always keep the tastiest treat in reserve in case you need to refocus your dog's attention back to the current training session. It is good to keep in mind that treating too close to meal times makes all treats less effective, so remember this when planning your training sessions. Obviously, if your dog is full from mealtime he will be less likely to want a treat reward than if he is a bit hungry, therefore your training session will likely be more difficult and far less effective.

What is In the Treats?

Before purchasing, look at the ingredients on the treat packaging, and make certain there are no chemicals, fillers, additives, colors and things that are unhealthy. Certain human foods that are tasty to us might not be so tasty to your dog, and he will tell you. Almost all dogs love some type of raw or cooked meats. In tiny nibble sizes, these treats work great to get their attention where you want it focused.

Many people like to make homemade treats and that is fine, just keep to the rules we just mentioned and watch what you are adding while you are having fun in the kitchen. Remember to research and read the list of vegetables dogs can and cannot eat, and note that pits and seeds can cause choking and intestinal issues, such as dreaded doggy flatulence. Remove the seeds and pits, and clean all fruits and veggies before slicing it into doggie size treats.

Bribery vs. Reward Dog Treating

The other day a friend of mine mentioned *bribery* for an action when he wanted his dog to shake his hand. I thought about it later and thought I would clarify for my readers. *Bribery* is the act of offering the food in advance to get the dog to act out a command or behavior. *Reward* is giving your dog his favorite toy, food, love, affection *after* he has performed the behavior.

An example of bribery would be, if you want your dog to come and you hold out in front of you in your hand a huge slab of steak before calling him. Reward would be giving your dog the steak after he obeyed the "come!" command.

Bribed dogs learn to comply with your wishes only when they *see* food. The rewarded dog realizes that he only gets his reward after performing the desired action. This also assists by introducing non-food items as rewards when training and treating. Rewards such as play, toys, affection, and praise can be substituted for treats.

Teething & Chew-Toys

First Guide Dog – *Following the first German Shepherd post WWI school for guide dogs that was located in Potsdam, Germany, Mrs. Harrison Eustis founded a school in Switzerland. From there, her first American client Morris Frank returned to America and founded "The Seeing Eye" in 1929, to train GSD dogs for use as guide dogs for the blind.*

Not only did he found the school, he and his dog "Buddy" became champions for seeing-eye dogs to assist blind people all over the world. Today "The Seeing Eye" dog school is the oldest existing guide dog school.

Between the third and sixth week your puppy will begin to feel the notorious baby teeth eruption. Puppy teeth are not designed to grind heavy foods, and consist of predominantly small, razor sharp canines and incisors. These new teeth number about twenty-eight, and during this painful and frustrating teething period, puppies will attempt to seek relief on anything within reach that they can clamp their little mouths down on. Later, when the baby teeth fall out and their adult teeth emerge, this will again cause discomfort, further increasing their drive to chew in search of relief. Usually by the end of six months, the intense chewing phase begins to wane. Although some variance exists by breed, adult dogs have forty-two teeth with the molars coming in last at around six to seven months of age.

Puppies are motivated to chew because of the discomfort that comes from teething, as well as to investigate new objects of interest. Chewing is a normal dog behavior that can be steered and directed toward owner approved toys and objects. Dogs certainly love to chew on bones, and they can spend hours gnawing until they feel that they have successfully scoured it clean, sometimes burying it for a later chew session, or solely as a trophy. Wood, bones and toys are some of the objects that occupy a dog during the activity of chewing. Chewing not only provides stimulation and fun, but it serves to reduce a dog's anxiety. It is our job to identify what our puppies can and cannot chew on, while gently establishing and enforcing the rules of chewing. This process begins by providing an ample amount of chew-toys for our puppy.

Chew-toys

A non-edible chew-toy is an object made for dogs to chew that is neither, consumable or destructible. Non-food items eaten by dogs are dangerous and can sometimes seriously harm your dog, so it is imperative to provide high quality and durable chew-toys. Choosing the type of chew-toy will depend upon your dog's individual preferences and chewing ability, so you may have to go through several to find the most appropriate. Some *super chewer* dogs can destroy a rawhide chew in a fraction of the time as others, so your dog's prowess and jaw power will dictate the types of chews that you will want to provide.

Edible chews such as pig ears, rawhide bones, Nylabones®, and other natural chew products are also available and appropriate for your puppy or adult dog. Beware that sometimes edibles can come apart in large chunks or pieces, thus having the potential to be swallowed, or possibly choke a dog. For safety, keep an eye on your dog whenever he is working away on an edible chew. While your puppy is discovering the variety and joy of chewing, take notice of the chews that he enjoys most.

KONG® and Petsafe® make plenty of top quality chew-toys, including those can be stuffed with food, such as kibble or cheese, to hold your dog's interest. KONG® products as well as the Petsafe® Busy Buddy® line are made from natural rubber and have a stellar reputation for durability. Many other brands are available to choose. When choosing chew-toys, take into consideration whether or not you are purchasing a natural or synthetic product, as well as keep in mind what your pal's preferences are. Usually, anything that you stuff with food will begin a puppy craving for that particular toy, but be aware that is not always the case.

Stuffing Chew-Toys

There are some basic guidelines to follow when using a stuffable chew toy. First, kibble is the recommended foodstuff when filling your puppy's chew-toy. Kibble assists in keeping your puppy at a normal weight, and if this is a concern, you can simply exclude the amount you used in the toy from his normal feeding portion. Secondly, you can use tastier treats, such as cooked meat or freeze-dried liver, but these should be reserved for special rewards. There are plenty of stuffing recipes available, but be cautious about the frequency you treat your puppy with special stuffing. Be conscious of when you reward your puppy, and avoid doing so when bad behaviors are exhibited. For example, if your puppy has been incessantly barking all afternoon, then if you provide a stuffed chew-toy do not reward him with something utterly delectable.

The art to stuffing chew-toys is that the toy holds your puppy's interest, and keeps him occupied. For your success, you will want to stuff the toy in a way that a small portion of food comes out easily, thus quickly rewarding your puppy. After this initial jackpot, the goal is to keep your puppy chewing while gradually being rewarded with small bits of food that he actively extracts. You can use a high value treat, such as a piece of meat stuffed deeply into the smallest hole, which will keep your dog occupied for hours in search of this prized morsel. With a little creativity and practice, the art of chew-toy stuffing will be acquired benefitting you and your canine friend. After trial and error, you will begin to understand what fillings and arrangements will keep your puppy occupied for longer and longer times.

Why Feed Dinner from Stuffed Chew-Toys?

Here is some advice that I gleaned off a friend of mine, and it does seem to pack some merit. As you are probably aware, the current practice indicates that puppies should be fed two to three times daily, from their bowl. There is nothing wrong with this, but it does raise a question as to whether perhaps they think that they are being rewarded for the non-acceptable behaviors that was possibly acted just prior to eating time. This should be taken into consideration, and feeding should be adjusted to avoid potential negative behavior reinforcement. The other item that I was made aware is that if you feed your puppy by stuffing his chew-toy, it will occupy more of his time and keep him from negatively acting out of boredom, excessive curiosity, or abundant adrenal stores.

The argument against bowl feeding is that it supplants the activity of searching for food, as they would in the wild, and as a result of the quick gratification in the easy meal, there remains an over-abundance of time remaining to satisfy the dog's mental and physical stimulation. To understand this better you have to put yourself into a puppy's paws. Besides sleeping and training, your dog has about twelve hours each day to fill with satisfying and rewarding activity. Resulting from an excess of unoccupied time, normal behaviors, such as grooming, barking, chewing, walking, and playing can become repetitive and unfulfilling. Sometimes an activity can lose its initial purpose and meaning, only to become a way to pass time instead of serving as a positive function of daily life. Obsessive and compulsive behaviors can come out of these long sessions of boredom. For example, vocalizing for alarm can become ceaseless barking, and grooming can turn into excessive licking or scratching, likely resulting in harm to the skin.

It falls upon us to instruct our puppies on healthy, calm and relaxing ways to pass the time of day. This is a critical part of training and socialization. Remember, that by stuffing the chew-toy full of kibble you can successfully occupy hours of your puppy's time, helping to reduce the possibility of negative behaviors overtaking your puppy. This can be accomplished by redirecting his attention to an activity that he enjoys, keeping his mind distracted from the potential of loneliness and boredom. Because of his time spent chewing the approved toy, he is kept calm and his time occupied, periodically rewarded by bits of kibble, and thus the possibility of developing any of the potential, aforementioned negative behaviors is minimized.

This feeding option is a method originally suggested by Dr. Ian Dunbar, a famed rewards-based trainer and SIRIUS® puppy-training pioneer. However, this method is not essential to maintain and train a healthy puppy; I felt it was worth mentioning since I was writing about chew-toys. Many people refrain from feeding their dog's kibble, utilizing the optional diet of raw foods, thus modification in the feeding method would be required here. Other factors when utilizing this method should take into consideration your dog's individual personality, as well as ability to withdraw food from the toy. Whichever feeding method you choose to use, be certain to feed your puppy the healthiest, least processed, non-chemical laden foods that you can find.

Bones

Later, as your puppy grows he will no doubt be interested in other types of things to chew on, as well as to eat. There exists some controversy as to whether raw bones, cooked bones, or any animal bones are at all good for dogs to chew. I do not want to state with certainty that bones are safe for your dog, as there are some obvious risks involved, but I do feed my dogs bones without problem. As a new dog owner, and with time and assessment, you can later determine what is best for your dog. Any concerns that surface can be solved by consulting your veterinarian, speaking with your breeder, and of course making a decision based upon your own findings and personal experience.

Recommendations are to provide your dog with bones that are sold specifically for chewing, which are often beef, or bison femur or hipbones, filled with satisfying marrow. Chicken bones and steak bones that have been cooked can splinter and pose a greater choking risk and should not be given to your dog. Some dogs that are intense chewers often chip a tooth, or splinter small pieces off the bones they are gnawing at, and because of this, it is good to supervise them. Be sure to avoid small bones in favor of larger raw bones. Present the bones on an easy to clean surface or somewhere outdoors. If you have more than one dog, it is important to separate them to avoid conflict. Also, be aware that dogs not who are not used to the rich, high calorie marrow inside of these bones could possibly have a bout of diarrhea after consumption.

Chew-toy Training

This is an option to controlling and shaping the chewing behavior. Something that I learned from other trainers is how to establish a chew-toy obsession for your puppy. When you bring your puppy home, you should immediately begin exposing him to chew-toys, always keeping them in close proximity, so you can effectively steer all of his chewing energies into these toys instead of your expensive leather shoes, flip-flops, or favorite slippers. Puppies love to chew on just about anything that they can get their mouths on, but depending upon your puppy's personality there exists some variance in the frequency and ferocity of the chewing. There is no reason to leave it to chance. By establishing an early obsession to chew-toys, you can be assured that all of your valuable human articles will be spared from the chewing machines we call *puppies.* As the owner of a new puppy, you will want to thoroughly puppy-proof your home. Until he has completely learned that his toys are the only acceptable objects for him to chew, everything in your house should be considered *at risk.*

Chew-toys provide puppies a focal point in which to channel their energy, and serve to keep boredom from setting up shop. It is a necessity to teach your puppy early on that the chew-toys you provide are fun and delicious. A good way to do this is to take advantage of the hollow toys, and stuff them with kibble, or other tasty treats of your choice. To bolster this training, you can keep your puppy's food bowl hidden for the first few weeks after his arrival, and serve all of your puppy's kibble from the stuffed toy, or a sterilized bone. Taking this action will support your puppy's quick understanding and connection between good things and his chew-toys. Remember, the goal here is to create an obsession to chew-toys, resulting in a dog that will leave all of the other non-chew toy items alone.

In order to reinforce his chew-toy obsession, you can use what is called, *the confinement program.* Through a process in which you narrow the choices of items your dog has available to chew, your puppy eventually will find a kind of solace in his own chew-toys. His association with his own chew-toys will grow as he grows, ultimately resulting in him craving to chew only his chew-toys, and nothing else.

The confinement program training begins by securing your puppy behind his gated area and providing him with plenty of chew-toys to occupy his alone time. Whether you do this prior to leaving the house or while you are in the house, do not forget to leave fresh water for your puppy. Additionally, every hour when you let your puppy out to relieve himself, begin to introduce chew-toy games. There a variety of games you can play, such as find the *hidden chew-toy, chew-toy tug-o-war,* and *fetch.* These games will reinforce his attachment to his chew-toys, and help create a positive obsession toward them. By providing your puppy with a singular choice that is stuffed with food, he will eventually develop a strong chew-toy obsession.

After your dog has formed his chew-toy habit, and has not had any other chewing mishaps, you can broaden his world by expanding his available confinement space to two rooms. As he proves his compliance as evidenced by not chewing items beyond his chew-toys, you can expand his roaming range of access to other rooms in the house, while gradually working up his access to the entire house.

If your puppy makes a chewing mistake, then return to the puppy confinement for 3-6 weeks, all depending upon his progress and the success of further confinement training. After a 3-week period, you will want to test the results of the behavioral modifications resulting from his confinement program. Grant him more access and see if your puppy has reverted to chewing objects on your *no chew list,* or if the program has been a success and it is time move on and enlarge his range. If he reverts again to chewing on objects other than his chew-toys, continue the confinement for a couple of more weeks then test again.

Because this training will be concurrently trained with housetraining, you will also need to monitor if, and when your puppy is having house-soiling accidents. Because your puppy is having accidents indoors, this may limit the house access that you can provide your puppy. It is recommended that in order for you to begin expanding his indoor range of access, your dog should be successfully housetrained, and beyond the possibility of a soiling accident. This training should not conflict with your house-training.

The benefits of making your dog's chew-toys an obsession is more than just for preventing household destruction. It also reduces barking and keeps him from running around the house, because while your puppy is chewing he is distracted, and thus unable to perform other activities. Another potential behavior issue that has negative implications is the separation anxiety that can occur because of your absence. Because chewing occupies your puppies down time, it assists in the prevention and development of separation anxiety. It acts like a blanket or a teddy bear to a child. Furthermore, it is pointed out that a chew-toy addiction is good for dogs that have Obsessive Compulsive Disorder. This addiction offers them an acceptable avenue to work out their obsessive compulsions. It is not a cure but instead a therapeutic device that can be used by them to obsess.

"Is this a good obsession for my puppy?"

Yes, it is, and additionally a good habit that is difficult to break. The benefits are that your puppy will not be chewing your personal items, and it works well towards keeping him away from compulsive behaviors, such as barking, digging, howling, anxiety from being alone, and a list of other undesirable behaviors.

The action of chewing also has a calming benefit, thus acts as a stress reliever. It turns out that a simple rubber chew-toy is an effective tool for controlling and shaping behaviors, as well as a therapeutic tool to occupy and sooth.

Crate Training

Dogs need their own safe place to call home and relax. An owner's house might be a place to roam, but it's not the den that dogs crave. The crate satisfies a dog's longing for a den, and along with its many other uses provides comfort to them. All puppies should be taught to enjoy residing in their crate and know that it is a safe haven for them, so it is important *never* to use it for punishment.

Before you begin crate training give your dog a couple of days to adjust to his new home and surroundings. Crate training can be trained for a dog of any age. A dog's love for their crate is healthy and assists you in taking care of him or her throughout their lifetime.

Try to limit your puppy's time in the crate to around one hour per session. Never leave your adult dog in a crate for longer than five hours without providing them time outside of the crate. As your puppy matures and has learned proper dog etiquette (not chewing everything in sight), is housetrained, and can be trusted to run freely around your house, you can then leave the door open so that they can use it for their private bungalow to come and go as they choose.

I have listed below the benefits of crate, things to avoid, types, furnishings, the steps to crate train your dog, and troubleshooting, Godspeed.

Benefits of the Crate

- It aids in housetraining because dogs are reluctant to soil their own sleeping area.

- Acts as a mobile doghouse for trips via car, airplane, train and then to be used at destinations such as motels, and foreign houses.

- The mobility can be utilized inside your own home by being moved throughout the house. *Especially beneficial during housetraining when you want your puppy near you.

- Can reduce separation anxiety.

- Keep your dog out of harm's way.

- Assists in chew-toy addiction.

- Aids your puppy in calming and quieting down.

Until he or she has learned that chewing, tearing, ripping of household and human items is forbidden, the crate keeps your dog shortly separated from destruction of those items.

Things to Avoid

- *Do not use the crate as punishment.* If used in this manner it will defeat the purpose and cause your dog to fear the crate instead of love it.

- *Avoid lengthy crating sessions.* Long periods in the crate defer socialization, exercise, and lend to doggy depression, anxiousness, and anxiety.

- Puppies have an issue holding their need to eliminate waste. Young puppies tend to go hourly, but as they mature, the time between elimination lengthens. Keep this in mind for puppies and adult dogs, and always schedule elimination breaks. Set a timer to remind you to let your dog outdoors.

A good rule of thumb for elimination intervals is as follows, up to six weeks of age - elimination every hour, at two months of age - around two to three hours, at three months - four hours, four months and up - around five hours. These times will vary with individual dogs.

If you are housetraining an adult dog, he or she might be able to hold their bowels longer, but have not yet learned that they are required to wait and go outdoors.

- *Soiled items.* Quickly remove and clean any soiled items inside the crate, and thoroughly clean the crate with a non-toxic cleaner that will erase any signs of elimination. Dogs are creatures of habit and will think it is okay to eliminate where they have previously eliminated.

- Avoid crating your dog when your dog has not recently eliminated waste.

- Avoid continued involuntary crating after your puppy is housetrained and he or she understands that damaging human property is forbidden; instead only use the crate when necessary.

Buying, Furnishing, and Preparing the Crate

The time has come for you to go crate shopping and you notice that they come in many sizes and design options. Let the shopper in you compare the advantages and disadvantages of the different styles to figure out which will be best suited for your usage and dog. A few types are as follows, collapsible metal, metal with fabric, wire, solid plastic, fixed and folding aluminum, and soft-sided collapsible crates that conveniently fold up easily for travel.

Regarding traveling be sure always to have your dog safely secured when in a motor vehicle. There are crates specially designed and tested for vehicle transportation.

"What size crate do I purchase?"

The crate should be big enough for your puppy to stand up, turn around, and lie down in. If you wish to hedge your bet, instead of purchasing multiple crates you can purchase a crate that will accommodate your puppy when full size, but this will require blocking off the end so that they are unable to eliminate waste in a section and then move to another that is apart from where they soiled.

In summary, per the criteria mentioned above, you need to cordon off the crate to accommodate your puppy's smaller size and then expand as he or she grows.

"What do I put into the crate?"

Toys, treats, blanket or mat and the entire home furnishings a young puppy needs and desires to be entertained. Avoid televisions, tablets, and radios. Seriously, you should provide an ample supply of natural material indestructible chew-toys, and things such as indestructible balls. All of the chews and toys should be large enough not to be swallowed, and tough enough to withstand tearing apart a portion that could be swallowed by your puppy. Treats will be occasionally required, and stuffing them into the chew-toys will occupy the young pup for hours.

Clean water is another essential item that all dogs must have regular access. You can utilize a small rodent type water dispenser attached to the side of the crate. If you know that your dog will only be in the crate under two hours, then he or she will probably be able to go without water.

"Where do I place the crate?"

It is a good idea to place the crate close to where you are located in the house. This keeps a puppy from feeling lonely and you able to keep an eye out for signs that he or she needs to eliminate waste. As housetraining is successful, the crate does not have to be located beside you, only near you, or in central location to where you are working or relaxing. Eventually the crate can be located at further distances, but you do not want your dog ever to feel isolated.

Introducing Your Dog to the Crate

These steps will help your dog to adjust to his crate and associate it with good things such as security, comfort, and a quiet place to ponder the meaning of life, things such as why he or she walks on four legs and humans on two, and how does my food magically appear.

Never force your dog into the crate by using physical means of persuasion. Crate training should be a natural process that takes place on your dog's time schedule. Curious dogs might immediately begin to explore the inner domain while others take some time, and possibly some coaxing by using lures such as toys and food. Let the process proceed in small steps and gradually your dog will want to spend more time in his new five-star luxury crate. This training can proceed very quickly or take days to complete.

Phase I

1. Set the crate in a common area and check that all of the crates goodies are inside, chew-toys, blanket or towel. Open and secure the door. If your dog does not mosey on over in his or her own accord, then place them near the crate entrance and give him a pep talk using your happy-go-lucky fun voice. Wait a bit and see if his curiosity kicks in and he begins to explore the inner domain.

2. If your pep talk and shining personality are not sparking his curiosity then go to plan B, food lures. To begin, you don't have to use anything fancy, just use his normal puppy food. Drop some in the back of the crate and a couple closer to the front door, and see if that gets his little tail wagging and paws moving. After you place the food inside step away and give him some room to make his own decisions. Do not force anything. Just observe throughout the day and see if your dog is venturing inside or near the crate. Do this a few times throughout the day.

3. If this does not work, try it again. If he is still disinterested, you can also drop a favorite chew-toy into the crate and ask him to find his toy and see if that lures him into the crate.

4. Continue doing this process until your dog will walk all of the way into the crate to retrieve the food or toy. This step is sometimes accomplished in minutes, but it can take a couple of days. Be sure to praise your dog for successfully entering. Do not shut the door. Observe whether they are calm, timid, or frightened.

5. Once your dog is regularly entering his crate without fear, you can move onto phase II.

Phase II

Phase II will help if your dog is not acting as though his crate is a place that he wants to enter and remain, and might be showing signs of fear or anxiety when inside. This phase will help warm him up to his crate.

By using feeding time, you can reinforce that the crate is a place that your dog should enjoy. During Phase II training, remain in the presence of your dog's crate or at least in the same room. Later you will begin leaving the room where he is crated.

1. Start by feeding your dog in front of his crate door. Feeding your dog near his crate will create a nice association with the crate. *If your dog already enters his crate freely, set the food bowl inside that he has to enter the crate to eat.

2. Next, place his food bowl far enough into the crate that your dog has to step inside to eat. Then each following time that you feed him place the bowl further inside.

3. When your dog will stand and eat inside his crate, and you know that he is calm and relaxed, then you can close the crate door while he eats his meal.

The first time, immediately open the door when he finishes his meal. Then after each successive meal, leave the door closed for longer durations. For example, after meal completion, two, three, four minutes, and then incrementally increasing until you reach ten to fifteen minutes. Stay diligent and if you notice your dog begins frantically whining or is acting anxious, back up and then slow down on the time increases.

4. If your dog continues whining the next time, then leave him in there until he calms. *This is important*, because you cannot reinforce that whining is a way out of the crate, or a way always to get your attention or manipulate.

5. Now that he is comfortable entering, eating, and spending some time in his crate, move onto Phase III, which explains about training your dog to enjoy spending more time in the crate with you around and out of the house.

Phase III

This is where you will continue increasing the time duration that your dog is crated. First, be certain that he is not displaying signs of fear or anxiety. Whining and whimpering does not always signify that anxiety is present. It is often a tool used when they want some attention from their mom or humans. It is a sympathy tool honed sharp when they were weaning on mothers milk.

If you choose at this point, you can begin issuing a command that goes with your crating action. For example, say "crate," "home," "cage," "cave," or whatever is simple and natural. Maybe cage sounds negative to us, but your dog does not know the difference.

1. Stand next to the crate with his favorite toy and then call him over to you and give the command "cave," while placing the toy inside. A hand signal that you choose can also be used along with this command, but make sure that you do not use the same hand signal for another command. As an option, you can use a favored treat instead of a toy.

When he enters, praise him, shut the door, and let him stay inside for duration of ten to fifteen minutes. You should remain close to the crate. Do this a few times separated by an hour or two. During dog training, gradually proceeding is always a good rule to follow.

2. Repeat the step above, but this time only stay nearby for about five minutes, and then leave the room for an additional ten to fifteen minutes. When you return, do not rush over to the crate, instead remain in the room for a few more minutes and then let your dog out of the crate. It is not necessary to physically remove him, just open the door.

Repeat this five to seven times per day and gradually increase the duration that your dog remains in the crate. Work your way up to 30-40 minutes when you are completely out of sight. *Do not forget to use your vocal command and physical cue every time that you want your dog to enter his crate.*

3. Continue increasing the time that he is crated while you are home. Work up to one hour.

4. Next, place the crate near your room and let him sleep the night inside the crate near where you are sleeping such as in the doorway or just outside your bedroom. At this time, you can also begin to leave your dog crated when you need to leave the house for short durations of under two hours.

A good way to begin is to leave your dog in his crate while you are outdoors doing yard work. Remember that when your return inside, to act casual and normal. Do what you need upon returning inside, and then open the crate door and then secure the opened door.

*Puppies usually need to eliminate waste during the night, thus you will need to make some late night trips outdoors.

As your dog becomes accustomed to his crate and surroundings, you can begin gradually to move the crate to your preferred location, but not to an isolated place.

Tips & Troubleshooting

• In the beginning, especially with puppies, keep the crate close to where you are in the house, and sleeping at night. As mentioned, you want to avoid any negative associations such as isolation that can result in depression or contribute to separation anxiety. This also strengthens your bond, and allows easy access for late night elimination trips.

Due to bladder and bowel control, puppies under six months should be kept crated for periods *under* four hours.

• Ignore whining unless your dog responds to your elimination command or phrase that you have been using when taking him to his elimination spot. If he does respond, then you know that he was whining for that and not simply for attention.

I know it is difficult to ignore whining, but it must be done so that your new dog or puppy understands that you are not at their disposal every time they seek attention. If you are bonding, socializing and practicing the other items suggested, then your puppy or dog should not need the extra attention.

• Before crating, take your dog outdoors to eliminate. There should be only 5-15 minutes between elimination and crating. *Best chance for success for your dog not to soil his crate.

• Don't forget to leave plenty of fresh water, chew-toys, and items that require problem solving, such as food stuffed toys.

• Don't place your dog into the crate for long periods before your departure from the house. Try to keep it under fifteen minutes or less.

Fluctuate the time between crating and departure.

- When soiling accidents occur inside the crate, thoroughly clean the crate and its contents with a *pet odor neutralizer*. Warning, do not use ammonia.

- *A couple of warnings* regarding crating - Avoid crating in direct sunlight or excessive heat, if your dog is sick with diarrhea or vomiting, or is having bowel and urine control issues. You can resume training once these are resolved.

- Always provide sufficient exercise and socialization.

- Never use the crate as a form of punishment.

- Quick review of approximate crating times per age, are as follows, 9-10 weeks 30-60 minutes, 11-14 weeks 1-3 hrs., 15-16 weeks 3-4 hrs., 17 + weeks 4-6 hrs.

- To thwart separation anxiety issues, never make a big emotional showing when you leave the house. Always act normal, because it is a normal thing for you to come and go. Do the same when you return, do not over dramatize your return, first do what you need to do then casually go over to his crate and open the door without making a big show of it. This aids your dog in understanding that all of this coming and going is a *normal* part of his life.

- After your dog is housetrained, and is no longer destructive, do not forcibly crate your dog, except when you absolutely need them crated. During other times, leave the door securely open and allow them to voluntarily come and go as they choose.

- Some reasons that your dog continues to soil his own crate are as follows. The crate is too large; there is a diet issue, health issue, too young to have control, suffering severe separation anxiety, or has drunk too much water prior to crating.

Another contributing factor could be the manner that your dog was housed prior to your acquiring him. If he was confined continuously to a small enclosure with no other outlet for elimination this will cause issues with housetraining and crating. If this is true for your dog, training will require more time and patience.

• Separation anxiety is an issue that cannot be solved using a crate. Consult the diagnosing and solving separation anxiety guidelines.

That wraps up crate training. I wish you well in crate and housetraining. I am sure that you will do wonderfully in shaping your dog's behaviors.

Housetraining Your GSD

Patience – Another of the foundational building blocks that you will carry forward. As mentioned, puppies and dogs have their own time schedules, and this requires applying a great deal of patience.

The fact is, dogs are a bit particular about where they "relief" and will invariably build a very strong habit. When housetraining your puppy, remember that whenever he relieves himself *somewhere* in the house, he is building a strong preference to that particular area. This is why preventing soiling accidents is very important; additionally thoroughly cleaning the area where the defecation occurred is important.

When your puppy does relieve his self in the house, *blame yourself*. Until your puppy has learned where he is supposed to do his business, you should keep a constant, watchful eye on him, whether he is in his crate, on a mat, beside you, or on the couch. While relief training, some people will *tether* their puppies to their waist or to a nearby object. This allows them to keep their puppies in eyesight.

- When your pup is indoors but out of the crate, watch for sniffing or circling, and as soon as you see this behavior, take him outdoors right away. *Do not hesitate.*

- If your pup is having accidents in the crate, the crate may be too big. The crate should be big enough for your puppy to stand up, turn around, and lie down in. If crate accidents occur, remove any soiled items from the crate and thoroughly clean it.

- Keep your puppy confined to their specific gated puppy area where accidents can be easily cleaned, such as section of bathroom, pantry, laundry, or similar. Do not leave your puppy confined to their crate for hours upon end. You want their crate to be an enjoyable place that they find safe and comforting.

- Set a timer to go off every hour so that you remember to take your puppy out before nature calls. With progress, you can increase the time duration between relief stops. Some Toy dogs need to go more frequently, around every thirty to forty-five minutes.

- A good rule of thumb for elimination duration is as follows, up to six weeks of age - elimination every hour, at two months of age - around two to three hours, at three months - four hours, four months and up - around five hours. These times will vary a little with individual dogs.

- If your pup does not do his *duty* when taken outdoors, bring him back indoors and keep a close eye on him. One option is to keep your pup tethered to your waist so that he is always in eyesight, then try again in 10-15 minutes.

- While you are away. If possible, arrange to have a person to take your puppy outside to eliminate.

Establish a Schedule

- You should take your puppy out many times during the day, most importantly after eating, playing, or sleeping. Feed your puppy appropriate amounts of food two or three times per day and leave the food down for around fifteen-minutes at a time, then remove. You can keep a pups water down until about eight at night, but then remove it from your puppy's reach.

- Puppies can generally hold for a good one-hour stretch. Larger breeds of dogs can hold their bladders longer than smaller dog breeds. Some small dogs cannot last the night before needing to go outside. Most adult dogs generally do not go longer than 8-10 hours between needing to urinate.

- Gradually, your puppy will be able to hold urinating for increasingly longer lengths of time, but until then keep to the every hour schedule. Keeping your puppy's excrement outdoors helps fast track your puppy's relief training success.

Consistency Is the Key to Prevention

Until your puppy is reliably housetrained, bring him outside to the same spot each time, always leaving a little bit of his waste there as a scent marker. This will be the designated relief spot. If you like, place a warning sign at that spot. Remember to use this spot for relief only, and not for play. Bring your puppy to his spot. When you see him preparing to relieve himself, say something like "relief time," "hurry up," or "now." As your pup is going, do not speak because it will distract him. Instead, ponder how much fun it will be when he is playing fetch and running back to you. When your puppy finishes, *praise, pet, give a top-notch treat,* and spend about five minutes playing with him. If he does not go potty, take your pup inside, keep an eye on him, and try again in 10-15 minutes.

If your puppy goes in the house, remember, that it is *your fault*. Maybe you went too quickly. If you see your puppy relieving himself in the wrong spot, quickly bring him outside to the designated relief spot so that he can finish, then when he is done, offer praise for finishing there. If you find a mess, clean it thoroughly without your puppy watching you do it. Use a cleaner specifically for pet stains so that there is no smell or evidence that you have failed him. This way it will not become a regular spot for your puppy and a new regular clean up chore for you.

Can I teach my puppy when to tell me when he needs to go out?

- Yes, you can! Hang a bell at dog level beside the door you use to let your dog outdoors. Put some easy cheese or peanut butter on the bell. When he touches it and rings it, immediately open the door. Repeat this every time and take him to the relief spot. Eventually, he will ring the bell without the easy cheese and this will tell you when he needs to go outside. Be careful here, your puppy may start to ring the bell when he wants to go outside to play, explore, or other non-relief reasons. To avoid this, each time he rings the bell, *only* take him out to the relief spot. If he starts to play, immediately bring him in the house.

Small Dogs often take longer time to soil train. I really do not know why, they just do. One way to help is to take them out more often than you would a larger dog. The longest duration I would go without taking a small dog to the relief spot is about 4 hours, and as a puppy maybe forty-five minutes instead of an hour. In addition, many small or toy dogs do well with a litter box. This way, they can go whenever nature calls and whatever the situation is, such as when there is an ice storm outside and they refuse to get their tiny little paws cold. Because many are easily chilled, some small dogs tend to dislike going outside during foul weather, or even cool conditions. Concurrently, we do not enjoy it either.

Clicker Response

Important - <u>Do not show your puppy the treat before pressing the clicker button,</u> and never deliver the treat prior to the clicker emitting a clicking sound. If you do this, your puppy will be responding to the treat and not the click, and this will undermine your training strategy.

Training should begin by simply observing your GSD puppy. What you are looking for is a desired behavior to reward. In other words, if your puppy is doing anything considered as an undesirable behavior, then do not reward. As long as your puppy is relaxed and behaving well, you can begin to train using this clicker response training.

What you are doing here is training your puppy to associate the clicker sound with doing something good. Whenever you click, your puppy will associate the sound with an acceptable performance, and will identify that he or she has a reward coming.

Timing is crucial when training your puppy. The essential technique when training your puppy with the clicker is by clicking precisely as the correct action takes place, followed by treating. It does not take long for your puppy to associate their behavior with the clicking sound, and subsequently receiving of a treat. Make sure that the treat is produced *immediately* following the clicking sound.

Crucial – *Never click without treating, and never treat without clicking. This maintains the connection and continuity between clicking and treating. This is the framework for achieving your desired outcomes.*

Steps

1. When your puppy is relaxed, you should stand, or kneel down at about an arm's length away, then click and give your puppy a treat.

2. Repeat this clicking and treating about 5-15 times. Pause a few seconds between clicks to allow your puppy to resume whatever he was doing. Do not click and treat if he seems to be begging for another treat. Find times throughout the day when he is performing a desired behavior, then click and treat. This teaches your puppy to associate the click with what you want him to do, and a tasty food treat.

When you click, and your puppy's head swings around in anticipation of a treat, then you know that your puppy has made the association between the clicking sound and a reward.

4. Repeat steps one and two the day following the introduction of clicker training. When your puppy quickly responds to the click, then you can begin using the clicker to train commands.

Teaching puppies to respond to this method can take several training sessions, but most commonly after about a dozen click and treats, they begin to connect the clicking sound with a treat. Usually, at the end of the first 5-minute session, puppies tend to swing their head around when they hear the clicker sound.

Important - After some dedicated training sessions, puppies tend to stop in their tracks and instantly come to you for a treat. At this time *refrain* from using this clicker technique to get your dog to come to you, but instead follow the instructions for teaching the "come" command.

Naming Your Puppy

After your puppy responds to the clicking sound, and he knows very well that treats follow the clicking sound, you can now begin teaching him commands and tricks.

Now, we are going to teach your puppy some specific things. Let's start with the base exercise that is teaching your puppy to respond to his or her *name*. I assume that you have already gone through the painstaking process of naming your puppy, and now when his or her name is spoken you want your puppy to learn to respond. This can be easy, fun, and satisfying when you finally get positive results.

Teaching your puppy his name is a basic and necessary objective that must be accomplished in order to gain and keep your puppies attention during all further training.

Before beginning training, be sure to gather an ample variety of treats. Put these treats in your treat pouch, or out of your puppy's reach.

1. Ignore your puppy until he looks directly at you, when he does, *click and treat* him. Repeat this 10-15 times. This teaches your puppy to associate the click with a treat, when he looks in your direction.

2. Next, when your puppy looks at you, begin adding your puppy's name, spoken exactly before you *click and treat*.

3. Continue doing this until your puppy will look at you when you say his or her name.

4. Gradually phase out clicking and treating your puppy every time that he or she looks at you. Decrease C/T incrementally; one out of two times, then one out of three, four, and then not at all. Try not to phase out the C/T too quickly.

After successful name recognition training, you should C/T on occasion, to refresh your puppy's memory and reinforce the association to hearing his name, and receiving a treat. Observe your puppy's abilities and pace during this training process, and adjust appropriately, when needed. The ultimate goal is to have your puppy obey all the commands via vocal or physical cue, *without a reward*.

Responding to his or her name is an important learned behavior, because it is the base skill for all future training. Therefore, you will want to give this training a considerable amount of attention, and thoroughly complete before moving forward.

I advise that you repeat this exercise in various locations around your home, while he is out on the leash, outside in the yard, or in the park. Eventually, make sure that you practice this while there are distractions, such as when there are guests present, his favorite toys are visible, food is available, and when he is amongst other dogs.

Always maintain good eye contact when you are calling your puppy's name. Keep on practicing this name recognition exercise until there is no doubt that when you speak your puppy's name, he knows whom you are referring to, and they respond appropriately.

It may sound odd, but also do this training when you are in different physical positions, such as sitting, standing, kneeling or laying down. Mix it up so that he gets used to hearing his name in a variety of areas and situations, and repeat this process frequently. No matter the situation, this command *must* be obeyed.

Name recognition will avoid trouble later on down the line. For example, if your puppy gets into something that he should not, such as chasing a cat or squirrel, you can simply call your puppy's name to gain his attention and then redirect him. You invariably want your puppy to come no matter what the distraction, so training "come" is also a crucial command to teach and regularly practice throughout the lifetime of your dog.

To be certain that you are able to grab your dog's attention in any circumstance or situation, continue to practice this training into adulthood to reinforce the behavior. When your puppy is appropriately responding to his or her name, I recommend moving forward to the "come" command.

The Jumper

Your dog loves you and wants as much attention from you as possible. The reality is that you are the world to your dog. Often when your dog is sitting quietly, he is easily forgotten. When he is walking beside you, you are probably thinking about other things, such as work, or anything but your loyal companion walking next to you. Sometimes your dog receives your full attention only when he jumps up on you.

When your dog jumps up on you, then you look at him, physically react in astonishment, maybe shout at him, and gently push him down until he is down on the floor. Then, you ignore him again, and make a mental note to teach your dog not to jump up onto you.

What do you expect? He wants your attention. Teaching your dog not to jump is essentially teaching him that attention will come only if he has all four paws planted firmly on the ground.

It is important not to punish your dog when teaching him not to jump up on you and others. Do not shout "no!" or "bad!" Do not knee your dog or push him down. The best way to handle the jumping is to turn your back and ignore your dog.

Importantly, since he loves you very much, your dog or puppy may take any physical contact from you as a positive sign. You do not want to send mixed signals; instead, you want to practice complete snubbing that consists of no looking or audio from you. If you do use a vocal command, use "sit," which your dog has probably already learned. Try not to use a command, and instead proceed with ignoring.

For jumping practice, it would be ideal if you could gather a group of people who will participate in helping you train your dog that jumping is unacceptable. You want to train your dog to understand that he will only receive attention if he is on the ground. If groups of people are not available, then teach him to remain grounded using his family. When your dog encounters other people, use a strong "sit stay" command to keep all four paws planted firmly on the ground.

Family

This is the easiest part, because the family and frequent visitors have more chances to help your dog or puppy to learn. When you come in from outside and your dog starts jumping up, say, "oops!" or "whoa," and immediately leave through the same door. Wait a few seconds after leaving and then do it again. When your dog finally stops jumping upon you as you enter, give him a lot of attention. Ask the rest of the family to follow the same protocol when they come into the house. If you find that he is jumping up at other times as well, like when you sing karaoke, walking down the hallway, or are cooking at the barbeque, just ignore your dog by turning your back and put energy into giving him attention when he is sitting.

Others

Prevention is of utmost importance and the primary focus in this exercise, especially with larger dogs. You can prevent your dog from jumping by using a leash, a tieback, crate, or gate. Until you have had enough practice and your dog knows what you want him to do, you really should use one of these methods to prevent your dog from hurting someone or getting an inadvertent petting reward for jumping. To train, you will need to go out and solicit some dog training volunteers and infrequent visitors to help.

- Make what is called a *tieback*, which is a leash attached to something sturdy, within sight of the doorway but not blocking the entrance keeping your dog a couple of feet or about a meter away from the doorway. Keep this there for a few months during the training period until your dog is not accosting you or visitors. When the guest arrives, hook your dog to the secure leash and then let the guest in.

Guests Who Want to Help Train

All of these training sessions may take many sessions to complete, so remain patient and diligent in training and prevention until your dog complies with not jumping on people.

- Begin at home, and when a guest comes in through the door, and the dog jumps up, they are to say "oops" or "whoa," and leave immediately. Practice this with at least five or six different visitors, each making multiple entrances during the same visit. If your helpers are jumped, have them completely ignore your dog by not making any eye contact, physical or vocal actions other than the initial vocal word towards your dog, then have them turn their backs and immediately leave.

- When you go out onto the streets, have your dog leashed. Next, have your guest helper approach your dog. If he strains against the leash or jumps have the guest turn their back and walk away. When your dog calms himself and sits, have the guest approach again. Repeat this until the guest can approach, pet and give attention to your dog without your dog jumping up. Have the volunteer repeat this at least five to seven times. Remember to go slowly and let your dog have breaks. Keep the sessions in the 5-7 minute range. For some dogs, this type of training can get frustrating. Eventually, your dog will understand that his jumping equals being ignored.

- Use the tie-back that you have placed near the door. Once your dog is calm, the visitor can greet your dog if they wish. If the guest does not wish to greet your dog, give your dog a treat to calm his behavior. If he barks, send your dog to his crate or the gated time out area. The goal is that you always greet your guests first, *not your dog*. Afterward, your guests have the option to greet or not greet, instead of your dog always rushing in to greet every guest. If he is able to greet guests calmly while tied back, then he may be released. At first hold the leash to see how your dog reacts, then if he is calm release him.

Another Alternative

1) For visitors that are not volunteers to help teach your dog and come visiting, there is another method. Keep treats by the door, and as you walk in throw them seven to nine feet (2.1 - 2.7 meters) away from you. Continue doing this until your dog begins to anticipate this. Once your dog is anticipating treats every time someone comes through the door it will keep him from hounding you or visitors that walk through the doorway. After your dog eats his treat and he has calmed down, ask him to sit, and then give him some attention.

2) Teach your dog that a hand signal such as grabbing your left wrist means the same as the command "sit." By combining the word "sit" with a hand on your left wrist, he will learn this. If you want to use another physical cue, you can substitute your own gesture here, such as holding your left elbow or ear.

Ask the guests that have volunteered to help train your dog to place their right hand on their left wrist and wait until your dog *sits* before they pet him or give any attention. Training people that meet your dog will help both you and your dog in preventing unwanted excitement and jumping up. Having your dog sit before he can let loose with jumps is proactive jumping prevention.

Barking

Surrender – *Remain lighthearted and avoid tunnel vision that has you overly fixated on things such as, "Why won't my dog learn this command?" or "Why does she still fear the lawnmower?" Let the process unfold naturally, not the way you envisioned.*

All dog owners know that dogs bark for many reasons, most commonly, for attention. Your GSD may bark for play, or because it is close to feeding time and he wants you to feed him. Dogs also bark to warn intruders and us, so we need to understand why our dog is barking. Not all barking is bad. Some dogs are short duration barkers, and others can go on for hours, our neighbors and we do not want that.

Whatever the case *do not* give your dog attention for barking. Do not send the signals that your dogs barking gets an immediate reaction from you, such as you coming to see why he is barking or moving towards him. As I mentioned in the opening paragraph, they do sometimes bark to warn us, so we should not ignore all barking, we need to assess the barking situation before dismissing it as nonsense barking.

When you know the cause is a negative behavior that needs correction, say, "leave it" and ignore him. While not looking at your dog go to the other side of the room, or into another room, you can even close the door behind you until your dog has calmed down. Make it clear to your barking dog that his barking does not result in any rewards or attention.

In everyday life, make sure you are initiating activities that your dog enjoys and always happening on *your* schedule. You are the alpha leader so regularly show your pup who is in charge. Also, make sure that he earns what he is provided. Have your pup *sit* before he gets any reward.

Your dog may bark when seeing or hearing something interesting. Below are a few ways to deal with this issue.

Prevention when you are at your residence

- *Teach your dog the command "quiet."* When your dog barks, wave a piece of food in front of his nose at the same time you are saying, "quiet." When he stops barking to sniff, *click and treat* him right away. Do this about four or five times. Then the next time he barks, pretend you have a piece of food in your hand next to his nose and say, "quiet." Always *click and treat* him as soon as he *stops* barking. After issuing the "quiet" command, *click and treat* him again for every few seconds that he remains quiet.

Eventually, as you make your way to five or ten seconds, gradually increase the time duration between the command "quiet," and *clicking and treating.*

- *Prevent it.* Block the source of sound or sight so that your dog is unable to see or hear the catalyst that is sparking his barking. Use a fan, stereo, TV, curtains, blinds, or simply put him in a different area of the house to keep him away from the stimulus.

- When your pup hears or sees something that would typically make him bark and he *does not bark*, reward him with attention, play, or a treat. This is reinforcing and shaping good behaviors instead of negative behaviors.

The Time Out

- Yes you can you can use a *time out* on your dog, but do not use it too often. When you give your dog a time out, you are taking your dog out of his social circle and giving your dog what is known as a negative punishment.

This kind of punishment is powerful and can have side effects that you do not want. Your dog may begin to fear you when you walk towards him, especially if you have the irritated look on your face that he recognizes as the *time out face*. The *time out* should be used sparingly. Instead, focus on teaching your dog the behaviors that you prefer while preventing the bad behavior.

Choose a place where you want the time out spot to be located. Make sure that this place is not the relief spot, crate, or his play area. Ideally it is a boring place that is somewhere that is not scary, not too comfortable, but safe. A gated pantry or the bathroom can work well.

Secure a 2-foot piece of rope or a short leash to your puppy's collar. When your pup barks, use a calm voice and give the command, "time out," then take the rope and walk him firmly but gently to the time out spot. Leave him there for about 5 minutes, longer if necessary. When your dog is calm and not barking, release him. You may need to do this two to a dozen times before he understands which behavior has put him into the time out place. Most dogs are social and love being around their humans, so this can have a strong impact.

Barking prevention when you are gone

- Again, prevent barking by blocking the sounds or sights that are responsible for your dog or puppy entering into barking mode. Use a fan, stereo, curtain, blinds, or keep him in another part of the house away from the stimulus.

- Use a Citronella Spray Collar. Only use this for when the barking has become intolerable. Do not use this when the barking is associated with fear or aggression.

Before using the spray, you will want to use this a few times while you are at home so that your dog understands how it works. Citronella collars work like this. The collar has a sensitive microphone, which senses when your dog is barking, when this happens it triggers a small release of citronella spray into the area above a dog's nose. It surprises the dog and disrupts barking by emitting a smell that dogs dislike.

Out walking

While you are out walking your dog, out of shear excitement or from being startled, he might bark at other dogs, people, cars, and critters. This can be a natural reaction or your dog may have sensitivities to certain tones, the goal is to try to limit the behavior and quickly cease the barking.

Here are some helpful tools to defuse that behavior.

- Teach your dog the *"watch me"* command. Begin this training in the house in a low distraction area. While you hold a treat to your nose, say your dog's name and "watch me." When your dog looks at the treat for at least one second give him a click and treat. Repeat this about 10-15 times. Then increase the time that your dog looks at you to 2-3 seconds, and repeat a dozen times.

- Then, repeat the process while pretending to have a treat on your nose. You will then want to incorporate this hand to your nose as your hand signal for *watch me*. *Click and treat* when your dog looks at you for at least one second, then increase to two or three seconds, and *click and treat* after each goal. Repeat this about 10-15 times.

- Increase the duration that your dog will continue to watch you while under the command. Click and treat as you progress. Try to keep your dog's attention for 5-10 seconds. Holding your dog's attention for this length of time usually results in the catalyst for him to move away from the area or to lose interest.

- Now, practice the "watch me" command while you are walking around inside the house. Then practice this again outside. When outside, practice near something he finds interesting. Continue practicing in different situations and around other catalysts that you know will produce your dog barking.

This is a great way to steer attention towards you and away from your dog's barking catalysts.

Other Solutions

- When you notice something that normally makes your dog bark and he has not begun to bark, use the "quiet" command. For example, your dog regularly barks at the local skateboarder. When the trigger that provokes your dog's barking, the skateboarder comes zooming by, use the command "quiet," and *click and treat*. Click and treat your dog for every few seconds that he remains quiet. Teach your dog that his barking trigger gets him a "quiet" command. Your dog will begin to associate the skateboarder with treats and gradually it will diminish his barking outbursts at the skateboarder.

- If he frequently barks while a car is passing by, put a treat by his nose, and then bring it to your nose. When he looks at you, *click and treat* him. Repeat this until he voluntarily looks at you when a car goes by and does not bark, continuing to *treat* him appropriately.

- You can also reward your dog for calm behavior. When you see something or encounter something that he would normally bark at and he does not, *click and treat* your dog.

Instead of treats, sometimes offer praise and affection.

- If you are out walking and your dog has not yet learned the *quiet* cue, or is not responding to it, turn around and walk away from whatever is causing your dog to bark. When he calms down, offer a reward.

- As a last resort use the citronella spray collar if your dogs barking cannot be controlled using the techniques that you have learned. Use this only when the barking is *not* associated with fear or aggression.

Your dog is Afraid, Aggressive, Lonely, or Territorial

Your dog may have outbursts when he feels territorial, aggressive, lonely, or afraid. All of these negative behaviors can be helped with proper and early socialization, but occasionally they surface. Many times rescue dogs might have not been properly socialized and bring their negative behaviors into your home. Be patient while you are teaching your new dog proper etiquette. If your dog is prone to territorialism, it can be a challenge to limit his barking.

- This is not a permanent solution, but is a helpful solution while you are teaching your dog proper barking etiquette. To allow your dog a chance to find his center, relax his mind and body, do this for about seven to ten days before beginning to train against barking.

As a temporary solution, you should first try to prevent outbursts by crating, gating, blocking windows, using fans or music to hide sounds, and avoid taking your dog places that can cause these barking outbursts.

Help

- Always, remain calm, because a relaxed and composed alpha achieves great training outcomes. A confident, calm, cool, and collected attitude that states you are unquestionably in charge goes a long way in training.

- If training is too stressful or not going well, you may want to hire a professional positive trainer for private sessions. When interviewing, tell him or her that you are using a clicker and rewards based training system and are looking for a trainer that uses the same type or similar methods.

It is important to help your dog to modify his thinking about what tends to upset him. Teach him that what he was upset about before now predicts his favorite things. Here is how.

- When the trigger appears in the distance, *click and treat* your dog. Keep clicking and treating your dog as the two of you proceed closer to the negative stimulus.

- If he is territorially aggressive, teach him that the doorbell or a knock on the door means that is his cue to get into his crate and wait for treats. You can do this by ringing the doorbell and luring your dog to his crate and once he is inside the crate giving him treats.

- You can also lure your dog through his fears. If you are out walking and encounter one of his triggers, put a treat to his nose and lead him out and away from the trigger zone.

- Use the "watch me" command when you see him getting nervous or afraid. *Click and treat* him frequently for watching you.

- Reward *calm* behavior with praise, toys, play, or treats.

Your dog is frustrated, bored or both

All dogs including your dog or puppy may become bored or frustrated. At these times, your dog may lose focus, and not pay attention to you. Here are a few things that can help prevent this:

- Keep him busy and tire him out with chew toys, exercise, play, and training. These things are a cure for most negative behaviors. A tired dog is usually happy to relax and enjoy quiet time.

- He should have at least 30 minutes of aerobic exercise per day. In addition to the aerobic exercise, each day he should have an hour of chewing and about 15 minutes of training. Keep it interesting for him with a variety of activities. It is, after all, the spice of life.

- Use the command "quiet" or give your dog a time out.

- As a last resort, you can break out the citronella spray collar.

Excited to Play

- Teach your dog that when he starts to bark, the playtime stops. Put a short leash on him and if he barks, use it to lead him out of play sessions. Put your dog in a time out or just stop playing with your dog. Reward him with more play when he calms down.

Armed with these many training tactics to curb and stop barking, you should be able to gradually reduce your dogs barking, and help him to understand that some things are not worth barking. Gradually you will be able to limit the clicking and treating, but it is always good practice to reward your dog for not barking. Reward your dog with supersized treat servings for making the big breakthroughs.

Nipping

Bite pressure is measured using pounds per square inch. GSD's are ranked number 7 for dogs with the most powerful bite and they can apply 238 pounds of bite pressure.

Rottweilers are number four with 328lbs. Number 2 is the Mastiff with 406 pounds, and number 1 is the livestock guardian Turkish Kandal with a scary 743 pounds of bite force. This compared to humans that can only apply approximately 86 pounds.

The highest ranked animal is the saltwater crocodile with a measured bite of 3,700 pounds per square inch.

Friendly and feisty, little puppies nip for a few reasons; they are teething, playing or they want to get your attention. If you have acquired yourself a nipper, not to worry, in time most puppies will grow out of this behavior on their own. Other dogs, such as some of those bred for herding, nip as a herding instinct. They use this behavior to round up their animal charges, other animals, family members, including those who are *human*.

While your dog is working through the nipping stage, you will want to avoid punishing or correcting your dog because this could eventually result in a strained relationship down the road. However, you will want to teach your puppy how delicate human skin is.

Let your dog test it out and give him feedback. You can simply indicate your discomfort when he bites too hard, by using and exclamation, such as, *"yipe!" or "youch!"* This in addition to a physical display of your pain by pulling back your hand, calf or ankle, will usually be enough for your dog to understand that it is not an acceptable behavior. After this action, it is important to cease offering any further attention towards your dog, because this offers the possibility that the added attention will reinforce the negative behavior.

If you act increasingly more sensitive to the nips, he will begin to understand that we humans are very sensitive, and will quickly respond with a sudden vocal and physical display of discomfort.

This is a very easy behavior to modify because we know the motivation behind it. The puppy wants to play and chew, and who is to blame him for this? Remember, it is important to give your dog access to a variety of chew-toys, and when he nips, respond accordingly, then immediately walk away and ignore him. If he follows you, and nips at your heels, give your dog a time out.

Afterward, when your dog is relaxed, calm and in a gentle disposition, stay and play with him. Use the utmost patience with your puppy during this time, and keep in mind that this behavior will eventually pass.

Preventing Nipping

- Always have a chew toy in your hand when you are playing with your puppy. This way he learns that the right thing to bite and chew is the toy, and is *not your hands, or any other part of your body*.

- Get rid of your puppy's excess energy by exercising him *at least* an hour each day. As a result, he will have no energy remaining to nip.

- Make sure he is getting adequate rest and that he is not cranky from lack of sleep. Ten to eleven hours per day is good for dogs.

- Constantly have lots of interesting chew toys available to help your puppy to cope during the teething process.

- Teach your kids not to run away screaming from nipping puppies. They should walk away quietly, or simply stay still. Children should *never* be left unsupervised around dogs.

- Play with your puppy in his gated puppy area. This makes it easier to walk away. This quickly reinforces his understanding that hard bites end play sessions.

- As a last resort, when the other interventions and methods discussed above are not working, you should increase the frequency of your use of a tieback to hold your dog in place, within a gated or time out area.

If your dog is out of control with nipping or biting, and you have not yet trained him that biting is an unacceptable behavior, you may have to use this method until he is fully trained. For example, you may want to use this when guests are over, or if you simply need a break. Always use a tieback while your dog is under supervision, and never leave him tied up alone. The tieback is a useful method and can be utilized as a tool of intervention when addressing other attention getting behaviors like jumping, and barking.

The best option during early training is to place him in a room with a baby gate in the doorway.

Troubleshooting

- Play with your dog and praise him for being gentle. When he nips say, *"yipe!"* mimicking the sound of an injured puppy, and then immediately walk away. After the nipping, wait one minute and then return to give him another chance at play, or simply remain in your presence *without nipping*.

Practice this for two or three minutes, remembering to give everyone present or those who will have daily contact with him a chance to train him through play. It is crucial that puppies *do not receive any reward for nipping*. After an inappropriate bite or nip, all physical contact needs to be abruptly stopped, and quick and complete separation needs to take place so that your puppy receives a clear message.

- After your puppy begins to understand that bites hurt, and if he begins to give you softer bites, *continue to act hurt, even if it doesn't* hurt. In time, your dog will understand that only the slightest pressures by mouth are permissible during play sessions.

Continue practicing this until your puppy is only using the softest of mouths, and placing limited tension upon your skin. It is best to avoid mouthing as it often re-escalates.

- Next, the goal is to decrease the frequency of mouthing. You can use the verbal cues of *quit* or *off* to signal that his mouth needs to release your appendage. Insist that the amount of time your puppy uses his mouth on you needs to decrease in duration, as well as the severity of pressure needs to decrease. If you need incentive, use kibble or liver to *reward after you command and he obeys.* Another reward for your puppy when releasing you from his mouth grasp is to give him a chew or chew-toy stuffed with food.

- The desired outcome of this training is for your puppy to understand that mouthing any human, if done at all, should be executed with the utmost care, and in such a manner, that without question the pressure *will not inflict pain or damage.*

- Continue the training using the verbal cue of *quit,* until *quit* becomes a well-understood command, and your dog consistently complies when it is used. Interject breaks every 20-30 seconds when playing and any type of mouthing is occurring. The calm moments will allow excitement to wane, and will help to reduce the chances of your dog excitably clamping down.

Practice this frequently, and as a part of your regular training practice schedule. The result from successful training and knowing that your dog will release upon command will give you piece of mind.

- If you have children, or are worried about the potential for injury due to biting, you can continue training in a way that your dog knows that mouthing is *not permitted under any circumstance.* This level of training permits you from having to instruct a permissible mouthing pressure. This will result in a reduction of your anxiety whenever your dog is engaged in playing with your family or friends. This of course nearly eliminates the potential for biting accidents to occur.

Remain vigilant when visitors are playing with your dog. Monitor the play, and be especially attentive to the quality of the interaction, being alert that the session is not escalating into a rough and potentially forceful situation in which your dog might choose to use his mouth in an aggressive or harmful way.

You will need to decide the rules of engagement, and it will be your responsibility that others understand these rules. To avoid harm or injury it will be necessary for you to instruct visitors and family prior to play.

Diggers

Some dogs are going to dig no matter what you do to stop it. For these diggers, this behavior is bred into them, so remember that these dogs have an urge to do what they do. Whether this behavioral trait is for hunting or foraging, it is deeply imbedded inside their DNA and it is something that cannot be turned off easily, or at all. Remember that when you have a digger for a dog, they will tend to be excellent escape artists, so you will need to bury your perimeter fencing deep to keep them inside your yard or kennel.

This trait is not easily altered or trained away, but you can shape the behavior into the direction of your choosing. To combat dog escapes you will need to bury your fencing or chicken wire deep into the ground. It is suggested that 18-24 inches, or 46-61cm into the soil below the bottom edge of your fencing is sufficient, but we all know that a determined dog may even go deeper, when in pursuit of quarry. Some dog owners will affix chicken wire at about 12 inches (30.5cm) up onto the fence, and then bury the rest down deep into the soil. Usually, when the digging dog reaches the wire, its efforts will be thwarted and it will stop digging.

Some dogs dig as an instinctive impulse to forage for food to supplement their diet. Because dogs are omnivorous, they will sometimes root out tubers, rhizomes, bulbs, or any other edible root vegetable that is buried in the soil. Even nuts buried by squirrels, newly sprouting grasses, the occasional rotting carcass or other attractive scents will be an irresistible aroma to their highly sensitive noses.

Other reasons dogs dig can be traced directly to boredom, lack of exercise, lack of mental and physical stimulation, or improperly or under-socialized dogs. Improperly socialized dogs can suffer from separation anxiety and other behavioral issues. Non-neutered dogs may dig an escape to chase a female in heat. Working breeds such as Border Collies, Australian Cattle Dogs, Shelties, and other working breeds can stir up all sorts of trouble if not kept busy. This trouble can include incessant digging.

It has been said that the smell of certain types of soil can also catch a dog's fancy. Fresh earth, moist earth, certain mulches, topsoil, and even sand are all lures for the digger. If you have a digger, you should fence off the areas where you are using these alluring types of soils. These kinds of soils are often used in newly potted plants or when establishing a flowerbed or garden. The smell of dirt can sometimes attract a dog that does not have the strong digging gene, but when he finds out how joyful digging can be, beware; you can be responsible for the creation of your own "digging machine."

Proper socialization, along with plenty of mental and physical exercises will help you in your fight against digging, but as we know, some diggers are going to dig no matter what the situation. Just in case your German Shepherd is an earnest excavator, here are some options to help you curb that urge.

The Digging Pit

A simple and fun solution is to dig a pit specifically for him or her to dig to their little heart's content. Select an appropriate location, and with a spade, turn over the soil a bit to loosen it up, mix in some sand to keep it loose as well as to improve drainage, then surround it with stones or bricks to make it obvious by sight that this is the designated spot.

To begin training your dog to dig inside the pit, you have to make it attractive and worth their while. First bury bones, chews, or a favorite toy, then coax your dog on over to the pit to dig up some treasures. Keep a watchful eye each time you bring your dog out, and do not leave him or her unsupervised during this training time. It is important to halt immediately any digging outside of the pit. When they dig inside of the designated pit, be sure to reward them with treats and praise. If they dig elsewhere, direct them back to the pit. Be sure to keep it full of the soil-sand mixture, and if necessary, littered with their favorite doggie bootie. If your dog is not taking to the pit idea, an option is to make the other areas where they are digging temporarily less desirable such as covering them with chicken wire, and then making the pit look highly tantalizingly, like a *doggie digging paradise*.

Buried Surprises

Two other options are leaving undesirable surprises in the unwanted holes your dog has begun to dig. A great deterrent is to place your dog's own *doodie* into the holes that he has dug, and when your dog returns to complete his job, he will not enjoy the gift you have left him, thus deterring him from further digging.

Another excellent deterrent is to place an air-filled balloon inside the hole and then cover it with soil. When your dog returns to his undertaking and then his little paws burst the balloon, the resulting loud "POP!" sound will startle, and as a result, your dog will reconsider the importance of his or her mission. After a few of these shocking noises, you should have a dog that thinks twice before digging up your bed of pansies.

Shake Can Method

This method requires a soda can or another container filled with rocks, bolts, or coins, remembering to place tape or apply the cap over the open end to keep the objects inside. Keep this "rattle" device nearby so that when you let your dog out into the yard you can take it with you to your clandestine hiding spot. While hidden out of sight, simply wait until our dog begins to dig. Immediately at the time of digging, take that can of coins and shake it vigorously, thereby startling your dog. Repeat the action each time your dog begins to dig, and after a few times your dog should refrain from further soil removal. Remember, the goal is to *startle* and to distract your dog at the time they initiate their digging, and not to terrorize your little friend.

Shake can instructions

1. Shake it quickly once or twice then stop. The idea is to make a sudden and disconcerting noise that is unexpected by your dog who is in the process of digging. If you continue shaking the can, it will become an ineffective technique.

2. Beware not to overuse this method. Remember your dog *can become desensitized* to the sound, and thus ignore the prompt.

3. Sometimes, it is important to supplement this method by using commands, such as "No" or "Stop."

4. Focus these techniques, targeting only the behavior (e.g. digging) that you are trying to eliminate.

5. Sometimes, a noise made by a can with coins inside may not work, but perhaps using a different container filled with nuts and bolts, or other items will. Examples are soda or coffee cans that are filled with coins, nuts, bolts, or other metal objects. You might have to experiment to get an effective and disruptive sound. If the noise you make sets off prolonged barking instead of a quick startled bark, then the sound is obviously not appropriate. If your dog does begin to bark after you make the noise, use the "quiet" command immediately after, and never forget to reward your dog when he or she stops the barking, thereby reinforcing the wanted behavior.

I hope that these methods will assist you in controlling or guiding your four-legged landscaper in your desired direction. Anyone that has had a digger for a dog knows it can be challenging. Just remember that tiring them out with exercise and games is often the easiest and most effective in curbing unwanted behaviors.

COMMANDS

"Sit"

Excitement – *Make sure that both you and your dog are having fun and enjoying your time together. Keep it lively!*

"Sit" is one of the basic commands that you will use regularly during life with your dog. Teaching your GSD to *sit* establishes human leadership by shaping your dog's understanding of who the boss is. This command can also help curb problem behaviors, such as jumping up on people. It can also assist in teaching polite doggy etiquette, particularly of patiently waiting for you, *the trusted alpha*. Teaching your dog to sit is easy, and a great way for you to work on your catalog of essential alpha behaviors touched upon in previous chapters.

- First, gather treats, then find a quiet, low distraction place to begin the training. Wait until your puppy sits by his own will, and soon as his hindquarter hits the floor, *click and treat*. Treat your pup while he is still sitting, then promptly get him up and standing again. Continue doing this until your pup immediately sits back down in anticipation of the treat. Each time he complies, be sure to click and treat.

- Next, integrate the verbal command of "sit." Each time he begins to sit on his own, say, "sit," then reinforce with a C/T. From here on, only treat your pup when he sits after being commanded to do so. Practice for 10-15 repetitions then take a break.

Do these variations

- Continue the training by adding the distraction of people, animals, and noises to the sessions. As with the come command, you want your dog to sit during any situation that might take place. Practice for at least five minutes each day in places with increasingly more distractions.

- Run around with your dog while you are sharing play with one of his favorite toys. After getting him worked up and excited, command your dog to *sit*. Click and treat your dog when he does.

- Before going outside, delivering food, playing with toys, giving verbal praise, petting, or getting into the car, ask your dog to *sit*. Having your dog sit before setting his food bowl down is something you can practice every day to help bolster his compliance to the sit command.

- Other situations where you can practice the sit command can be when there are strangers present, or before opening doors for visitors. In addition, other excellent opportunities to work on the sit command is when there is food on the table, when you are barbequing, or when you are together in the park.

Keep practicing this command in all situations that you may encounter throughout the day. I recommend a gradual increase to the level of distraction exposure during this training. Sit is a powerful and indispensable command that you will utilize throughout the life of your dog. Later, we will add the command of "sit-stay" in order to keep your dog in place until you release him.

-It is important eventually to phase out the clicking and treating every time that he obeys the "sit" command. After his consistent obedience to the command, you can begin gradually to reduce C/T by treating every other compliance, then once out three times, followed by once out of four, five, six, and then finally cease. Be sure to observe your dog's abilities and pace, making sure not to decrease C/T too rapidly. The overall goal of this training is to have your dog obey all commands without a reward, and only by a vocal or physical cue.

-Take advantage of each day, and the multiple opportunities you have to practice the sit command.

Now move forward to other commands.

"Come"

Simplicity – *Avoid overloading your dog with extended repetitions and long training sessions; keep the sessions at ten to fifteen minutes and reorder the commands being taught.*

After your puppy recognizes, and begins responding to his name being called, then the "come" command takes priority as the first command to teach. *Why, b*ecause this one could save his life, and save your sanity.

If by chance, he is checking out the olfactory magic of the trash bin, the best way to redirect your dog is firmly command him to *"come,"* followed immediately by a reward when he complies. Petting, verbal praise, or play is an appropriate reinforcement and an effective redirecting incentive during this type of situation.

In order to grab your dog's attention, no matter what activity he is engaged in, it is necessary to implement an effective verbal command. Unfortunately, the word *"come"* is a commonly used word that is spoken regularly during daily life, thus making it difficult to isolate as a special command word, so I suggest that a unique and infrequently used word be chosen for this. For example, say "Skipper & *Zam,"* which replaces the standard, "Skipper *come,"* or "Skipper *here."* When your dog hears a special cue word such as *zam*, he will recognize it as the word associated with the command to return to you and receive a special treat. However, if you find it effective and natural, there is nothing wrong with simply using "come" as your command word.

Note: Choose a command word with one or two syllables, and one that you can easily say, because it will be difficult to change the substituted "come" command word later.

Here is what to do-

- If you have chosen to use a unique "come" command, you can begin here. We will not use the clicker at this time. First, gather your assortment of treats such as bits of steak, bacon, cheese, or whatever your dog most covets.

Start with the tastiest treat in hand, and speak the new command word, immediately followed by a treat. When your dog hears this new word, he will begin to associate it with a special treat. Keep repeating this exercise, and mix up the treats that you provide. Remember to conclude each training session by providing a lot of praise to your dog. Repeat for about ten repetitions then proceed onto the next step.

- Gather your clicker and treats, and then find a quiet, low distraction place so that both of you can focus. First, place a treat on the floor and walk to the other side of the room. Next, hold out a hand with a visible treat in it. Now, say your dog's name to get his attention, followed by the command "Come." Use a pleasant, happy tone when you do this.

When your dog begins to move towards you, press the clicker, and praise him all the way to the treat in your hand. The objective of this is for him to ignore the treat on the ground and come to you. When he gets to you, *treat* him from your hand and offer some more praise and affection. Be sure and not click again, only give the treat.

Each time your dog comes to you, pet or touch his head and grab a hold of his collar before treating. Sometimes do this on top of the collar, and sometimes beneath his head on the bottom of the collar. This action gets your dog used to being held, so that when you need to grab a hold of him by the collar he will not shy away or fight you.

Do this 10-12 times, and then take a break. Make sure that your dog accomplishes the task by walking the complete distance across the room to you, while wholly ignoring the treat that you placed on the floor.

- For the next session, you will need the assistance of a family member and will not use the clicker. First, situate yourselves at a distance of about 5-6 paces opposite each other, and place a treat on the floor between the two of you. Each of you show your dog a treat when you say his name followed by "come." Now, take turns calling your dog back and forth between the two of you. Treat and praise your dog each time he successfully comes all of the way to either of you, *while ignoring the treat*. Repeat this about a dozen times. The objective of this exercise is to reinforce the idea that coming when commanded is not only for you, but is beneficial to him as well.

- This time, grab your clicker. As before, put a treat on the ground, move across the room, and then call your dog's name to get his attention, but this time hold out an empty hand and give the command. This will mess with him a little, but that's okay, he is learning. As soon as he starts to come to you, give him praise and when he reaches you, *click and treat* by using the opposite hand that you were luring him.

If your dog is not completing the distance to you, press the clicker as he begins to move closer to you, and the first time he completes the distance, give him a supersized treat serving (7-10 treats). Each additional time your dog comes all of the way to you; reward your dog with a regular sized treat serving. Do this about a dozen times, and then take a break. Cease using the clicker as a lure, and only use the hand signal, then C/T when he comes all of the way to you.

- Keep practicing this exercise, but now call your dog using an empty hand. Using this technique over several sessions and days should eventually result in a successful hand signal command.

Following your dog's consistent compliance with this hand signal training, you can then take the training to the next step by phasing out the hand signal by using only a verbal cue. When shifting to the verbal cue training, reduce treating incrementally, first by treating one out of two times, then one out three times, followed by one out of four, five, six, and lastly without treating at all.

Note: It is important to treat your dog periodically in order to reinforce the desired behavior that he is exhibiting, as well as complying with the command you are issuing. Make sure your dog is coming when commanded; this includes all family members and friends. By the end of this section, your dog should consistently be obeying the hand signal and the verbal *come* command successfully.

Adding Distractions

- Now, by adding distractions we will begin to make obeying commands a more difficult task for your dog. The outcome of this training should result in better control over your canine in times when there is distracting stimulus.

First, find somewhere where there are sights, sounds, and even smells that might distract your dog. Almost anything can serve as a distraction here. You can intentionally implement distractions, such as having his favorite toy in hand, by having another person present, or even doing this training beside the steaks cooking up on the BBQ.

Indoors, distractive aspects of daily home life, such as the noise of the television, the doorbell, or friends and family coming and going can serve as distractions.

Then move to calling your dog from different rooms of the house, meanwhile gradually introducing other distractions such as music from the stereo, groups of people and combinations of the sort. Of course, the outdoor world offers a plethora of potential interruptions, commotions and interferences for your pal to be tantalized and diverted by.

- During this training exercise, I find it helpful to keep a log of not only how your dog is progressing, but also accounting for the different kinds and levels of distractions your dog is encountering.

Now, in the high stimulus setting, resume training using the previous set of learned commands. As before, begin with treats in hand, because in this instance, when necessary, the snacks will act as a lure for your dog to follow in order to help him focus, rather than as a reward. The goal is to dispense with the treats by gradually phasing them out, eventually only using the vocal command.

When you are outdoors, practice calling the command "come." Practice when you and your dog are in the yard with another animal or person, and then followed by increasing and more complex distractions. Such as a combination of a person and animal together, then with multiple people conversing or while children are running around, and then you can even throw some toys or balls into the mix.

Eventually, move out onto the streets and sidewalks, introducing even busier locations, remembering to keep track of your dog's progress as the situations become more and more distracting. The goal is that you want your dog to come every time you call "come," no matter how much noise and movement is happening around him.

If your dog consistently begins to return to you seven or eight times out of each ten commands, regardless of the distractions, this shows that the two of you are making very good progress, and that you are well on your way to the ideal goal of nine out of ten times compliant. If your dog is sporting ten out of ten times, you may consider paying a visit to MENSA, because you have got yourself one special canine there.

We all want a dog that comes when you use the "come" command. Whether he is seven houses down the road, or just in the next room, a dog that comes to you no matter what he is engaged in, is a dog worth spending the time training.

Interrupting Fetch Exercises, Hide & Seek, and the Decoy Exercise

Practice all of the following exercises with increasing distractions, both indoors and outdoors. Focus on practicing one of these exercises per session, eventually mixing up the order of the exercises as your dog masters each. Remember it is always important to train in a safe area.

- Interrupting Fetch Exercises

Get an ample-sized handful of your GSDs favorite treat. Then, lob a ball or a piece of food at a reasonable distance, and as your dog is in the process of chasing it, call him by issuing the *come* command. If he comes *after* he gets the ball/food, give your dog a little reward of one piece of treat. If he comes *before* he gets the ball/food, give your dog a supersized (7-10) serving of treats.

If your dog is not responding to your "come" command, then throw the ball and quickly place a treat down towards his nose height while at the same time saying, "come", when he comes to you click and supersize treat your dog. Then, begin phasing out the treat lure.

After you have thrown the ball/food over several sessions, it is time to change it up. Like the exercise prior, this time you will fake throwing something, and then call your dog. If your dog goes looking for the ball/food before he comes back to you, give a small treat. If he comes immediately after you say, "come," give the supersized treat portion. Repeat this exercise 7-10 times.

- Hide & Seek

While you are both outside, and your dog is distracted and does not seem to know you exist, quickly *hide* from him. When your dog comes looking for you, and eventually finds you, *click and treat* your dog in addition with lots of love and praise. By adding a little drama, make it seem like an extremely big deal that your dog has found you. This is something that you can regularly practice and reward.

- *The Decoy*

One person calls the dog; we will call this person the *trainer*. One person tries to distract the dog with food and toys; we will call this person the *decoy*. After the trainer calls the dog, if the dog goes toward the decoy, the decoy person should turn away from the dog and neither of you offer rewards. When the dog goes towards the trainer, he should be rewarded by *both* the trainer and the decoy. Repeat 7-10 times per session.

Help

- Let your dog know that his coming to you is always the best thing ever, sometimes offering him supersized treat rewards for this behavior. Always reward by treating or praising, and when appropriate you can add play with a favorite toy or ball.

- Never, call your GSD for something he might find unpleasant. To avoid this disguise the real purpose. If you are leaving the field where he has been running, call your dog, put on the leash, and play a little more before leaving. If you are calling your dog to get him into the bath, provide a few minutes of affection or play instead of leading him straight into the bath. *This will pacify and distract from any negative association with coming to you.*

- You are calling, and your puppy is not responding. What do you do now? Try running backwards away from your dog, crouch, and clap, or show your dog a toy or food. When he comes, still reward him even if he has stressed you out. Running *towards* your dog signals to play *catch me*, so avoid doing this.

- If your dog has been enjoying some unabated freedom off lead, remember to give him a C/T when he checks in with you. Later you can phase out the C/T and only use praise.

- You should practice "come" five to ten times daily, ongoing for life. This command is one of those potentially life-saving commands that helps with all daily activities and interactions.

The goal is that your dog will come running to you, whether you are in or out of sight, and from any audible distance. As owners, we know that having a dog that obeys this command makes life less stressful.

"Leave it"

Rin Tin Tin *has twenty-eight acting credits ranging from the years 1922-1931. Rinty starred in over twenty-six pictures, had his own private chef, eighteen dog stand-ins, and ate daily lunches of tenderloin steak while listening to classical music. Not a bad life for a movie star dog.*

The goal of the *leave it* command is to steer your GSDs attention away from any object before it ends up in his mouth, making it a proactive command.

A proficiency in this command will help to keep him safe from dangerous items, for example objects such as dropped medications, broken glass, trash, wires, chemical tainted rags, or that treasured item you spy your dog about to place into his mouth.

A simple "leave it" command can thwart those especially smelly, frequently dead things that dogs find irresistible and often choose to bring us as offerings of love and affection." We all know that our dogs love to inspect, smell, taste, and in some cases roll in what they find. You can begin to teach the leave it command as soon as your dog recognizes his own name.

- Start with a treat in each fisted hand. Let him have a sniff of one of your fists. When he eventually looks away from the fist and has stopped trying to get the treat, click and treat, but treat your dog from the opposite hand that he sniffed. Repeat this exercise until he completely refrains from trying to get the treat from you, as evidenced by showing no interest in your fist.

- Next, open your hand with the treat, and show him the treat. Close your hand if he tries to get the treat. Do this until he simply ignores the treat in the open hand, known as the decoy hand. When he ignores it, click and give your dog the treat from the other hand. Keep doing this until he ignores the treat in the open hand from the start of the exercise.

When you have reached this point, add the command "leave it." Now, open the decoy hand, say "leave it" just once for each repetition, and when your dog does, click and treat him from the other hand.

- Now, put the treat on the floor and say, "leave it." Cover it with your hand if he tries to get it. When your dog looks away from the treat that is lying on the floor, click and treat your dog from the other hand. Continue issuing the command "leave it" until your dog no longer tries to get the treat that is on the floor.

-For the next exercise, put the treat on the floor and say, "leave it," and then stand up. Click and treat if he obeys. Now, walk your dog by the treat while he is on his leash and say, "leave it." If he goes for it, prevent this by restraining him with the leash. C/T him only when he ignores the treat. Lastly, increase the length of time between the leave it command and the C/T.

Teaching your dog to leave it using a treat first, will allow you to work up to objects such as toys, animals, pills, spills, and even people. Once he gets the idea in his head that leave it means rewards for him, you both can eventually work towards more complex situations involving more difficult to resist items. Begin with a low value item such as a piece of kibble, then move to a piece of hard to resist meat, his favorite toy, another animal, or people.

- After your dog is successful at leaving alone the treat and other items, take the training outside into the yard, gradually adding people, toys, animals, and other hard to resist distractions. Next, head to the dog park, or any other place with even more distractions.

Remember to keep your puppy clear of dog parks until at least after his seventh week, preferably no sooner than his tenth week, and certainly only after his first round of vaccines. Some veterinarians and experts suggest even waiting until after the second round of vaccinations before your dog is exposed to other animals.

Continue practicing daily until your dog has this command down pat. This is another potential lifesaving command that you will use regularly during the life of your dog.

- At this point, you both can have some real fun. Try placing a dog biscuit on your pups paw, snout, or head and say, "leave it." Gradually increase the time that your pup must leave the biscuit in place. Try this when he is in the sitting and other down positions. Have some fun and be sure to reward your dog the biscuit after he leaves it undisturbed. ~ Enjoy!

- Gradually phase out clicking and treating your dog every time that on command he obeys "leave it." As with prior commands, begin gradually reducing treating by one out of two times, one out three times, then one out of four, five, six, and finally none. Remember not to decrease too quickly or it will undermine your training. Keenly observe your dog's abilities and pace at all times. The goal is that your dog will obey all the commands without a reward, eventually with only a vocal or physical cue.

"Drop it"

Looking for action - *GSD bitches are in heat twice yearly, with a heat cycle lasting anywhere from one to twenty-one days. The mating phase resides somewhere between twelve and twenty-one days.*

Teaching your GSD to *drop it* is very important because if you have ever had a young puppy, you know that it is one giant mouth gobbling up whatever is in sight. Puppies are clueless in regards to what might do them harm. Sometimes valuable and dangerous things go into that mouth, and the command to "drop it" may save your family heirloom, over even perhaps your dog's life.

If you teach your dog correctly, when you give the command "drop it," he will open his mouth and drop whatever is in there. Most importantly, he will not only drop the item, but he will allow you to retrieve it without protest. When teaching the *drop it* command you must offer a good trade for what your dog has in his mouth. You need to *out-treat* your dog by offering a better treat of higher value in exchange for what he has in his mouth. In addition, it is a good idea to stay calm and not to chase your puppy, as this elicits a play behavior that can work against your desired training outcomes.

If this command is successfully taught, your puppy will actually enjoy hearing "drop it." This command will also build trust between the two of you. For example, if you say, "drop it," then you retrieve the item, and afterward you give a treat, he will know that you are not there simply to steal the thing he has found. Because of the trust that will develop, he will not guard his favorite toys, or food. Negative behaviors, such as guarding, can be avoided with this, and socialization types training.

Training

- Gather a variety of good treats, and a few items your dog might like to chew on, such as a favorite toy, or a rawhide chew. With a few treats in hand, encourage your dog to chew on one of the toys. When the item is in his mouth, *put a treat close to his nose* and say, "drop it!" As soon as he opens his mouth, *click and treat* him as you pick up the item. Then, return the item to your dog.

At this point, your dog may not want to continue to chew on the item because there are treats in the area, and his mouth is now free to consume. If he appears now to be distracted by the treats you possess, rather than the chew-toy, you can take this as an opportunity to pause the training.

Be sure and keep the treats handy though, because throughout the day when you see him pick something up, you both can practice the *drop it* command. Do this at least ten times per day, or until this command is mastered.

In the event that he picks up a forbidden item you may not want to give back to him, instead, give your puppy an extra tasty treat, or a supersized serving as an equitable exchange for the item that you confiscate. You want your puppy to be redirected, and he should be properly rewarded for his compliance.

- Once you have done the treat-to-the-nose *drop it* command ten times, try doing it *without* holding the treat to his nose. Continue to use your hand, but this time it should be empty. Say the command, and when he drops the item, *click and treat*. Make sure the first time he drops it, when you are not holding a treat to his nose, that you give him a supersized treat serving from a different hand. Practice this over a few days and training sessions. Do not rush to the next step until his response is consistently compliant, and training is successful.

- This next part of the *drop it* training will further reinforce the command, in particular during situations where a tug-of-war between you may ensue. This time you will want to use a treat that your dog might find extra special, like rawhide, making sure that it is something that cannot be consumed quickly. Next, hold this new chewy in your hand and offer it to your dog, but this time *do not let it go*. When your dog has the chewy in his mouth, say, "drop it." When your dog drops it for the *first time*, C/T, being sure to give your dog extra treats, and then offer the chew back to him to keep.

Because better treats are available, he may not take the chewy back. Recognize this as a good sign, but it also signals a time for a break. Later, repeat this training about a dozen times before you move on to the next phase of "drop it." If your dog is not dropping it after clicking, then the next time use a higher value treat.

- For the next phase of the "drop it" command training, repeat the exercise above, but this time do not hold onto the chew, just let him have it. As soon as your dog has it in his mouth, give the command "drop it." When your dog drops the chewy, C/T a supersized portion, then be sure to give the chew back to him to keep. Your dog will be thrilled by this exchange. Once you have successfully done this a dozen times, move onto the next step.

During this exercise, if your dog does not drop the chewy, it will be necessary to show the treat first, as incentive. Once he realizes that you hold treats, you will want to work up to having him drop it before the treat is given. This in actuality is *bribery*, and I do not suggest utilizing this action as a short cut elsewhere during training. *Remember,* only use this method as a last resort, and discontinue it quickly. - Try this command with the things around the house that he is not supposed to chew on, such as pens, chip bags, socks, gloves, tissues, or shoes.

After you and your dog have achieved success indoors with this command, try the exercise outside where there are plenty of distractions. To hold his attention when you are moving into further distracting situations, be sure and have with you the best of treats. Keep in mind that your goal is to have the drop it command obeyed in any situation.

- Practice the drop it command when playing fetch, and other games. For example, when your dog returns to you with his ball, command "drop it," and when he complies, offer up the magic duo of praise, plus a treat.

- Gradually phase out the clicking and treating of your dog every time that he drops something on command. Progressively reduce treating by first treating one out of two times, then one out three times, followed by one out of four, five, six, and finally not at all.

Always remain aware of your dog's abilities, and his individual pace, being sure not to decrease treating too rapidly. The desired outcome of this training is that your dog will obey *all* commands by a vocal or physical cue, without a reward.

Help

- If your GSD already enjoys trying to incite games of grab and chase with you, it is best to curb this behavior from the onset by teaching your dog that you *will not* chase after him if he thieves and bolts. If your dog grabs and runs, *completely* ignore him. For you to be effective here, it means that you do not indicate your disapproval with any sort of eye contact, body language, or vocalization. He will quickly get bored, and drop the item on his own.

- If your dog refuses to drop an item, you may have to retrieve it manually. You can do this by placing your hand over the top of your dog's muzzle, and with your index finger and thumb placed on either side of his upper lip, firmly pinch it into his teeth. Before utilizing this technique, it is best to attempt to calm your dog's excitement as much as possible. In most cases, your dog will open its mouth to avoid the discomfort, and at this time, you can retrieve the item.

This may take a couple of practices to get the correct pressure and the most effective location to apply it. In the rare instance that this fails, you can simply use both hands and try to separate the jaws by slowly pulling, *not jerking*, the upper and lower jaws apart.

-Another trick for distracting your puppy's attention is by rapping your knuckles on a hard surface, emulating a knock at the door. Often, a puppy will want to investigate what he perceives as a guests arrival, thus dropping whatever is in his mouth to greet the nonexistent visitor.

"Down"

Super Smart *– GSD's are known for their high intellect and ranked the third smartest breed. To earn this spot they had to learn a command after only five repetitions, and properly obey commands the first time that a command is issued, at a rate of ninety-five percentile.*

Teaching your GSD to lie down not only helps to keep him in one spot, but also offers a calming timeout, in addition, it is a useful intervention to curtail, or even prevent barking. When paired with the stay command, you can keep your dog comfortably in one place for long periods. Down not only protects your dog in potentially hazardous situations, but it also provides you with peace of mind that your dog will remain in the place where you commanded him to stay. This is yet another essential command that you will utilize daily, throughout the lifetime of your dog.

Training

- Begin training in a quiet place with few distractions, and bring plenty of treats. Wait for your dog to lie down of his own will, and then *click and treat* while he is in the lying down position. Toss a treat to get him up again. Repeat this until he begins to lie down immediately after he gets the treat. His compliance means that he is starting to understand that good things come to him when he lies down, so in anticipation of this, he lays right back down.

- Now, augment the training with the addition of the verbal command, "down." As soon as your dog starts to lie down, say "down," and *click and treat*.

From here on, only *click and treat* your dog when he lies down after your command.

- Next, practice this in a variety of areas and in situations of various distractions. Begin the practice indoors, then take it outside into your yard, and then wander into the neighborhood, and beyond. Remain patient in the more distracting locations.

Situations to command your dog to lie down could be times when there are strangers present, when there is food nearby, or when the stereo or television is on. Anytime you are outdoors barbequing, having a party, in the park, or during your walks together are also excellent opportunities to practice this command. Maintain diligence with this training, and attempt to find situations of increasing levels of distraction where you might need to use the command "down." Remember that you are looking for consistent compliance.

The power and importance of the command "down" will prove to be one of the most useful of all to train and maintain during the life of your dog. After your success with the training of "down," you can then move to the combination command of "down-stay," which should be trained in order to keep your dog in place until you release him.

Imagine the ease and joy when your pooch accompanies you to the local café, and he lies quietly, as well as *obediently*, at your feet while you drink your morning beverage. Having an obedient companion is a very attractive and respected attribute of any responsible dog owner.

It is important to monitor and track your partner's progress by taking notes during his training, especially as you increase the distractions, highlighting where and when he needs more work, or attention.

- Gradually phase out clicking and treating your dog every time that he obeys the "down" command. Reduce the treats to one time out of two compliances, followed by one out of three, then one out of four, five, six, and finally stop altogether. Do not decrease the treats too rapidly and be sure to observe closely, your dog's abilities and pace. The goal of the training is to have your dog obey *all* commands with only a vocal or physical cue, *without a reward*.

Troubleshooting

- If your dog will not comply with the down command, you need to return the training to a low distraction area, such as a bathroom. There is not much to distract him in the bathroom and little room to other things beside sit or lie down.

- If your dog does lie down, but pops right back up, be sure that you are only treating him when in the lying down position. In this way, your dog will sooner understand the correlation between the command, action, and the subsequent treat. Remember the **P** in PRICELESS.

"Stay"

Pregnancy - *GSD bitches are pregnant for approximately 60 days before giving birth to their puppies.*

St*ay* is perhaps a command that you have looked forward to teaching, after all, it is up there on top of the list, as one of the most useful and used *essential* commands. This command can be paired with *sit* and *down*. With these combination commands obeyed, daily life with your companion will be made easier.

Teaching your dog restraint has practical uses, as well. By reinforcing the wanted behavior of remaining in place, your dog will not end up in potentially dangerous situations, such as running out the door and into the street. This command also limits the possibility of your dog putting you in embarrassing or inconvenient situations, such as jumping up on people, or chasing the neighbor's pet. Furthermore, it is a valuable command that teaches compliance, which facilitates better control of your dog. Stay not only teaches your dog patience, but also reinforces his understanding of who is in charge of the decision-making. After you have taught your dog *sit* and *down*, the stay command should be next on your training agenda, as they make for useful pairings.

- To begin, find yourselves a quiet low distraction place, and bring plenty of treats. Give the sit command, and after he obeys, wait two-seconds before you *click and treat*. Continue practicing while gradually extending the duration of time between his compliance and his receiving the click and treat, thus reinforcing the length of time he is in the sit position. Work up to 10-15 seconds of sitting before clicking and treating.

- Next, you can begin to issue the combination *sit-stay* command, and this time you can add a hand signal to the mix. While you issue the command, the signal can simply be your flat hand directed towards his fuzzy little face, at about 12 inches (30cm). You can also choose a unique hand signal of your own to use in conjunction with sit-stay. Continue practicing while increasing the time he is in the sit position. Gradually increase the sit-stay time to one minute before you C/T.

- If your dog gets up during this training, it means you are moving too quickly. Try again with a shorter stay time goal, and then slowly increase the time your dog is to remain completely still. *In addition, your dog may be anticipating the time, so mix up the sit-stay times.

Continue practicing until your dog will stay for longer intervals. A good way to keep track of your dog's progress through each training session is by starting a training log. This is helpful for many reasons, including monitoring his compliance, goals, outcomes, as well as wanted and unwanted behaviors.

- Test your progress.

Now, say "sit-stay," and take one big step away from your dog, then C/T him for his obedience. Keep practicing this until you can take two big steps in any direction, away from your dog without him moving. It is essential that you return to treat your dog at the exact spot in which he stayed in place. Refrain from treating him if he rises, or if he comes to you.

Keep progressing with this exercise until you can take several steps away, eventually moving completely out of sight of your dog, while he stays stationary. Work towards the goal of him staying motionless for two full minutes while you are in his sight, followed by an additional two minutes that you remain out of his sight.

By gradually increasing the stay-time interval during this training, you reinforce the stay-response behavior to the point that your dog will stay put *no matter what is going on*. Often dogs will simply lie down after a number of minutes in the stay position. Usually, after about five minutes my dog just lies down until I release him.

- Lastly, begin increasing the distractions, while practicing all that has been trained up to this point. As previously instructed, begin the practice indoors, and then take it outside into the yard, and then move away from the familiarity of your house and neighborhood. For obvious reasons, be patient in the more distracting locations. It is important to maintain a practice routine of at least five minutes per day, particularly in places with increasing distraction. During your training sessions, continue to add other people, animals, all in a variety of noisy and increasingly distracting environments. The desired outcome of this training is to have a dog that remains in place in any situation you both may encounter during your time together.

Now, repeat the above steps chronologically using the command "*down*."

- Gradually phase out clicking and treating your dog every time that on command he obeys. As previously instructed, phase out treating by reducing it gradually, first by treating one out of two times, then once out three times, followed by once out of four, five, six, and then finally refrain all together. Be sure not decrease the treats too quickly. Observe and take notes of your dog's abilities and pace. The goal is to have a dog that will obey all of the commands without reward, and only by a vocal, or physical cue.

When finished with this section you should have the commands "sit-stay" and "down-stay" obeyed by your dog. Take care not to train both commands in the same training sessions.

Help

- *Always* reward your dog in the location where he has remained in place. It is important to refrain from releasing him with a C/T while using the *come* command. This will invariably confuse the outcome of the training, and diminish the importance of the come command. Keep it clear and simple.

- Note when your dog decides not to participate. It could be that the training is getting too difficult, too quickly. Put variation in the stay-time, as well as in the location, when giving commands to your dog. Give the pup a chance to learn at his own pace.

- Practice the command of *stay,* particularly before he meets a new person. Practice this also before he follows you out the door, or into the car, or in the course of feeding, *before* you put down his food bowl.

- If you encounter any difficulties, back up a step, or calmly resume later. Be aware that each dog has his own pace of learning, so your ongoing patience is crucial. It is best to simply laugh, smile, and roll with your dog's own natural abilities while enjoying the process of teaching and learning together. After all, this is all quality time spent while hanging out with your new best friend.

"Go"

"Go" is a great cue to get your GSD into his crate or onto his mat or rug. This is a very handy command to send your dog to a specific location and keep him there while you tend to your business. Before teaching, "go," your dog should already be performing to the command, *down-stay*.

While training the following steps, do not proceed to the next step until your dog is regularly performing the current step.

- Find a quiet low distraction location to place a towel or mat on the floor and grab your treats. Put a treat in your hand and use it to lure your dog onto the towel while saying, "Go." When all four paws are on the towel, *click and treat* your dog. Do this about ten to fifteen times.

- Start the same way as above, say "go," but this time have an empty hand, act as though you have a treat in your fist while you are luring your dog onto the mat. When all fours are on the mat *click and treat* your dog. Do this ten to fifteen times.

- Keep practicing with an empty hand and eventually turning the empty hand into a pointed index finger. Point your finger towards the mat. If your dog does not understand, walk him to the mat then click and treat. Do this about ten to fifteen times.

- Now, cue with "go" *while pointing* to the towel, but do not walk to the towel with him. If your dog will not go to the towel when you point and say the command, then keep practicing the step above before trying this step again. Now proceed practicing the command "go" while using the pointed finger and when your dog has all four paws on the mat, click, and then walk over and treat him while he is on the mat. Do this about ten to fifteen times.

- Now, grab your towel and try this on different surfaces and other places, such as grass, tile, patio, carpet, and in different rooms. Continue to practice this in more and more distracting situations and don't forget your towel or mat. Take the mat outdoors, to your friends and families houses, hotel rooms, the cabin, and any other place that you have your trusted companion with you.

Next Step – "Settle"

In accordance with "go" This is an extra command you can teach. This is a single word command that encapsulates the command words go, down, and stay all into one word. The purpose is to teach your dog to go to a mat and lie on it until he is released.

This is for when you need your dog out from under foot for extended lengths of time, such as when you are throwing a party. Pair it with "down and stay" so your dog will go the mat, lie down, and plan on staying put for an extended period of time. You can substitute your own command, such as "settle," "rest," or "chill," but once you choose a command stick with it and remain consistent.

This command can be used anywhere that you go, letting your dog know that he will be relaxing for a long period and to assume his peaceful posture. You can train this command when your pup is young and it will benefit you and him throughout your life together.

- Place your mat, rug, or what you plan using for your dog to lay.

- Give the "go" command and C/T your dog when he has all four paws on the mat. While your dog is on the mat, issue the command "down stay," then go to him and C/T while your dog is still on the mat.

- Now, give the "settle" command and repeat the above exercise with this "settle" command. Say, "settle," "go" and C/T your dog when he has all four paws on the mat. While your dog is on the mat, issue the command "down stay," and C/T while your dog is still on the mat. When your dog understands the "settle" command it will incorporate go, down, and stay.

Practice 7-10 times per session until your dog is easily going to his mat, lying down, and staying in that position until you release him.

- Next, give only the "settle" command and wait for your dog to go to the mat and lie down *before* you *click and treat* your dog. Do not use any other cues at this time. Continue practicing over multiple sessions, 7-10 repetitions per session, so that your dog is easily following your one word instruction of "settle."

- Now, begin making it more difficult; vary the distance, add distractions, and increase the times in the settle mode. This is a wonderful command for keeping your dog out of your way for lengthy durations. You will love it when this command is flawlessly followed.

Help

-While you are increasing the time that your dog maintains his relaxed position, click and treat every 5-10 seconds.

- You can also shape this command so that your dog assumes a more relaxed posture than when you issue "down stay." When your dog realizes that the "settle" command encompasses the super comfortable posture that he would normally use under relaxed conditions, he will understand that he will most likely be staying put for a lengthy period and your dog might as well get very comfortable.

Leash Training

Training your GSD to the leash will probably be one of the hardest things you will do. However, in the end, it is very rewarding and can serve to strengthen the trust and bond between you and your dog. A leash, or lead, is simply the rope that tethers you to your companion. Though a strong, good quality leash is crucial, a feature of greater significance is the collar, or harness. There is a variety of collars to choose from, and it is up to you to do some research to determine which one is best fit for your dog. Head collars and front attachment harnesses are a couple of choices. Make sure it is a good fit and that your dog is comfortable wearing it.

Keep in mind some general guidelines suggested when choosing a collar. If you are small and your dog is large, or if your dog tends to be aggressive or powerful, you will need to exert the greatest control, so the sensible choice should be a head collar. Front attachment collars are an excellent choice for any dog or activity. Head and frontal attached collars should be used with leashes with a length of six feet (1.82 meters), or less. The reason for maintaining a shorter leash is that a longer lead length could allow your dog, if he bolts, to gain enough speed to injure himself when the lead runs out and becomes suddenly taut.

The main goal here is to get your dog to walk beside you without pulling against the leash. An effective method during training is simply to stop moving forward when your dog pulls on the lead, turn and walk the opposite direction. Then, when he obediently walks beside you, reward with treats, praise and affection to reinforce the wanted behavior. The following steps will help you train your dog to have excellent leash manners. Remember, *loose leash walking is the goal!*

Before moving forward to the next instructional step, please make sure that your dog consistently performs the target action of the training step that you are teaching. His consistent compliance is necessary for the success of this training, so do not be inclined to hurry or rush this training.

Walking with you

Start by donning your dog with a standard harness fastened with a non-retractable leash that is about ten to twenty feet (3-6 meters) in length. Before starting the training session, remember to load up your pouch or pockets with top-notch treats and head out to the back yard or another familiar, quiet, low distraction outdoor spot. It is best if there are no other animals or people present during this initial phase.

First, decide whether you want your dog to walk along on your left or right side. It is at this side that you will treat your dog, and when you do, treat at your thigh level. Eventually, your dog will automatically come to that side because that is where the goodies can be found. Later, you can train your dog to walk on either side of you, but for now, stick with one side. In the future, training for both sides allows you the flexibility to maneuver your dog anywhere, whether out of harm's way, or for a more practical application, like easily walking on either side of the street.

- Place a harness or collar on your dog and attach the leash. Begin the training by randomly walking about the yard. When your dog decides to walk along with you, *click and treat* on the chosen side, at the level of your thigh. To "walk along with you" specifically refers to an action where your dog willingly joins you when you move along, in full compliance, and in a manner without applying any resistance to the lead. If he continues to walk on the correct side, and calmly with you, give him a *click and treat* with every step, or two, that you take together, thus reinforcing the desired behavior. Keep practicing this until your dog remains by your side, more often than not.

At this time, do not worry about over-treating your trainee; you will eventually reduce the frequency of delivery, eventually phasing out treats completely upon his successful mastering of this skill. If you are concerned with your companion's waistline, or girlish figure, you can deduct the training treats from the next meal.

- Repeat ambling around the yard with your pal in-tow, but this time walk at a faster pace than your prior session together. As before, when your dog decides to walk with you, give him a *click and treat* at thigh level of the chosen side. Keep practicing this until your dog consistently remains by your side, at this new pace. This leash training should occur over multiple sessions and days.

There is no need to rush any aspects of training. Remember to be patient with all training exercises, and proceed at a pace dictated by your dog's energy level, and his willingness to participate.

Let's go

Keeping your dog focused on the training at hand. Teaching him that you are in control of the leash is crucial.

This time, start walking around the yard and wait for a moment when your dog lags behind, or gets distracted by something else. At this time say, "let's go" to him, followed by a non-violent slap to your thigh to get his attention. Make sure you use a cheerful voice when issuing this command, and refrain from any harsh tactics that will intimidate your pooch, which can certainly undermine any training. When he pays attention to you, simply walk away. By doing this, it isolates the cue connected to this specific behavior, thus moving closer to your dog's grasp of the command.

- If your dog catches up with you *before* there is tension on the leash, *click and treat* him from the level of your thigh on the chosen side. *Click and treat* him again after he takes a couple of steps with you, and then continue to reinforce this with a C/T for the next few steps while he continues walking beside you. Remember, the outcome of this training is *loose leash walking*.

If your dog catches up *after* the leash has become taut, *do not treat him*. Begin again by saying, "let's go," then treat him after he takes a couple of steps with you. Only reinforce with C/T when he is compliant.

- If he does not come when you say, "let's go," continue moving until there is tension on the lead. At this point, stop walking and apply firm, but gentle pressure to the leash. When he begins to come toward you, praise him as he proceeds. When he gets to you, *do not treat him*, instead say, "let's go," and begin walking again. Click and treat your dog if he stays with you, and continue to C/T your dog for every step or two that he stays with you.

Keep practicing this step until he remains at your side while you both walk around the yard. If he moves away from you, redirect him with pressure to the lead and command cue of "let's go," followed up with a C/T when he returns to the appropriate position of walking obediently in tandem with you.

Do not proceed forward to subsequent steps of the training until your dog is consistently walking beside you with a loose leash, and is appropriately responding to the "let's go" command. It can sometimes take many days and sessions for your dog to develop this skill, so it is important for you to remain patient and diligent during this time. The outcome of this training is well worth your time and effort.

Sensory Overload

Just like you, your dog is going to want to sniff things and eliminate waste. During these times, you should be in control. While your dog is on the leash, and when he is in anticipation of his regular treating, or at about each five minute interval, say something like, "go sniff," "go play," "free time," or some other verbal cue that you feel comfortable saying, followed by some self-directed free time on the leash.

Keep in mind that this is a form of reward, but if he pulls on the leash, you will need to redirect with a "let's go" cue, followed by your walking in the opposite direction, quickly ending his free time. If your dog remains compliant, and does not pull on the leash before the allotted free time has elapsed, you are still the one that needs to direct the conclusion of free leash time, by saying, "let's go," coupled with you walking in the opposite direction.

Increase Movement

Using steps one through three, continue practicing leash walking in the yard. During the course of the training session, gradually shorten the lead until 6-foot (1.8meter) length remains. Now, change the direction and speed of your movements, being sure to *click and treat* your dog every time he is able to stay coordinated with the changes you have implemented.

As loose leashed walking becomes routine and second nature for your companion, you can start phasing out the click and treats. Reserve the C/T for situations involving new or difficult training points, such as keeping up with direction changes, or ignoring potential distractions.

Streets

Now, it is time to take your dog out of the yard and onto the sidewalk for his daily walk. You will use the same techniques you used in your yard, only now you have to deal with more distractions.

Distractions can come in all forms, including other dogs, friendly strangers, traffic, alarming noises, sausage vendors, feral chickens, taunting cats and a host of other potential interruptions and disturbances. It is during these times that you might want to consider alternate gear, such as a front attachment harness, or a halter collar, which fits over the head offering ultimate control over your companion.

Arm yourself with your dog's favorite treats, apply the utmost patience, and go about your walk together in a deliberate and calm manner. Remember to utilize the "let's go," command cue when he pulls against his leash, or forgets that you exist. In this new setting, be sure to treat him when he walks beside you and then supersize the portions if your dog is obedient and does not pull on the lead during a stressful moment, or in an excitable situation. Lastly, do not forget to reward with periodic breaks for sniffing and exploring.

Stop and Go exercise

Attach a 6-foot lead to the collar. With a firm hold on the leash, toss a treat or toy at about twenty feet (6 meters) ahead of you and your dog, then start walking toward it. If your dog pulls the leash and tries to get at the treat, use the "let's go" command and walk in the opposite direction of the treat. If he stays beside you without struggle while you walk toward the treat, allow him have it as a reward.

Practice this several times until your dog no longer pulls toward the treat and stays at your side, waiting for you to make the first move. The other underlying goal is that your dog should always look to you for direction and follow your lead before taking an action such as running after the toy while he is still leashed.

Switching Sides

After your dog is completely trained to the specific side chosen, and with a few months of successful loose leash walking practice under your belt, then you can begin the training again, targeting the opposing side that the two of you have previously trained towards. There is no need rush, so proceed with the training of the opposite side when you know the time is right, and you are both comfortable with changing it up a bit. As previously mentioned, a dog that is able to walk loose leashed, on either side of you is the desired, target outcome of this training. This skill is essential for navigating your dog, with ease and safety, in the outside world.

Troubleshooting

- If your dog happens to cross in front of you during your time together, he may be distracted, so it is important to make your presence known to him with a gentle leash tug, or an appropriate command.

- If your dog is lagging behind you, he might be frightened or not feeling well, instead of pulling your dog along, give him a lot of support and encouragement. If the lagging is due to normal behavioral distractions, such as scent sniffing or frequent territorial marking, keep walking along. In this case, it is appropriate to pull gently on the leash to encourage his attention to the current task.

- The reinforcement of wanted behaviors necessitates you delivering numerous rewards when your dog walks beside you, or properly executes what it is you are training at that time. During your time together, pay close attention to your dog's moods, patterns and behaviors. You want to pay close attention to these things so that you can anticipate his responses, modify your training sessions, or simply adapt whatever it is you are doing to assure that his needs are being met, and you are both on the same page.

Being conscious of your dog's needs will assist in maintaining a healthy, respectful bond between the two of you. Make an effort to use playful tones in your voice, with a frequent "good dog," followed by some vigorous petting, or some spirited play. Try to be aware of when your dog is beginning to tire, and attempt always to end a training session on a high note, followed by plenty of treats, play, and praise.

Heel

You will find this command indispensable when you are mobile, or perhaps when you encounter a potentially dangerous situation. There will be times where you will need to issue a firm command in order to maintain control of your dog in order to keep the both of you out of harms-way. *Heel* is that command.

During your time together exploring the outside world, things such as another aggressive dog, the busy traffic, a construction site, a teasing cat, or that irresistible squirrel may warrant keeping your dog close to you. If trained to the heel command, your dog will be an indispensable asset in helping to avert possible hazardous circumstances. The heel command is a clear instruction, trained to assure that your dog remains close beside you, *until you say otherwise*.

- Begin this training inside of your back yard, or in another low distraction area. First, place a treat in your fist on the side you have decided to train. Let him sniff your fist, then say "heel," followed by a few steps forward, leading him along with the fisted treat at thigh level. Click and treat him as he follows your fist with his nose. The fist is to keep your dog close to you. Practice for a few sessions.

- Next, begin the training as before, but now with an empty fist. With your fist held out in front of you, give the "heel" command, and then encourage your dog follow by your side. When he follows your fist for a couple of steps, *click and treat* him. For each subsequent session, repeat this practice a half dozen times, or more.

- Continue to practice heel while you are moving around, but now begin to increase the length of time *before* you treat your dog. Introduce a new direction in your walking pattern, or perhaps use a serpentine-like maneuver, snaking your way around the yard. You will want to continuously, but progressively challenge him in order to advance his skills, and to bolster his adaptability in various situations.

During all future outings together, this closed-empty-fist will now serve as your non-verbal, physical hand cue instructing your dog to remain in the heel position. From here on out, remember to display your closed-empty-fist at your side when you issue your heel command.

- Now, move the training sessions outside of the security of your yard. The next level of teaching should augment his learning by exposing him to various locations with increasingly more distractions. The implementation of this new variation in training is done to challenge, as well as to enhance your walking companion's adaptability to a variety of situations and stimulus.

Continue to repeat the *heel* command each time you take your dog out on the leash. Keeping his skills fresh with routine practice will ease your mind when out exploring new terrain together. Knowing that your dog will be obedient, and will comply with all of your commands, instructions and cues will be satisfying; in addition, it will keep you both safe and sane.

Out in the crazy, nutty world of ours there are plenty of instances when you will use this command to avoid unnecessary confrontations or circumstances with potentially dangerous outcomes. If by chance you choose to use a different verbal cue other than the commonly used *heel* command, pick a word that is unique, and easy to say, and does not have a common use in everyday language. This way you avoid the possibility for confusion and misunderstanding."

Mentally Stimulating Activities for Your GSD

Schutzhund *translates into English as "protection dog" – This sport was developed as a suitability test specifically for the GSD. The first competition was in 1901. Schutzhund was begun to assess the working ability of the GSD herding dog, testing its temperament and working ability to find reliable dogs containing the proper qualities sought after in the GSD breed, and then using the finest dogs for breeding. Today, the competition continues to build positive character and confidence in the participatory dogs, and helps breeders produce the desirable traits for working dogs used in the many services worldwide.*

Below are some items to keep your GSD fit and mentally healthy.

- Treibball is a relatively new dog sport where dogs gather and move large balls that represent a flock of animals.

- Retrieval games are physically and mentally stimulating.

- Agility games that are physical, but primarily mental, you can turn your household items into a course.

-Tracking, this uses dog's natural scenting abilities to find hidden objects.

- Herding trials or tests allow dogs to use their natural or trained herding abilities.

- Free play with other familiar dogs assists in socialization, energy release, and stimulation.

- Trick performance that is rewarded with access to your dog's highly valued items.

- Obedience classes.

- Flyball for physical activity.

- Hide and Seek with family members is good physical exercise for all.

- Working livestock is challenging both mentally and physically for dogs.

Grooming

Oral maintenance, clipping, and other grooming will depend upon you and your dog's activities. Most people never clip their GSD's unless the footpads or ears have some issue, or the coat is severely matted. However, we all know our dogs love to roll and run through all sorts of possible ugly messes, and put obscene things into their mouths, and this requires us to do our part in keeping them looking their best.

Most basic care can easily be done by you at home, but if you are unsure or uncomfortable about something, seek tutelage and in no time you will be clipping, trimming, and brushing like a professional.

Some Equipment - Longhaired dogs need pin brushes, short, medium, and some longhaired dogs require bristle brushes. Slicker brushes remove mats and dead hair. Rubber Curry Combs polish smooth coats. Some of the grooming tools available are clippers, stripping knives, rakes, and more.

German Shepherd Dogs are not considered high maintenance, but if you prefer your dog to have a shiny luxurious coat, good breath, white teeth, and look his or her best, then regular maintenance is necessary.

Adorable GSD puppies have a fuzzy puppy coat that will eventually be replaced at around four months. The GSD coat consists of a thick soft undercoat and a coarse longer outer coat. This coat combination allows the GSD to withstand and work while enduring harsh climate conditions. The coat can be either the shorter *stock coat* or the *stock long coat* with both shedding daily and heavily twice annually.

The original GSD had the longhaired coat, but then the shorthaired version was introduced into breeding, and now both exist. The AKC standard sites that the ideal GSD coat is a medium length double coat consisting of close lying dense, straight, harsh hair that is allowed to be slightly wavy and wiry.

Brushing

Puppies of all coat lengths should be brushed daily. This not only helps with their coat but also allows for *handling* practice. Use gentle pressure, a soothing tone of voice and praise while you attend to your puppies coat. Reward their good behavior with a treat, and gradually increase the time of grooming sessions.

Whichever coat length your GSD has, daily brushing helps to control the amount of loose hairs floating around your house and vehicle, however it is not essential unless you have a longhaired GSD. During the heavy shedding periods, it is recommended to brush daily, and throughout the rest of the year the short coat only requires brushing a couple of times per week.

The longhaired coats tend to mat, tangle, accumulate debris, burrs, and mud easier. Be observant and tend to these issues promptly. To remove mats you can use a comb, fingers, and if necessary a specialized comb.

- When brushing, first place your dog into a comfortable position for him and you. You can either have him lie down on this side, or stand if he does not mind. Begin brushing at the head and brush in the direction that the coat flows all the way to the tail tip. If your dog is lying down, then roll them to the others side and repeat.

- Next, follow the same instruction beginning at the head, but use a shedding blade that will pull out the dead hairs.

- Finish by using a slicker brush over the entire coat, and then using a damp cloth to pick up any straggling dead hairs. Now you will have a dog with a shiny coat and a big bag of dog hair to dispose of.

Bathing

Your *GSD puppy* will not require bathing, but it is a good idea to get them accustomed to the process. Placing your GSD into the tub every week and then wetting him will familiarize him to the process and help conquer any fears that might surface. It is not necessary to soak him each time, but only introduce him to having warm water being poured over him. This is crucial, because it will be difficult to have a grown GSD that refuses to be bathed. Afterward, be certain that you thoroughly dry your puppy.

German Shepherd Dog's do not require frequent bathing. If they are regularly brushed, they can require as few as three or four baths per year. When they are blowing their coats, many people bathe their GSDs to loosen up excess hairs. If the weather and water is warm you can easily bathe your dog outdoors, but the bathtub is best during chilly weather and often is the most convenient.

1. Supplies – Dog specific shampoo, 3-4 towels, nonslip bathmat for inside the tub.

2. Shampoo – Use a dog shampoo made specifically for sensitive skin. This helps avoid any type of potential skin allergy, eye discomfort, and furthering pre-existing skin conditions.

3. Coax your dog into the tub and shut the door (just in case he is not in the mood, or decides to bolt outside while still wet). We have all experienced this.

4. Use warm water, not hot. Hot water tends to irritate the skin and can cause your dog to itch and then scratch. Do not use cold water on your dog.

5. Apply enough shampoo to create lather over the body, but take care not to use so much that rinsing is difficult and time consuming. Rub into lather, avoiding the eyes and ears.

6. Bathe the head area last.

7. Rinse repeatedly and thoroughly to avoid skin irritation.

8. Thoroughly towel dry your dog. If it is cold outside you will want to finish by using a low setting hair dryer. Additionally, a slicker brush can be used while drying, remembering to brush in the direction of the hair growth.

Natural coat oils are needed to keep your dog's coat and skin moisturized. Never bathe your dog too frequently.

Nails

For optimal foot health, your dog's nails should be kept short. There are special clippers that are needed for nail trimming that are designed to avoid injury. If you start trimming when your dog is a puppy, you should have no problems. However, if your dog still runs for the hills or squirms like an eel at trimming time, then your local groomer or veterinarian can do this procedure.

Recommended nail trimming is every 3-4 weeks, however dogs that do a lot of hard surface walking, such as on cement, will keep their nails naturally shorter and require less trimming. If you notice the tap, tap, tap of your dog's nails upon your floor, then he is due for a trimming.

Again, begin early so that your puppy is used to the process and tolerates it without a fuss. Follow the instructions in "Handling" *paws* and occasionally cutting a bit from the ends of your puppy's nails, followed by a quick filing.

Dog's nails are composed of a hard outer shell named the *horn* and a soft cuticle in the center known as the *quick*. The horn has no nerves and thus has no feeling. The quick is composed of blood vessels and nerves, and therefore needs to be avoided. Because GSD's have black nails the quick is harder to identify. Furthermore, the quick grows with the nails, so diligent nail trimming will keep the quick receded.

If you have a dog with white nails, the quick is easy to see because of its pink coloring. Dogs that spend a lot of time walking and running on rough surfaces tend to have naturally shortened quicks.

1. Identify where the quick is located in your dog's nails. The object will be to trim as close (2mm) to the quick as possible without nipping the quick and causing your dog pain and possibly bleeding.

2. To identify the quick, begin cutting small pieces from the end of the nail and examine underneath the nail. When you see a uniform gray oval appear at the top of the cut surface, then stop further cutting.

Behind the gray is where the quick is located, if you see pink then you have passed the gray and arrived at the quick. If you have done this, your dog is probably experiencing some discomfort. *The goal is to stop cutting when you see the gray.*

3. File the cut end to smooth the surface.

4. If you accidentally cut into the quick, apply styptic powder. If not available, cornstarch or flour can be substituted.

5. Do not forget to trim the dewclaws.

6. If your dog challenges your cutting, be diligent and proceed without verbal or physical abuse, and reward after successful trimming is completed. If you encounter the occasional challenge, your diligence should curtail the objection. If you manage never to cut into your dog's quick, this helps prevent any negative associations with the process, but some dogs simply do not enjoy the handling of their paws or nail trimming.

Ears

You will notice that your GSD puppy has folded ears. As they grow, the cartilage in their ears will grow and stiffen into erect open ears. Until then your puppy will have floppy ears for the first several months. GSD ears are prone to accumulation of debris.

- Inspect them every few days for bugs such as mites and ticks.

- To tell if your dog has an ear infection you can use your sense of smell. Whiff your dog's ears. Ear infections emit a strong odor that is easily identifiable. Other symptoms are if the ear is red, inflamed, producing large amounts of horrible smelling wax, and possibly discharge.

- Some causes of infection can be dirty water, trapped debris, and allergies.

- For cleaning German Shepherd Dog ears, use a non-alcoholic ear cleaner. If you have never done it, you should first seek instruction from a trained professional. There is no reason to risk damaging or hurting your dog.

- Fill your dog's ear canal with cleaner and then massage the base of the ear for about 30 seconds. This will loosen, soften, and then release any ear muck that is trapped. Then take a cotton ball to wipe out the loosened debris, and then absorb the excess fluid. Repeat this process until all of the muck and debris has disappeared. This process usually requires action twice daily during infections. Afterward it is okay to let your dog shake his head.

- Twice weekly inspections and cleanings are recommended for dogs that swim often and or do a lot of outdoor work.

- Lastly, keep a keen eye on the infection and if you think it has moved from the outside to the inside, do not hesitate to seek veterinary assistance.

Eyes

Whenever you are grooming your dog, check their eyes for any signs of damage or irritation. Other dog signals for eye irritation are if your dog is squinting, scratching, or pawing at their eyes. You should contact your veterinarian if you notice that the eyes are cloudy, red, or have a yellow or green discharge.

Use a moist cotton ball to clean any discharge from the eye. Avoid putting anything irritating around, or into your dog's eyes.

Teeth and Gums

In the chapter titled "Handling," the practice outlined in that chapter helps with oral care. Keeping your dog's teeth and gums healthy throughout his or her life will help you with doggy breath, and them to avoid painful gum diseases such as gingivitis. Dental hygiene and maintenance is easily assisted by regularly providing your dog with hard rubber toys and other indestructible items to chew.

I recommend non-fluoride natural compound toothpaste specifically for dogs.

If you can already lift your dog's lips and touch the brush to his or her teeth then you can begin to brush your dog's teeth with a brush. If not start with a finger brush, which is a rubber knobbed cap that fits over your finger. Gently insert your finger brush to touch and stroke your dog's teeth and gums. After your dog is used to that, then place a dab of toothpaste on your finger and let you dog taste it. Next, add toothpaste to your finger brush and brush the teeth and gums.

When without objection you are able to touch and brush all of your dog's teeth with the finger brush, you can graduate to the normal dog toothbrush. Angle the brush at about a forty-five degree angle toward the gum line and brush away either in a circular or sawing motion.

Pick up a specially designed canine tooth brush and cleaning paste. Clean your dog's teeth as frequently as daily. Try to brush your dog's teeth a few times a week at a minimum. Now that he is comfortable with your finger, repeat with the brush. In addition, it is important to keep plenty of chews around to promote the oral health of your pet. When your dog is 2-3 years old, he or she may need their first professional teeth cleaning.

Anal sacs

These sacs are located on each side of a dog's anus. If you notice your dog scooting his rear, or frequently licking and biting at his anus, the anal sacs may be impacted. You can ask your veterinarian how to diagnose and treat this issue.

Dog Nutrition

As for nutrition, humans study it, practice it, complain about it, but usually give into the science and common sense of it. Like humans, dogs have their own nutrition needs and charts to follow, and are subject to different theories and scientific studies, as well.

In the following, we will look at the history of dog food, as well as the common sense of raw foods, nutrient lists, and what your dog might have to bark about regarding what he is ingesting.

In the beginning, there were wild packs of canines everywhere and they ate anything that they could get their paws on. Similar to human survival, dogs depended upon meat from kills, grasses, berries, and other edibles that nature provided them. What is the great news? Many millennia later nature is still providing all that we need.

Some History

In history, the Romans wrote about feeding their dogs barley bread soaked in milk along with the bones of sheep. The wealthy Europeans of the 1800's would feed their dogs better food than most humans had to eat. Meat from horses and other dead animals was often rounded up from the streets to recycle as dog food for the rich estates on the outskirts of the city. Royalty is legendary for pampering their dogs with all sorts of delicacies from around the world. Meanwhile, the poor and their dogs had to fend for themselves or starve. Being fed table scraps from a pauper's diet was not sufficient to keep a dog healthy, and the humans themselves often had their own nutrition problems. To keep from starving dogs would hunt rats, rabbits, mice, and any other rodent or insect type creature that they could sink their teeth.

Other references from the 18th century tell of how the French would mix breadcrumbs with tiny pieces of meat to feed their dogs. It is also written that the liver, heart, blood, or all, were mixed with milk or cheese and sometimes bread was a manmade food source for domestic canine. In England, they would offer soups flavored with meat and bone to augment their dog's nutrition.

In the mid to late 1800's a middle class blossomed out of the industrial revolution. This group started taking on dogs as house pets and unwittingly created an enterprise out of feeding the household pets that were suddenly in abundance. This new class with its burgeoning wealth had extra money to spend.

Noting that the sailor's biscuits kept well for long periods, James Spratt began selling his own recipe of hard biscuits for dogs in London, and shortly thereafter, he took his new product to New York City. It is believed that he single-handedly started the American dog food business. This places the dog food and kibble industry at just over 150 years old, and now is an annual multi-billion dollar business.

All the while we know that any farm dog, or for that matter, any dog that can kill something and eat it will do just that. Nothing has changed throughout the centuries. Raw meat does not kill dogs, so it is safe to say that raw food diets will not either. If you are a bit tentative about the idea of raw foods, cooking the meats you serve your dog is a viable option.

Feeding Your Puppy and Adult Dog

To check if your puppy is having his proper dietary needs met, check to make sure that your puppy is active, alert, and is showing good bone and muscle development. To understand the correct portion ask the breeder to show you the portion that he or she feeds their puppies. Observe whether your puppy is quickly devouring his food and then continuing to act as though he wants and needs more. If so, then increase the portion a little until you find the correct portion. If your puppy is eating quickly and then begins to just nibble, and in the end leaves food in the bowl, then you are over-feeding your puppy. As you adjust the food portion to less or more; observe whether your puppy is gaining or losing weight so that you can find the proper portion of food to serve during feeding times. Very active puppies tend to burn lots of energy and this is one reason that a puppy might need a little extra food in his bowl. The suggested portions are on the food containers, but this is not a one-size fits all world that we live in. Observation and note keeping is needed to determine the correct portion for you individual dog.

Many breeders and trainers state that puppies should not leave their mothers until they are at least eight weeks old. This allows their mother's milk to boost their immunity by supporting antibodies and nutrition that is needed to become a healthy dog. Around three to four weeks old puppies should begin eating some solid food in conjunction with their mother's milk. This helps their digestion process begin to adjust to solid foods making the transition from mother's milk to their new home and foods easier.

When choosing your puppy's feeding times, choose the times that you know will be the best for you to feed your puppy. Feeding on a regular schedule is one part of over-all *consistency* that you are establishing for your puppy to know that as the alpha you are reliably satisfying their needs. After setting the feeding schedule, remain as close to those times as possible. For example, 7am, around noon, and again at 5pm. An earlier dinnertime helps your puppy to digest then eliminate before his bedtime.

Puppies are going to eat four times a day up until about eight weeks. At eight weeks, they can still be fed four times a day, or you can reduce to three times. Split the recommend daily feeding portion into thirds. Puppies' nutritional requirements differ from adult dogs so select a puppy food that has the appropriate balance of nutrients that puppies require. Puppy food should continue to support healthy growth, digestion, and the immune system. Supplying your growing puppy with the correct amount of calories, protein, and calcium is part of a well-balanced diet.

During the three to six month puppy stage, teething can alter your puppies eating habits. Some pups may not feel like eating due to pain, so it is your responsibility to remain diligent in your job to provide them all of their nutritional requirements and confirm that they are eating. *Hint*: Soaking their dry food in water for 10-15 minutes before feeding will soften it and make it easier for your puppy to eat. This avoids suddenly introducing new softer foods to your puppy, and avoids the unknown consequences of doing so.

At six months to a year old, your puppy still requires high quality nutritionally charged foods. Consult your breeder or veterinarian about the right time to switch to an adult food. When you switch to an adult food, continue to choose the highest quality food that has a specified meat, and not only by-products. Avoid unnecessary artificial additives. In many cases, higher quality foods that you feed your dog allow you to serve smaller portions because more of the food is being used by your dog and not just flowing through. Fillers are often not digested and this requires feeding your dog larger portions.

Additionally, follow the alpha guideline that states that *humans always eat first*. This means that the humans finish their meal entirely and clear the table before feeding their dogs, or feed your dog a couple of hours before you and your family eat. This establishes and continues the precedence that all humans are above the dog in the pecking order.

Help Identifying Dog Food Quality

- The first ingredient, or at a minimum, the second should specify *meat* or *meat meal*. NOT by-product.

- *"What is a by-product?"* Unless specified on the label, a by-product can be left over parts from animals and contain parts of hooves, feet, skin, eyes, or other animal body parts.

- Beware of ingredients that use wording such as *animal* and *meat* instead of a specific word such as beef or chicken.

- "Meal" when listed in ingredients is something that has been weighed after the water was taken out, an example would be *chicken meal*. This means it has been cooked with a great amount of water reduction occurring in the process, and thus it is providing more actual meat and protein per weight volume.

- As an example, if the dog food only states "beef" in the ingredients, it refers to the pre-cooking weight. This means that after cooking, less meat will be present in the food.

- A label that states "beef" first then "corn meal" secondly, is stating that the food probably contains a lot more corn than beef. Corn is not easily digested nor does it offer much in the way of nutrients that are vital to a dog's health. Furthermore, it has been linked to other health issues, and dogs are not designed to eat corn and grains in high doses. Try your best to avoid corn, wheat, and soy in your dog's food. The higher quality more expensive foods are often worth the cost to advance your dog's health.

- If you decide to change dog food formulas or brands, a gradual change over is recommended, especially if your dog has a sensitive stomach. This is done by mixing some of the old with the new, and then throughout the week gradually increasing the amount of new.

An example schedule of changing dog foods

Day 1-2 Mix ¼ new with ¾ old food

Day 2-4 Mix ½ new with ½ old

Day 5-6 Mix ¾ new with ¼ old

Day 7 100% of the new dog food

The Switch - Moving From Puppy to Adult Food

When your puppy is ready to make the switch from puppy to adult dog food, you can follow the same procedure above, or shorten it to a four to five day switch over. During the switch, be observant of your dog's stools and health. If your dog appears not to handle the new food formula then your options are to change the current meat to a different meat, or try a different formula or brand. Avoid returning to the original puppy food. If you have any concerns or questions, consult your veterinarian or breeder.

Raw Foods

Let us take a look-see at the raw food diet for canines. First, remember that our dogs, pals, best friends, comedy actors, were meant to eat real foods such as meat. Their DNA does not only dictate them to eat dry cereals that were concocted by humans in white lab coats. These cereals based and meat-by products may have been keeping our pets alive, but in many cases possibly not thriving at optimum levels.

There are many arguments for the benefits of real and raw foods. Sure it is more work, but isn't their health worth it? It is normal, not abnormal to be feeding your dog, a living food diet; it is believed that it will greatly boost their immune system and over-all health. A raw food diet is based off pre-dog food diets and is a return to their wild hunting and foraging days.

There are different types of raw food diets. There are raw meats that you can prepare at home by freeze-drying or freezing that you can then easily thaw to feed your dog, commercially pre-packaged frozen raw foods, or offering up an entire whole animal. All of these diets take research and careful attention so that you are offering your dog all that they need, and something that their bodies can easily tolerate. Correct preparation of raw foods diets needs to be understood, for example, it is suggested that vegetables are cut into very small pieces or even pureed.

Raw food diets amount to foods that are not cooked or sent through a processing plant. With some research, you can make a decision on what you think is the best type of diet for your dog. For your dog's health and for their optimal benefits it is worth the efforts of your research time to read up on a raw foods diet, or possibly a mix of kibble and raw foods. *All foods,* dry, wet, or raw contain a risk, as they can all contain contaminants and parasites.

Known benefits are fewer preservatives, chemicals, hormones, steroids, and the addition of fruits and vegetables into their diet.

Physically your dog can have firmer stools, reduced allergies, improved digestion, healthier coat and skin, and over-all improved health.

Some of the negative attributes are the lack of convenience versus kibble and potential bacterial contamination. However, dogs are at a lowered risk for salmonella and E. coli than humans are. A dog's digestive system is more acidic and less prone to such diseases; the greater risk is to the preparer. Many experts state that the overall risk of a *properly prepared* raw food diet is minimal.

There is a process named HPP (High Pressure Pasteurization) which most pre-prepared raw food brands utilize in their processing that does not use heat but eliminates harmful bacteria without killing off good bacteria.

Rules of thumb to follow for a raw food diet

1. Before switching, make sure that your dog has a healthy gastro-intestinal track.

2. Be smart, and do not leave un-refrigerated meats for prolonged periods.

3. To be safe, simply follow human protocol for food safety. Toss out the smelly, slimy, or the meat and other food items that just do not seem good.

4. Keep it balanced. Correct amount of vitamins and minerals, fiber, antioxidants, and fatty acids. Note any medical issues your dog has, and possible diet correlations.

5. A gradual switch over between foods is recommended to allow their GI track to adjust. Use new foods as a treat, and then watch stools to see how your dog is adjusting.

6. Take note of the size and type of bones you throw to your dog. Not all dogs do well with real raw bones, because slivers, splinters, and small parts can become lodged in their digestive tracks. Always

provide the freshest bones possible to dogs. Never give dogs cooked bones.

7. Freezing meats for three days, similar to sushi protocol, can help kill unwanted pathogens or parasites.

8. Take note about what is working and not working with your dog's food changes. Remember to be vigilant, and take note of your observations when tracking a new diet. If your dog has a health issue, your veterinarian will thank you for your thorough note taking.

9. Like us humans, most dogs do well with a variety of foods. There is no one-size-fits-all diet.

10. Before switching over please read about raw foods diets and their preparation, and follow all veterinary guidelines.

Vitamins – Minerals -Nutrients

According to nutritional scientists and veterinarian health professionals, your dog needs twenty Amino Acids, ten of which are essential. At least thirty-six nutrients and a couple of extra may be needed to combat certain afflictions. Your dog's health depends upon the intake of the following nutrients. Read labels and literature to take stock of the foods you provide your canine.

36 Nutrients for dogs:

1. 10 essential Amino Acids – Arginine, Histidine, Isoleucine, Leucine, Lysine, Methionine, additionally Phenylalanine, Threonine, Tryptophan, and Valine.

2. 11 vitamins – A, D, E, B1, B2, B3, B5, B6, B12, Folic Acid, and Choline.

3. 12 minerals – Calcium, Phosphorus, Potassium, Sodium, Chloride, Iron, Magnesium, Copper, Manganese, Zinc, Iodine, and Selenium.

4. Fat – Linoleic Acid

5. Omega 6 Fatty Acid

6. Protein

The Vitamins

Vitamin A - This is necessary for normal vision, good eye health and night vision, crucial for reproductive health, helps itchy and dry skin. Additionally it is essential for the normal growth and development of puppies.

Vitamin B1 (Thiamine) - Promotes normal functioning of the nervous system and is necessary for the bulk of cellular reaction in the body. B1 also increases good metabolism and alertness.

Vitamin B2 (Riboflavin) – Works to regulate certain hormones, and helps prevent cataracts in the eyes. It is vital to energy generation, and nerve and blood development.

Vitamin B3 (Niacin) – Works to produce proper energy metabolism and circulation, creates healthy skin and normal functioning of the nervous system.

Vitamin B5 (Pantothenic Acid) - This is critical for the process of converting food to energy, helps wound healing, relieves stress and fatigue.

Vitamin B6 (Pyridoxine) – Is necessary for the functioning of the nervous system and the immune system by helping the metabolism.

Vitamin B7 (Biotin/Vitamin H) – Is critical for normal growth and development, and improving the skin and coat.

Vitamin B9 (Folic Acid) – Is essential for the growth and reproduction of all body cells, and is needed for the creation of DNA in pregnant bitches.

Vitamin B10 (PABA) – Supports growth.

Vitamin B12 (Cyanocobalamin) - Stimulates growth and cell development and potentially improve a dog's appetite.

Vitamin C – Supports the immune system, strengthens joint function, and maintains healthy skin.

Vitamin D – Is paramount for healthy bones, teeth, nerve and muscle function, and metabolizes calcium and phosphorus.

Vitamin E – Works as a strong antioxidant. It boosts the efficiency of the heart, circulatory system, acts as a mild anti-inflammatory, and helps to maintain good footpads.

Vitamin K – Is essential for normal blood clotting and kidney function.

The Minerals

Calcium - Keeps bones, teeth and gums healthy, needed for blood coagulation and a regular heartbeat, also keeps nerves and muscles functioning well.

Chloride - Helps maintain the proper acid/alkali balance in the body. Chloride is also necessary for the production of hydrochloric acid in the stomach, which helps in the digestion of protein. Chloride is often found in sodium chloride (salt). Sodium aids the transfer of nutrients and removal of waste products. Sodium and Chloride aid in balancing the fluids of individual cells.

Copper – Is necessary for bone growth and maintenance, absorption of iron, development of red blood cells.

Iodine – Is essential for proper functioning of the thyroid gland, supports normal growth, and regulates metabolism.

Iron - Is necessary for carrying oxygen in the blood and maintaining a healthy immune system.

Magnesium – Is necessary for absorption of certain vitamins and minerals, and helps in the formation of teeth, bones and supports a healthy heart.

Manganese – Is necessary for the proper use of protein and carbohydrates, reproduction, and the actions of many enzymes that are responsible for producing energy and making fatty acids.

Phosphorus – Is needed for producing and maintaining healthy bones, teeth, kidneys, heart and metabolism.

Potassium – Is necessary for many normal functions of the body, essential for a healthy heart and kidneys, and maintains fluid balance in cells.

Selenium – Is an important mineral with antioxidant properties that functions in conjunction with Vitamin E and other enzymes that together protect cells.

Sodium - Sodium aids in the transfer of nutrients and removal of waste products. Sodium and Chloride aid in balancing the fluids of individual cells.

Zinc – Is necessary for the production of enzymes and is important for a healthy coat and skin.

The Antioxidants

Beta-Carotene - A vital antioxidant that can protect against certain forms of cancer and might enhance the immune system.

Green Tea Extract - Is a powerful antioxidant that protects cells from free radical damage.

Lecithin – Is an antioxidant and has the potential to improve cognitive disorders.

Selenium – Is an important mineral that contains antioxidant properties.

The Amino Acids

One or more chains of amino acids form proteins. Proteins are a group of complex organic macromolecules that contain carbon, hydrogen, oxygen, nitrogen, and in most cases sulfur. When proteins are consumed they must be broken down into the separate amino acids so that the body can then reassemble them to build, replace, and rebuild cells which are the foundation for creating tissues, enzymes, organs, hormones, antibodies, and more. For these reasons, *protein* is an important part of any dog's diet and food.

Having the correct amount and balance of protein in your dog's food is essential. A protein source, or a combination of protein sources, is considered balanced when it contains both non-essential and essential amino acids in the correct proportions for a dog's body. It is vital that the protein sources are highly digestible so that the maximum amount of the serving is digested and able to be broken down inside the dog's body and be utilized for its purpose. Good examples of highly digestible proteins are eggs, organ and muscle meats. These should be the main ingredients in quality foods. Other lesser providers of protein are grain and vegetable byproducts. Sometimes it is easier to provide dogs these proteins in the correct high-quality portions when given a properly prepared raw foods, combination, or cooked foods diet.

Some large and very large breeds should maintain a moderate protein diet during their growth period. This allows their growth to develop slowly and strengthens their bone and joint structures hence avoiding future orthopedic problems that stem from rapid development. After their growth period, normal protein diets can begin.

It is widely agreed that a high protein diet offers many benefits including providing excess energy. Dogs fed deficient protein diets can develop poor growth, decreased appetite, weight loss, poor coat conditions, and lowered immune function. In breeding animals, decreased milk production and lower reproductive drive can surface.

Protein requirements differ in growing puppies and for senior dogs, both requiring lower amounts of protein and higher carbohydrates in their food. It is always a good practice to consult top breeders and veterinarians about when to change amounts of protein for your dog. A dog's activity levels can change its requirements. Additionally, a bitch during her gestation and lactation period has specific requirements. Evidence shows that other food ingredients can alter the amount of amino acids required by dogs. Some preservatives effect the requirement by interfering with the processing of amino.

Arginine – Functions in metabolic processes that help heart disease and high blood pressure. It is believed to help in the prevention and fighting of cancer in dogs. It does this by converting into nitric oxide and it then assists immune cells to fight cancer. However, arginine can also turn into L-ornithine, and if this occurs, it is believed that it assists cancer in growing. Studies show that arginine in conjunction with fish oils have created remission in canine cancers therefore extending their lives.

Histidine – Is an essential amino acid that is very important for adult dogs, especially females. It helps build plasma, muscle, and many other metabolic functions.

Lysine - Is an essential amino acid that stimulates gastric juice secretion, and bone growth in puppies. It is found in high quantities within muscle tissues, connective tissues, and collagen.

Isoleucine, Leucine, and Valine – These essential amino acids are part of the branched-chain amino acids that are obtained from dairy products, meat, and legumes. Branched-chain refers to their chemical structure. These amino acids stimulate the building of protein in muscle, and potentially help reduce muscle breakdown allowing for increased performance during exercise and sports.

Methionine - Is an essential amino acid that assists the gall bladder, balances urinary tract pH levels, treats and prevents urinary stones. It is also involved in neurotransmitter metabolism.

Phenylalanine – Is an essential amino acid building block of protein that comes in three forms, D - Phenylalanine, L - Phenylalanine, and a combination that is made in the laboratory named DL - Phenylalanine. The primary sources of L-phenylalanine are eggs, cheeses, milk, and meats. It is used to manufacture chemical messengers, but the exact working process is unknown. It assists in mood elevation, skin pigmentation, adrenaline production, and thyroid hormones.

Threonine – Is an essential amino acid that *works in conjunction with phenylalanine* in mood elevation, skin pigmentation, adrenaline manufacturing, and thyroid hormones.

Tryptophan - Is an essential amino acid that produces serotonin to aid in sleeping, and aids in clotting blood. There are studies that indicate a concurrent lack of tryptophan and methionine can cause hair loss.

Fatty Acids

Essential fatty acids (EFA's) are fats that the body cannot produce. Therefore, they must be acquired through diet. Fatty acids are essential for the growth and functioning of cells, muscles, nerves, organs, and processes performed by hormone type substances. Insufficiencies of fatty acids can cause health issues such as, cancer, diabetes, heart disease, and more.

Essential fatty acids are divided into Omega-3 and Omega-6. Many food makers do not add these to their foods in sufficient quantities and there is some issue with Omega-3's quickly spoiling without the addition of expensive preservation techniques. Quality foods contain a ratio of at least 2.2% Omega-6 and 0.3% Omega-3, or close to that ratio. Some variance in ratios are quoted by different experts. Additionally, the ratio might vary depending upon your breed, dog, and any health conditions affecting them.

High levels of Omega-3 have been shown to fight inflammatory disease, improve cardiovascular diseases, shield against the development of cancer cells, boost immune system, and reduce joint stiffness and allergic dermatitis. Good sources of Omeg-3's are flax seed oil, and fresh or canned fish that has preferably been cooked. Dogs prone to kidney disease should use fish and not flax oil. Because Omega-3's spoil quickly, use a supplement that has vitamin E added.

Omega-6 Fatty Acids

Arachidonic acid – Is an Omega-6 that is found in lean meat, egg yolks, some fish oils, and the body fat of poultry.

Dihomogamma linolenic acid – Is an Omega-6 that is metabolized from gamma linolenic acid. They are found in organ meats such as the kidney, spleen, heart, and adrenals.

Gamma linolenic acid – Is an Omega-6 that is found in borage oil, black currant seed oil, and evening primrose oil.

Linoleic acid – Is an Omega-6 that is found in sunflower, safflower, canola, soy, and corn oils. It is also found in whole grains, and the body fat of poultry. It helps maintain a healthy skin and coat.

Omega-3 Fatty Acids

Alpha linolenic acid – Is an Omeg-3 that is found prominently in flaxseed oil. To a lesser extent, it is found in canola, soy, and walnut oils.

Docosahexaenoic acid – Is an Omeg-3 that is found in cold-water fish and their oils.

Eicosapentaenoic acid - Is an Omeg-3 that is found in cold-water fish and their oils.

We realize it may take time to understand what kind of diet your dog requires to thrive. Do your best to include in your dog's daily diet, all thirty-six nutrients mentioned here. All of which can come from fruits, veggies, kibble, raw foods, cooked foods, and yes, even good table scraps. You will soon discover that your dog has preferred foods. For your dog to maintain optimum health, he needs a daily basis of a GI track healthy, well-rounded diet combined with a good balance of exercise, rest, socializing, care, and love.

This is just a short summary about some of the processes and science involved in vitamin, nutrient, and protein nutrition. As a dog owner, you owe it to yourself and your dog's livelihood to provide them with the most balanced nutritious diet that will bring out their vibrancy and boost their constitution enabling them to fight off potential diseases and physical ailments. I recommend further investigation into your dog's health and diet. I wish you and your dog a long healthy vivacious life.

Conclusion

Evolution - *As the two of you continue to practice commands and shape behaviors, the successes will grow and lock in confidence between the two of you.*

Thank you for joining me in this German Shepherd dog training adventure. I am confident that by now, you and your dog have both learned much and that your dog is obeying commands while looking to you as his or her *alpha leader*. Furthermore, I presume that the PRICELESS MINDSET is part of your everyday personality and is second nature. I hope that the two of you have had fun, laughed, and played along the way. When spending time with my dog I often shake my head, smile, and laugh at one of us. Aren't dogs great? Dogs have truly enriched my life.

There is always more to learn and improve upon so please continue to read, watch videos, and practice. I hope that you were never too judgmental of your own skills and that the PRICELESS mindset was a consistent helpful reminder of how you should act during interactions with your dog.

Time and practice will enable you to continually improve your skills, and for your dog to improve his adept response to your commands while continuing to learn more tricks and commands. These beautiful intelligent dogs are capable of learning and performing a myriad of sports, tricks, and tasks.

Keep in mind that training and owning a dog is a lifelong commitment. Please remain a committed alpha that always has his or her dog's welfare in the forefront of his or her mind.

I wish you well in training, fun, health, and the enjoyment of each other's company.

About the Author

Daniel Vega enjoys training and studying dog behaviors. He is dedicated to causes that promote humane treatment for all animals.

Legal Disclaimer:

The author of the *"German Shepherd Puppy Training The Complete German Shepherd Puppy Training Guide for Caring, Raising, and Training German Shepherd Puppies"* dog training book, Daniel Vega is in no way responsible at any time for the action of your pet, not now or in the future. Animals, without warning, may cause injury to humans and/or other animals. Daniel Vega is not responsible for attacks, bites, mauling, nor any other viciousness or any and all other damages. We strongly recommend that you exercise caution for the safety of self, the animal, and all around the animals while working with your dog. We are not liable for any animal or human medical conditions or results obtained from training. While all attempts have been made to verify information provided in this publication, neither the author nor the publisher assume any responsibility for errors, omissions or contrary interpretation of the subject matter contained herein. The publisher and author assume no responsibility or liability whatsoever on the behalf of any purchaser or reader of the material provided. The owner of said dog training guide assumes any, and all risks associated with the methodology described inside the dog-training guidebook.

Content Attributions

Photos: We wish to thank all of the photographers for sharing their photographs via Creative Commons Licensing.

BIO -CLOSE UP GSD PUPPY https://www.flickr.com/photos/blumenbiene/14253534264/, CC License 2.0 Generic https://creativecommons.org/licenses/by/2.0/legalcode, Puppy, By Maja Dumat, no changes made

Puppy Training Prep - PUPPY GSD TONGUE OUT LOOKING UP, https://www.flickr.com/photos/marilynjane/2358902018/in/photostream/, License 2.0 Generic https://creativecommons.org/licenses/by/2.0/legalcode, Kim 8 weeks, By Marilyn Peddle, cropped pant leg out of right side of photo

PUPPY PROOF HOME -BLACK GSD PUPPY https://www.flickr.com/photos/blumenbiene/14689079482/, CC License 2.0 Generic https://creativecommons.org/licenses/by/2.0/legalcode, Black Puppy, By Maja Dumat, no changes made

NAMING -GSD PUPPY SITTING TONGUE OUT https://www.flickr.com/photos/blumenbiene/14299122625/, License 2.0 Generic https://creativecommons.org/licenses/by/2.0/legalcodeAufgeregt, By Maja Dumat, no changes made

DOWN - PUPPY GSD PONDERING LIFE LAYING DOWN https://www.flickr.com/photos/blumenbiene/14273972373/, License 2.0 Generic https://creativecommons.org/licenses/by/2.0/legalcode, Geigein, By Maja Dumat, no changes made

ACTIVITIES - GSD JUMPING OBSTACLE https://pixabay.com/get/8e2f87fe89d0473214ca/1447911282/dog-826804_1920.jpg?direct, Pixabay CC License https://creativecommons.org/publicdomain/zero/1.0/deed.en, no changes made

SIT -GSD WITH PIG IN MOUTH https://pixabay.com/en/german-shepherd-dog-young-animal-710174/, www.localpuppybreeders.com, CC License 2.0 Generic https://creativecommons.org/licenses/by/2.0/legalcode, no changes made

CONCLUSION - PAIR OF GSD'S SITTIN IN GRASS TONGUES OUT https://pixabay.com/en/dogs-homemade-animals-888415/, https://creativecommons.org/publicdomain/zero/1.0/legalcode, no changes made

Printed in Great Britain
by Amazon

ALSO BY RR HAYWOOD

EXTRACTED SERIES

EXTRACTED

EXECUTED

EXTINCT

Block-buster Time-Travel

#1 *Amazon* US

#1 *Amazon* UK

#1 *Audible* US & UK

Top 3 Amazon Australia

Washington Post Best-seller

In 2061, a young scientist invents a time machine to fix a tragedy in his past. But his good intentions turn catastrophic when an early test reveals something unexpected: the end of the world.

A desperate plan is formed. Recruit three heroes, ordinary humans capable of extraordinary things, and change the future.

Safa Patel is an elite police officer, on duty when Downing Street comes under terrorist attack. As armed men storm through the breach, she dispatches them all.

'Mad' Harry Madden is a legend of the Second World War. Not only did he complete an impossible mission—to plant charges on a heavily defended submarine base—but he also escaped with his life.

Ben Ryder is just an insurance investigator. But as a young man he witnessed a gang assaulting a woman and her child. He went to their rescue, and killed all five.

Can these three heroes, extracted from their timelines at the point of death, save the world?

ALSO BY RR HAYWOOD

THE UNDEAD

"The best series ever..."

THE UK's #1 Horror Series

The Undead. The First Seven Days (compilation edition)

The Undead. The Second Week (compilation edition)

Day Fourteen to Day Twenty-One (individual books)

The Undead Twenty-Two

The Undead Twenty-Three

CHAPTER ONE

Sunday Afternoon

I wake quickly. Transitioning from sleep to awake in an instant to find I'm bathed in sweat and sitting bolt upright in bed. Fleeting images of torn bodies ease back from my mind as the dream fades and disappears, leaving me momentarily confused.

I'm at home. Not my home in Boroughfare. My parent's house. Why am I here? A few seconds to blink as the memories of the last two days come crashing back. The world is over. Everyone is either dead or infected and one of those things.

One of those things. What are those things? Zombies are from the movies, and it feels weird to even think of them like that. This is real. This is happening.

Too many thoughts too soon from wakening and I blink at the window, seeing it's light outside.

Anyway, zombies are dead, and dead bodies don't bleed. Those things certainly bleed. Especially when Dave cuts their heads off and they spray blood all over the place. I cut a few open like too, but that was more by accident than design. Dave was something else, the way he was killing them. The speed of him, and I think, on reflection, that I am more of a blunt trauma man. The axe was good. Nice and heavy and easy to split skulls open, and if you get the swing right you can easily lop arms and legs off.

What else did I use? Oh yeah, the sledgehammer. That was amazing, but really only a one-trick weapon, great for an overhead smash but too heavy and tiring.

Then there were the two lump hammers, again they were effective at one on one, or even a couple of them at a time, but against several undead zombie things they lack the range. The chainsaw was bloody amazing, really, truly amazing and I regret not bringing it with us. A few people armed with chainsaws could destroy tons of undead, but again they are heavy and too reliant on fuel. If one part breaks or jams it would be rendered useless. Good point. I'll stick with the axe until we find some guns.

Guns? What the fuck. I'm a supermarket manager, not a soldier. What do I know about combat or fighting techniques? Dave, on the other hand, is not all he seems. He said he was in the Army for fourteen years, but he wouldn't say anything else about his time in the service. I've met loads of ex-service people; quite a lot of them had seen action in the Middle East. Some had physical scars, others had scars that weren't so noticeable. Post traumatic stress disorder they called it.

But Dave doesn't betray any feelings or emotions. The only time I have seen him give anything away was last night in the supermarket, when I told him he could do what he wanted. He clearly had nowhere to go, no family or friends. The thought of taking away his routine must have scared him. He could have run or even closed the doors; every staff member is shown how to close and shut off the automatic doors, in case of emergency. Dave didn't shut them though; he stayed on the shop floor. He even killed the rest of the staff as they were turned into undead. I wonder if any of them fought alongside him until they were taken down. If they did then Dave didn't hesitate but killed them too. Blimey. Would he do that to me if I get bit?

Routine must be important to him, as well as having someone in a position of authority – of *perceived* authority, anyway. Fourteen years of Army life must have moulded him. But then, other long-serving military people I have known weren't like that.

Anyway. What now? What's next? My parents clearly haven't got back, so from that I can only assume they are not coming back. Shit, that hurts. A pang inside. Deep and raw. The thought of them going out to look for me and getting hurt by those things brings back that rage I had yesterday. That searing, driving energy that made me attack and kill. I've never felt anything like that. Not even close. What I felt was something else, something deeper, a base state of being, an instinct to exact revenge and hurt those that hurt me.

To be honest, I didn't even know people could have such feelings. Other than maybe serial killers.

Am I a serial killer? Crumbs. That's a bit worrying. No, but hang on, those things aren't people. The bodies are just carriers for the infection inside. An infection that just happens to make them want to eat other people.

Whoa. That's a bit alarming. If they can bleed and what possesses them is an infection, then maybe they will recover. What if it's just a forty-eight hour bug? Jesus, they might recover of their own accord, and I've already slain shitloads of them, plus I burnt down a village. What will I say if they all go back to normal?

Oops ... sorry about that. I thought you were all zombies. My mistake. Never mind – no harm done.

I banish such thoughts away and finally get off the bed to look out the window at a gorgeous summer day. The air almost looks hazy with the scorching sun. I glance at my watch; it's almost 3 p.m. I've had a few hours of sleep but my body is hurting like hell from all the physical exertion. My legs hurts, my arms too. Actually, pretty much everything hurts.

I head downstairs, pausing to flick the light switches a few times while remembering the power went off as I fell asleep. I always thought it would last longer if like the world ended or something. Shows you what I know.

I reach the kitchen to see Dave sitting at the counter drinking what looks like coffee. I cross to the fridge and open the door, but the light doesn't come on.

'Power's gone,' he says in that dull monotone voice.

'How did you make the coffee then?' I ask, somewhat gruff and somewhat sleepy while somewhat squinting.

'Gas.'

'Gas?' I look over to the gas hob with a nod of realisation. A saucepan of water steaming away and I spot a bottle of milk in a bowl of water. A few seconds of staring, of looking from the pan and milk to Dave sitting silently at the breakfast bar. An urge to say something and fill the silence. Instead I just nod again and make coffee while feeling spaced out. Like there is no order or sense to my thoughts.

Coffee made and I lean back against the counter to sip the hot liquid, holding the mug two handed while studying Dave and how he looks so clean and freshly shaved. Even his top is tucked in. I glance down to see I'm just in boxer shorts and suddenly feel very self-conscious that I'm in my undies with a man I hardly know. The fact we slaughtered a raging horde of infected zombie things together doesn't really register. What happened to my clothes? I squint, frown, think on this and then spot them neatly folded on top of the tumble dryer. I remember we stripped off and put them onto wash then in the tumble dryer before I went to sleep.

I look at Dave. He stares back. 'At least the clothes dried before the power went off then,' I say casually, which just sounds weird and forced.

'Almost. I put them outside.'

'What, in the garden? On the washing line? Bloody hell, Dave ... thank you.'

'That's okay, Mr Howie.'

'Dave, you don't have to call me Mr Howie anymore, Howie is fine.'

'Okay.'

He won't call me Howie, I know that.

I head into the lounge to dress. The thought of getting dressed in front of him feels weird. Mind you, everything feels weird. I stand up from tugging my shoes on and spot Dad's road atlas on the bookshelf. My dad loved technology and would always have the latest gadget: new computer, latest phones, but despite all of that, he would lecture me that society has become too over-reliant on technology.

'... it has its uses and should be enjoyed, but not taken for granted.'

I listened but never really took it in. Looking at the atlas now reminds me of what a careful and prepared man he was. Then I get an idea and take the atlas into the kitchen and start flicking the pages. Dave doesn't say a word but sits in silence.

I find the south east and rest my finger on my location now. Brighton is east of here, London is north; about two hours on a good day. But then the roads are empty now, so reaching London should be easy, however, getting *through* London will be an entirely different matter. Bloody hell, you'd need a tank.

'Dave?' I ask. He looks at me but stays silent. 'Nothing,' I say, feeling stupid for a second. 'Where could I get a tank from?' I ask, deciding that feeling stupid is the least of my worries right now.

He doesn't even flinch. 'Salisbury.'

'Where's that?'

'I don't know, Mr Howie.'

'Are they hard to drive?'

'I don't have a licence.'

'They must be hard, how about those armoured vehicles?'

'APCs.'

'Yeah, them. They must be like cars to drive.'

'I don't know, Mr Howie.'

'Do they have those APC things at Salisbury too?'

'Yes.'

'Okay, so we need to get into London to get my sister, but I heard an emergency broadcast that said London is infested and to stay away, so I reckon we should get to Salisbury, nick an APS and get going.'

'An APC.'

'What?'

'You said APS – it's an APC. Armoured Personnel Carrier.'

'Oh, right ... sorry. We get an APC and try for London. Oh hang on. I mean *I* need to go to London, I didn't mean to assume that you were coming with me.'

'I'll come with you, Mr Howie,' he says in that flat way.

'Okay. Great,' I say into the slightly awkward silence. 'Er, so Salisbury is here and we are here. It should take us around two hours to get there, I think, and it's 3 p.m. now. It gets dark at about half nine –so if we leave now, we should make it before nightfall.'

'Okay.'

No questions. No anything.

I nod and finish my coffee.

CHAPTER TWO

Half an hour later and we stand outside staring at the blood and gore smeared over the front of the Tesco home delivery van. Should have washed it off really.

However, I did think ahead and fill some bags with food from the kitchen. Snack food and a few tins. Dave then put some bedding from the spare rooms in the back of the van then found a gas lamp from the garage. I should have thought of that really and chide myself to start thinking properly.

I grab my two new axes and with a last look back at the house, I get into the front of the van and slot the axes down next to me as Dave gets in with a load of knife handles poking from the top of his rucksack. Another second of silence as I look at them then at him.

'I like knives,' he says.

I nod and start the engine. Not quite knowing what you say to that. I pull off and start driving away then realise I don't know where my sister actually lives. 'Arse,' I mutter, bringing the vehicle to a stop then selecting reverse to go back as the air fills with the reversing alarm. 'Need my mum's address book,' I tell Dave, but Dave doesn't appear to wish to chat.

I rush back into the house and find Mum's old address book. Hard-backed and brightly coloured with a flowery pattern. The sight of it brings forth a rush of pain inside. I remember this book from childhood and the sight of my mother's handwriting is almost too much to see.

I quickly flick to 'S'. There it is, 'Sarah – London'. I kiss the book and offer a silent prayer to my mother, still taking care of me. Back outside and into the van; the book goes into my rucksack and then I think better of it, and give it to Dave.

'Can you look after this please, mate, my sister's address is inside and I can't afford to lose it, her name is Sarah – her address is under Sarah, London. If anything happens to me ...'

He takes the book like I'm passing him a priceless antique, staring at it for a second before taking a small hand towel from his knife-loaded bag that he wraps the book in like it's a valuable relic.

'Ready?' I ask.

He looks at me, devoid of expression, devoid of anything. 'Yes, Mr Howie,' he says simply, and we set off.

It feels wrong to be heading away from my sister. If a little coastal town like Boroughfare can amass a few hundred undead, then think what a city centre will be like? I think of my own town and the first night and that cash in transit van driving past my house. Who was that? It worked though. Luring them away like that.

Then I think on the way the infection things group together. It was the same in Littleton, they all grouped together in the village square. Maybe that was the last place they took a survivor down so they stayed there, hopeful of another one, or maybe a survivor got away from there and they stayed in the last place of contact, like when I ran through the precinct into the nightclub – they stayed outside those doors for a long time.

But then, in Boroughfare, it looked like more were joining the crowd. There must be something that passes between them, an alert state? So if one senses prey then they all join in, and the signal passes, until they are coming from all around. Can that even happen?

This might be something we could use; draw them together and create a safe passage – like the *cash in transit* driver – but on a bigger scale ... a much bigger scale. How would we do that? I don't know the roads in London well enough to know where to draw them to; we could easily get ourselves trapped or stuck in a far worse situation if we start pissing about, trying to be clever.

I look up at the sky and realise we won't have enough time to get to Sarah today – by the time we have found a suitable vehicle and then get into London it could be late evening. We don't have satellite navigation, so finding her address in the city will be hard enough. If only I could get a message to her, tell her to wait. Hang on, sat nav might work ... the mobile networks are down but do sat navs use the same network systems as mobiles? They all work off satellites and something to do with GPS – maybe they are still online?

I go through the radio stations in the van, flicking through all of the preset ones first, and then manually through the frequencies ... the message is gone. I didn't make a note of the frequency setting from the Micra. I check FM, MW, and LW but get only static and so we drive on in a slightly awkward silence. Moving from the town into the countryside, passing fields and meadows. Trees overhead and long winding country lanes. Birdsong heard outside and the summer sun bearing down. The odd house or turning for a tiny village. An idyllic Home Counties' type of setting, worthy of picture postcards.

'You hungry?' I ask, opening one of the bags of food. I take an apple and start eating while thinking on this and that, on the infection inside the people, on satellites and London and all manner of things. I still feel spaced out and achy, but the normalcy of driving and eating sooths my nerves.

I cast the remains of the apple out the window and catch Dave glancing at me. A few seconds later I take a banana and scoff that too before flinging the skin out the window, which earns me another sharp look as he takes the waste bag he was using and pointedly places it on the seat between us.

'Sorry mate, I wasn't thinking. I'm leaving a trail behind us, aren't I?' I say while glancing at the wing mirrors and looking about out the windows. 'They'll be able to follow us...I guess you learnt that in the Army?' I look back at him to see his face is still devoid of all expression while somehow managing to imply I am a dick.

'Keep Britain Tidy,' he says, facing the front again.

'Right,' I say slowly. 'Sure...er, Dave, what you said to me before, about keeping a firm grip, strike and move. How do you know that stuff? And the way you use those knives, you must have studied martial arts or something?'

'No.'

'Where did you learn it then?'

He pauses for a few seconds.

'The Army.'

'Wow, why did they teach you all that? I thought it was more about guns and stuff.'

Silence.

'So, like, they teach you hand to hand combat and things then?'

Silence.

I nod and take a breath. 'Dave, the army has probably fallen mate. Christ, I think the whole country has fallen, probably the whole world...what I mean is that I'm sure it will be okay if you tell me.'

'I can't, Mr Howie.'

'Why not?'

'I'm not allowed to say.'

'Eh? You're not allowed to say why you can't tell me or are you just not allowed to say anything?'

'Yes.'

'What the fuck?' I ask, shaking my head at the confusing answer as a sudden cramping hits my stomach with an urgent message being passed from bowel to brain that I really need an urgent poo.

I cast about thinking I really don't want to squat anywhere Dave can see me and spot the entrance to a lane up ahead. That'll do. I stop the van. Grab some wet-wipes and start rushing out as the cramping comes back harder.

'Mr Howie ...' Dave calls. I turn back to see him holding one of the axes out. I grab the handle, offer a wan smile and leg it off into the lane entrance while trying to clench my bum cheeks. A few yards in. A quick look about. All clear. I tug my trousers and boxers down and squat at the side of the road. The smell is disgusting; my stomach must be upset from the extreme lifestyle of the last couple of days, plus the sporadic eating. I guess the copious fruit we just ate hasn't helped matters either.

However, and despite the smell, and the thought of taking a crap in broad daylight in a country lane, the feeling of relief is amazing and I'm moaning with the pleasure. I almost sound like one of the infected, and that makes me try and mimic their noise. Groaning while pooing in a country lane at the same time as pondering of zombies need to shit. I bet they just poo in their pants. Dirty undead.

A noise behind me and I twist round to see an entrance a few metres into the lane that was concealed by the bushes when I first looked. A shuffle. Footsteps maybe then I spot something in the darkness of the shadows and grab the wipes to start cleaning my arse. It might be the end of the world and I understand we all have to make sacrifices and change our normal behaviour in this new world, but walking around with a shitty arse isn't one of mine.

Then the sound comes closer so I think stuff it and yank my trousers up as a black and white farm dog emerges out of the entrance. I freeze and go stock still with my mind filling with images of being chased by a zombie dog, but then my eyes adjust to the gloom and I can see it looks normal. It doesn't have red eyes anyway and it's head keeps flicking from me to something else set back that I can't see. I swallow, blink a few times then call out.

'Hello boy, who's a good doggy. You're a good doggy.'

I love dogs, always have done. We had dogs when I was younger, ones from rescue shelters – so we had a good mix of crosses and mongrels.

The growl coming low and deep makes me stop and as the view opens up, so I gain sight of a very fat middle aged infected man shuffling slowly towards me in rubber boots looking every inch the stereotypical farmer. He just needs one of those long sticks with the crook at the end. I imagine his wife making apple pies and Sunday roast dinners.

Dave comes around the corner, obviously concerned that I have been gone for too long. I point at the entrance, guessing that he can't see them from where he is. He comes down further and joins me, then stops on seeing the infected and silently draws a knife from his belt.

'I don't think the dog will let you near him, mate. Mind you, he doesn't look aggressive either…maybe we can try and get him out of that lane, his farm must be close.'

Dave looks at me.

'Most farms have shotguns don't they…'

He nods and walks a bit closer to the dog, who crouches lower and growls more. Dave stops and waits for the undead to make his way out of the entrance. The dog keeps glancing at his master, then moves position, edging closer to Dave who backs away, just a little at a time.

I drop the axe head onto the raised verge and lean on the handle. Despite the horrible circumstances, the lane is pleasant and quiet. Sunlight dapples through the canopy, causing shadows to dance across the surface of the road. It feels like it is getting hotter and there is no wind; the air is very close.

That makes me look back at the dog and the big tongue hanging out the side. Poor thing must be so hot.

'Wait here a sec,' I say to Dave and rush back to the van to find a bottle of water and a mug and run back to see them all pretty much in the same position.

'You thirsty?' I ask the dog, crouching down to pour water into the mug. The dog watches me closely, eyeing the water while glancing back to his owner. 'Good boy...come on...get some water...'

We back away enough for the dog to feel safe and watch as it rushes forward to lap thirstily at the water in the mug.

We skirt them both and go wide to get behind and into a narrow track rutted with wheel marks and head off moving slowly uphill. Minutes later and I'm sweating from the heat and exertion while Dave looks as fresh as anything.

The lane ends at a metal five-bar gate, which is wedged open. A rusty cattle grid lies just beyond the gate; the dark metal poles are evenly spaced, with weeds growing up between them. A few hundred metres to some buildings; some of them are sheds and barns, long and low with corrugated roofs. Plant machinery dotted about, things that farmers attach to tractors.

Our raised position means that we can see the fields beyond the buildings. We both wait and stare at the view.

Finally, Dave looks at me and nods and we go through the gate and onto the driveway. There is a herd of black and white cows standing at the gate in a field adjacent to the buildings. As we get closer, I can see that the udders look full. I had heard that cows will get so used to the routine of milking they will wait at the gate. I also heard that cows explode if they don't get milked – so I watch them as we pass, ready to duck, in case of bovine explosion.

The cows haven't been bitten and the dog was okay too. The farmer would have access to all types of animals, but they look unharmed.

I had thought of using rotting flesh, or an animal carcass to lure them away in London, but it appears the infected people only crave human flesh. If we are going to use meat as a trap, then it has to be human meat – and alive too. I force the thought away, disgusted that I'm even thinking of it.

We reach the farmhouse, circling it quietly while looking for entry points or signs of movement. The windows all have heavy net curtains inside, in order to prevent the farmhands looking in the house, I guess.

The front door is dark wood and inward opening. I slowly push the handle down and the door opens a fraction. I look at Dave, nod, and then slowly start to step forward. The axe bangs noisily on the lower half of the door, which remains closed. I look at Dave with an apologetic grimace.

'Sorry ... it's a stable door.' I reach in and unlock the bottom half of the door and we proceed.

The floor is made from flagstones and there is a flight of exposed wooden stairs ahead of us.

Dave taps me on the shoulder and motions for me to stay still; he moves off to the right into a doorway and is gone from view for a few seconds. He returns and gives me a *thumbs up* signal, then motions with his hand towards the door on the left. He goes first, easing each foot down, treading carefully.

He gets to the door, pushes it open and leans his head in. Without looking at me, he takes both knives in his left hand and raises his right to the side of his head. He makes a fist and then extends two fingers, giving me the V. He makes a fist again and then extends one finger, pointing it to the room, then a fist and again he extends a finger and points into the room – more off to the side this time. Then he makes a flat hand and runs it across his throat; next he extends all his fingers out straight and reverses his hand so that the palm is facing towards the door, then more palms and fingers are waved about.

I have no idea what this all means.

I think he is telling me that there is someone in there ... the rest leaves me clueless. He looks back at me and I shrug my shoulders, and, again, even though his face wears the usual *devoid of expression* look, I could swear he is wondering why he got stuck with me. He then points two fingers directly at his own eyes and motions for me to look. He eases back and I peek inside; there are two undead in the room.

Ah ... so that's what he meant, two of them. Then the hand across the throat must have implied they are dead, or undead. I get it, anyway, even though I have no clue what the rest of the waving and pointing was about.

One of the undead is a fat woman, a *really* fat woman. She must be the farmer's wife, all jolly and large, wearing a white apron over a flowery dress. The other undead is an adult male, wearing dirty and stained overalls tucked into rubber boots.

They are standing side by side with their backs to the door, facing out the window. The farmer's wife has a huge chunk torn out of her meaty upper arm with dried blood splattered all down her dress.

There are bloodstains on the male too, but I can't see any injury from here. They're in the kitchen area in front of the sink. There is another closed door opposite me; there must be more rooms beyond it as the house extends further than the size of this room.

I ease back and gently pull the door closed. Dave motions with his head for me to follow him and he starts climbing the stairs. I climb up behind him, looking back at the kitchen door to make sure that I closed it and walk into the back of Dave with my head nudging his backside.

'Sorry,' I whisper.

He doesn't reply or even look back.

'I didn't know you had stopped,' I add.

He stays still for a second, doesn't look back, and then carries on going up. I wait for a gap to form between us then start to follow him to the landing and a corridor stretching off with closed doors on either side.

Dave motions for me to stay put, then goes left, gingerly working his way down the corridor. I watch how he walks; swinging each foot slow and purposefully, the heel going down first in an almost exaggerated manner, then he slowly moves forward and puts his weight onto the front foot then repeats the movement, in complete silence.

He stops at the first door and listens, craning his head, and then leans in closer, until his ear is almost touching the door, his mouth open.

He eases the door open, steps inside and is back out within seconds. He repeats the action until all of the rooms on that end are clear. Then he creeps back to me and motions for me to move forward; I think he wants me to check my end.

I start forward a few steps, copying his movement and putting my heels down first. It seems to take ages to work my way down. At the first door I stop and listen, but I can't hear anything above my heart hammering away in my chest.

I lean into the first door, but still can't hear anything. I take hold of the handle and twist it back. The handle squeaks really loudly and I stop twisting. I look back at Dave who nods for me to carry on. I keep twisting the handle – which sounds like it's screaming in protest. The door suddenly gives and I push it open too fast, almost tripping in and banging the axe against the frame.

This time I don't look back. I'm too embarrassed to face him. I know that his face will be blank, but he still manages to convey a message through that vacant gaze. I peer into the room – it's all clear.

I move off down the corridor, treading carefully and trying to show that I can do this too.

At the next door, I grasp the handle and hold my breath as I twist. Silence.

I breathe a sigh of relief and start to push the door open, which creaks loudly on the hinges.

For fuck's sake, this is a conspiracy. How did he get all of the silent handles and doors?

I keep pushing slowly, the hinges creaking and groaning. I stop. Pushing slowly is making it worse. If I push it open quickly the hinges won't grate so much. I heave with force to a cacophony of metallic screams. At least the room is clear.

The final door at the end facing the corridor and again I take hold of the handle and push. It opens into a large bathroom: white tiles, white bath and white shower curtain around the bath, nice and bright – apart from the large pool of blood on the floor and the infected woman in the white nightdress standing in the middle of it.

She is fat, incredibly fat, quite possibly one of the fattest people that I have ever seen, and the sight isn't helped by the fact her white nightdress as thin sleeves, which only serve to accentuate the rolls of fat on her upper arms. She's got very long dark hair with a wooden-handled hairbrush tangled in the flowing locks.

She slowly turns round to face me and I see the red, bloodshot eyes. Her wrist has been bitten deeply, leaving a nasty gaping wound.

I look back at Dave and raise my hand to the side of my head, making a fist. He nods, then I extend one finger and point into the room, again he nods. Then I puff out my cheeks, hold my arms out and waddle slightly on the spot, while motioning to the door behind me – he just stares at me.

I keep waddling on the spot, holding my arms out and pretending to rub my big belly. Dave looks so serious and, after the tension of creeping down the corridor, I let go and start giggling like a school-boy. Then I pretend to brush my hair and extend one finger and point it into my pretend hair. Within seconds, I am trying to stifle my laughter but the undead farmer's daughter starts waddling towards the door and I back away.

She is taller than me and the girth of her is amazing, puffed cheeks making her mouth look small and pouty.

I back off down the corridor, still trying to stop myself laughing. She makes it to the doorway and gets stuck face on; too fat to get through. She keeps pushing forward though, grunting and straining against the effort.

That's it; I'm gone. Tears of laughter are falling down my face and I'm leaning against the wall. All of the stress of the last few days have built up and the sight of the fat woman unable to walk through the door has finished me off.

I try to be quiet at first, but knowing that we have to be silent makes it worse and I can't stop myself from howling. Within minutes my stomach is hurting. I manage to get myself under control, then look back at her wedged in the doorway with her stomach pushing through, but her shoulders and arms can't fit and she is sort of leaning back and trying to get through belly first. I'm off again, sliding down the wall onto the floor. The laughing is hurting but I can't stop. I try to look at Dave but the tears have misted my eyes. I imagine him standing there, stony-faced.

It takes many minutes, but eventually I get myself under control and get back up. Dave is standing there, impassive as ever, but I swear there is a glint in his eye.

CHAPTER THREE

We make our way down the stairs and stare at the kitchen door; there was no sign of a gun cabinet anywhere upstairs. The only place left to check is the kitchen and the room on the other side, but that means going through the room containing two infected people.

'What do you reckon?' I ask. 'We could lead them out again.'

Dave nods and I check my watch.

'It's gone 5 p.m. already. Shit ... We really have to get going.'

'Okay.'

He walks straight past me into the kitchen, disappearing round the door with two loud thumps following within seconds.

'What the...' I rush in behind him to see the farmer's wife now almost decapitated with her spinal column showing through her severed neck. 'Fuck,' I gasp and blanch as Dave drags the dead infected male on top of the farmer's wife, showing his OCD for tidiness again and the humour from a few minutes ago disappears instantly.

The brutal yet reserved nature of this man is staggering. His mind must be so straightforward when he is completing a task, whether it's filling shelves at Tesco or severing the head of a zombie farmer's wife.

A second for my brain to try and catch up as I blink and widen my eyes. Dave stands back, looking down at his work then over to me. Silence again. I swallow and nod then head through the other door into a utility area. An old, stained kitchen top with a deep, white ceramic sink. Dirty pairs of rubber boots up against the wall and overalls hanging from rails. There are two washing machines labelled: HOUSE and FARM.

There is a back door to the right. To the left is the promised bounty: a large, metal cabinet fixed on the wall, complete with a massive padlock hanging from a clasp. The padlock has a thick, metal loop, and the clasp has multiple strong rivets securing the cabinet.

'I bet the farmer has the key in his pocket,' I say quietly. Dave doesn't reply.

We start searching the area, checking drawers and the pockets of the overalls. We find keys, but none of them fit. 'Cock it,' I mutter while staring at the padlock, figuring we'll have to break it open. I take a step back and reverse the axe so that the blunt end will be used.

'Watch out, mate.'

Five minutes later and I'm out of breath with the metal cabinet bashed and dented but still holding firm and decidedly locked. I even try wedging the blade of the axe into the gap of the cabinet door, but I can't get enough leverage.

'Fucking thing, any suggestions, mate?'

I look around, but Dave is gone and the back door is open. I step over half thinking he's probably seen sense and legged it as far away from me as possible, but there he is, coming back with a sledgehammer and a big metal spike. He walks in without saying a word, hands me the sledgehammer and sticks the pointy end of the spike into the gap between the cabinet and the padlock clasp and looks at me with an air of expectation. Not that his expression changes. I heft the big sledgehammer and look at the spike, then back at Dave, then at the cabinet all covered in dinks and dents.

'Um, maybe we should swap....' I suggest, thinking I'm highly likely to miss and bludgeon Dave to death.

We move places in the confined space as I take the spike and realise just how close I am to the cabinet, and start thinking maybe this is a bad idea because Dave could now bludgeon me to death. Then Dave swings and hits the spike, making me yelp and flinch and half pull back while waiting for the pain to explode. None comes and I open my eyes to see the spike has been driven in an inch. He hits it again with near on surgical precision. It's a big heavy hammer too and he doesn't show any signs of exertion either. A few hits later and the padlock falls away as I step back rubbing my arm now tingling from the energy transference sent through my hand.

I watch Dave as he takes the weapons out and recognise three shotguns from having two big barrels and big wooden bases, or stocks, or bottom bits. Whatever they're called.

There is also a long camouflage bag in the cabinet holding a rifle that looks very slim compared to the shotguns.

'What is it?' I ask.

'Lee Enfield point three, zero three, bolt action rifle.'

'Is that good?'

'Yes.'

Ask a question. Get an answer. Within seconds the gun is separated into parts with Dave's hands working like machines. He checks the separate sections and then puts it back together and pulls the bolt back several times, listening to the sound. Satisfied, he turns to the shotguns and takes them out of the cabinet, laying them on the worktop.

Two of them have barrels side by side, the other one also has two barrels but one on top of the other; they are heavy and feel alien to hold.

I push the wooden end of one into my shoulder and look down the barrel. There are two triggers, one in front of the other. I guess it's one trigger for each barrel.

There is a lever where the metal barrel meets the wooden bit. I push this over and the shotgun bends in the middle. I remember that shotguns have cartridges, not bullets. The cartridges must just slot in the holes; close the barrel and pull the triggers. I've seen it done on television and movies and it looks simple enough.

There are boxes of bright, red cartridges in the cabinet. They are marked *12 Gauge*. I've heard of that but don't know what it means.

Dave has found a shoulder strap for the rifle and has fitted it on, checking the length and making adjustments until he seems satisfied. I guess he has chosen the rifle then. After my debacle in the corridor upstairs he probably wouldn't trust me with a paintball gun.

He next takes a box of shiny bullets, picks up the shotgun with the two barrels on top of each other, and heads out of the back door. I take the other two shotguns and boxes of the shiny, red cartridges and follow him out into the bright sunshine.

He stops in the middle of the central yard area and I look about at the outbuildings and barns nearby then watch as Dave holds the rifle and looks down the sights, aiming into the empty barn; he pulls the trigger and listens to the noise – I'm sure they call it *dry firing*.

Dave takes a strip of bullets, all stuck together in a line, and presses them into a hole in the top of the gun. Then he raises it to his shoulder and pulls the bolt back and forth once. He aims into the barn and fires; the sound is really loud, and I was expecting him to be jerked back from the recoil, but he hardly seemed to move. He quickly slides the bolt and a shiny bullet case springs out. He fires again and repeats the action with the percussive bangs rolling out across the quietness of the land.

'You try,' he says, holding the rifle out,

He shows me how to pull the bolt back, push the strip of bullets in and how to use the bolt to get the first bullet ready. Then he pushes the butt of the rifle into my shoulder and extends my left hand, so it is holding the rifle on the wooden frame underneath the barrel. He then aligns my finger to the trigger and steps back.

'Squeeze gently.'

I pull the trigger; the recoil feels awful, jerking my shoulder back with a violent push. I have no idea where I am aiming for. I do the bolt thing and try again, repeating the action.

The recoil frightens me and I feel myself bracing in readiness. I end up closing my eyes. I fire three times and hand the rifle back, trying to do what he did and point the rifle down to the ground.

'I'm no good at it mate, you use it. We'll just waste bullets if I keep trying.'

He nods and picks up one of the shotguns, breaks it and pushes a red cartridge into each hole, slamming the barrel closed.

He steps forward and again raises the gun into his shoulder. His finger pulls the first trigger, then drops back and pulls the second one. Both times, there is a loud bang, but he hardly moves from the recoil. I pick up another shotgun and copy his actions, breaking the gun, pushing the red cartridge in and snapping it closed.

I brace my feet and fire. The first blast feels almighty and slams me backwards – I'm more prepared for the second barrel and the recoil doesn't feel so bad. I try again, loading and firing, readying for the recoil and getting used to it.

'Mr Howie,' Dave gets my attention, pointing off to a male infected shuffling from one of the outbuildings, drawn by the noise and action. He is also fat, but this one clearly works and has big, meaty shoulders and arms.

'I thought farmers led healthy lives?' I murmur.

Dave just shrugs and takes the rifle back out of the bag, pushes in another strip of bullets and raises it to his shoulder. He fires and the infected man is thrown backwards, hitting the side of the building and slumping down with the back of his head spread across the peeling boards with bits of brain and bone dripping down.

The sight makes me feel weird. Like my heart is thumping too hard. I just saw a man getting shot dead right in front of me. We've killed countless with hand weapons, but nothing like this. It was so easy; Dave just lifted the gun and pulled the trigger.

For the first time in my life, I realise why firearms are so talked about; their power is staggering. I've watched hundreds of war films and seen news reports of war footage, but I guess that I became desensitised over the years. It was just make-believe or footage from somewhere far away. The sheer brutality of it: point and shoot and you make someone die. I'm suddenly very uncomfortable here and I want to leave, I want to be back in the safety of the van and moving away.

We load up and head back down the lane, stopping halfway so that I can hop into the bushes and open my bowels again.

Dave looks a little rosy in the cheeks when we reach the van, but I'm melting with sweat coming off me in buckets. We load the weapons, clamber in and get going with the lovely air-conditioning kicking in. I want to eat but my stomach is still gurgling away, so I just drink lots of water instead.

Back to the motion of driving. To the normalcy of it and my minds starts thinking how the shotguns are really quite heavy and cumbersome. The rifle is good, and Dave handles it beautifully, but I won't be fast enough to keep breaking the shotguns open if we get trapped. That makes me think I'll need to keep my axe with me at the same time as the shotgun.

I start imagining ways to fit the axe head to the end of the shotgun so I can fire, then reverse it and chop them. I wonder if anyone has invented one. I could have patented it and made a fortune selling it to the crazy survivalists who kept going on about the end of the world.

Mind you ... they weren't so crazy, were they? Are they feeling self-righteous and pious, walking round their communes, patting each other on the back? Maybe one of them even started it? A mad scientist, a fundamentalist – end of world theorist – doing it on purpose to prove they were right ... cleansing the Earth of all the sin, while they sit back and gloat at the genocide they have created.

Fucking fundamentalists.

They're just mentalists, no *funda* about it.

CHAPTER FOUR

We are in a town. I was too busy thinking of my new *shotgunaxe* invention to realise we were out of the country; I was just following the road, and without looking at the map I can tell we're in grimy Portsmouth. I should have been paying better attention and avoided the city area.

I've been here a few times; the old part of Portsmouth, with the historic ships, is nice but the rest just looks horrible with old, grey buildings and graffiti everywhere.

We used to come shopping here and I've been for a few nights out with friends, but everyone seemed so aggressive and angry: blokes with tattoos and earrings; and barely clad women with scraped back hair, big-hooped bangles and mouths like sailors. Portsmouth is just a small city in the Home Counties and I could never understand why they all tried talking like *mockney* Londoners; walking about with bandy swaggers.

We are on a wide road with crappy-looking shops on either side; the metal shuttering on some of them has already been forced open or wrenched off. There are windows smashed and debris litters the place. We spot a few people too, running in and out of the smashed windows, taking armfuls of gear. They look furtive and scared, staying low or hunkering down out of sight until we pass.

We move further into the city seeing more signs of civil breakdown. Bodies scattered in the road. Burnt out cars and vans. Some of the bodies are clearly infected, sadly a lot of them look like normal people. We pass cars still alight and others smouldering with thick, black smoke coiling up into the hot summer air already stinking of burning rubber and chemicals.

I feel myself tensing up at the sight of it all. At the sinister vibe hanging in the air, at the weird silence where there should be noise and life. A noise to my side and I snap my head over to see Dave pushing a fresh strip of bullets into the rifle and ramming the bolt back. He grabs the shotguns next, breaking them in turn to load with cartridges.

I stare front and think that places like Portsmouth were always on the brink of civil collapse anyway. Hard places full of hard people.

Dave pulls his Tesco fleece out of the bag and puts it on. It's roasting weather and I can't understand why he's doing that. He zips it and then loads more of the ammunition clips into the pockets of the fleece. Next, he takes an empty plastic bag and puts shotgun cartridges into it; he leans over and threads the handles through my belt, tying them off. He makes a small, hand-sized hole in the top of the bag. I look down at the bag and feel for the hole with my left hand while slowing down to navigate the obstacles in the road. Cursing myself for coming this way and feeling a growing sense of dread in my gut. Silence in all directions. I look about, trying to see through the smoke to the smashed in stores as we pass through a narrow gap underneath a concrete footbridge going over the road.

'Ambush,' Dave says, his voice still flat but more urgent, harder maybe. I snap my head up to see the top of the bridge alive with kids and teenagers leaning over launching rocks and stones that thud on the bonnet and sides. 'Go,' he says, motioning ahead of us. I push my foot down to speed up and hear the sides scraping the debris as we get through.

'Shit,' I spot the barricade ahead running flush to the walls of the junction beyond it. Vehicles parked end on end and more stuff puled on tip, wheelie bins, sofas, beds, cabinets and all manner of furniture, worse than that however is the huge horde of infected gathered between us and the barricade. There must be hundreds of them.

I clench my jaw while my heart starts racing, cursing myself for coming this way and getting trapped between a huge horde of infected and a bunch of nasty kids chucking missiles about.

The van is strong and the infected are slow moving, but if they mass in front of us there will be no way through, and too many to go over. I look back at the bridge and see the children running down the walkways towards the van with more missiles in their hands.

'Shit. Look at that lot...' I say as Dave leans forward, peers into the wing mirror, grabs a shotgun and drops out to run down the side of the van while lifting the gun to aim.

'Dave!' I rush out and round the van to see him aiming towards the teenagers, his face so passive it sends a chill running down my spine. 'Don't shoot them...' I blurt the words out, thinking he'll do it, or that the kids will keep coming and he'll have to bloody do it. Another noise comes to the fore at that same second from the horde of infected all groaning as they turn and start moving towards us as the tension ramps and the first missiles start getting lobbed towards us, but the distance is too great to risk harm and the bricks and rubble they chuck just bounces off the road.

We have to get out of here. I glance about, thinking the safest thing will be to drive back under the bridge and hope we don't get hurt by them throwing things down. Maybe Dave could fire a warning shot? Would that work? I twist back to the barricade beyond the infected and realise that someone must have built it, and a barricade is used to keep somewhere safe, which must mean there is a safe place behind it.

'Dave,' I say, pointing to the closest building near the edge of the barricade. 'See those doors, maybe we can get through?'

He shakes his head at me. 'We'll lose the vehicle and the weapons.'

'Well we can't bloody stay here...' I trail off as one of the doors set in the wall next to the barricade slams open and in that split second I figure someone is trying to help us. 'Dave, see that...quick...' I set off as a group of people rush through the door. A woman struggling between two men gripping her arms. She screams out, loud and terrified, fighting hard to break free and get back inside and even from this distance I can see the men cast fearful looks at the horde as they throw her out, sending her sprawling over the ground. She hits hard, grazing her knees and hands but springs back up and runs back as the men get through the door and slam it closed.

She pounds hard. Screaming and shouting as the closest infected people start shuffling back towards her, then more and more. She's empty handed too with no way to fight them.

'PLEASE!' she screams out, hammering on the door. Her voice cracking with fear and panic. 'PLEASE...IT WAS FOR MY KID...I SWEAR IT...'

'Fucking hell, she'll get torn apart,' I mutter the words, Dave at my side as more of the horde start turning back towards her as she thrashes and begs to be let back in. Screaming that she's sorry.

'I SWEAR! IT WAS FOR MY BABY...'

'We can't just leave her,' I say. I don't know what she's done but that is wrong, just plain wrong.

I run back to the van and shove more cartridges into the plastic bag and grab the other shotgun before running back to Dave.

'Dave, you go for her, I'll draw them away,' I say quickly. 'OI! OVER HERE...' I shout loudly as Dave runs behind me.

'Don't shoot me, Mr Howie.'

As if I would. It does make me pause and think though, and also realise that if I fired now I'd be shooting towards the woman. 'OI... COME ON...' I shout at the horde and start moving to the side, leading them on. 'HEY...STOP SHOUTING...LOVE! LET ME GET THEM AWAY...'

I scream out for the woman to stop shouting but she doesn't hear me, locked in her cycle of panic and terror, hammering on the door and still drawing the infected towards her.

'STOP SCREAMING. STAY QUIET.'

Holy shit. That came from Dave. A full on proper *parade square* voice roaring out. I look over, amazed that such a quiet man can produce such a noise. Mind you, it does the job though and she spins about, seemingly stunned at the sight of me and Dave.

'Stay still and be quiet, let me draw them off,' I call over. She looks terrified and doesn't show any sign of understanding me, but then she doesn't start screaming out again either. 'HEY! THIS WAY...COME THIS WAY...' I shout out again, trying to draw them away. A few turn and head my way but many still keep going towards her, fixed on their prey.

There's nothing for it. She can't get back in the house and she's too scared to think to run. Instinct inside. Nothing but pure instinct and I lift the shotgun, aim at the infected and pull the first trigger then watch as the first person is blown back off their feet. I move the aim a little and pull the second trigger, taking another one down. My heart booms and my hands shake when I start reloading, doing what Dave taught me: lever, break, cartridges out, cartridges in, closed, raise and fire.

I don't notice the recoil this time, or the noise. I just see bits of undead body flying off as the pellets strike them. And at such close range the effect is devastating.

I move back and keep drawing them away from the woman, not watching my sides enough as an infected man looms at me from the side. An instinctual reaction again and I slam the butt into his face, making him staggers back as Dave steps in and slices through his jugular with a knife. The rifle on his back, hanging from the strap.

No time to think. No time for thought and I reload to fire again. Filling the air with shotgun blasts and watching as the infected get blown away. Gunning them down one after the other. Another reload and I glance over to see Dave fighting through the infected that had almost reached the woman, his knife slicing necks, severing arteries and spraying bright red blood across the pavement. I reload and notice that the cartridges are the same colour as the blood.

I keep firing into the crowd.

An undead goes down just as I fire; the pellets spread out and knock several undead over behind him.

Beautiful.

A gap in the horde and I spot Dave reaching the woman, but she seems frozen to the spot, looking down at the bloody bodies lying at her feet. I start running over, veering around the slow infected and jumping over bodies either shot down by me or killed by Dave. Blood everywhere. Thick pools of it on the ground and a few crawlers too, pawing their over the road with legs all shot to bits from pellet blasts.

'Is she okay?' I call out as the door opens again with one of the men reaching out to grab a fistful of hair and yank the woman back inside. Brutal and harsh. 'HEY!' I shout out as Dave lunges at the door, getting his body into the gap before it slams shut. More infected in front of me and I veer while running, catching sight of Dave pushing hard to get inside then suddenly he's gone and the door slams shut behind him.

Shit.

'Dave?' I shout out, reaching the door. 'DAVE?' I kick at it then spin to see the rest of the horde all aiming in towards me. Hundreds of them. I aim and fire, sending a few spinning away then use the butt to hammer on the door.

'Dave ... Open up!'

A woman screams from inside, then I hear muffled thuds and male voices yelling. It goes quiet and I start hammering again as the door opens, spilling me inside as Dave slams it shut behind me.

A front room stripped of furniture. Like someone's lounge emptied out and that awful droning groan of the horde fades away as I look about at the bodies. Men lying on a faded carpet with their throats cut open with huge pools of blood already forming.

'What the fuck?' I gasp, looking from them to Dave standing

perfectly still with his hands at his sides and not a drop of blood on him. Even the knife looks clean. 'Seriously...what the fuck?'

'They tried to grab me,' he says in that flat voice.

'Right,' I say, not knowing what else to say. 'Are they all dead?' I ask, which is a dumb question considering most of them are nearly decapitated.

'Yes,' he says as calmly as ever.

I spot the woman cowering at the far end of the room, her hands covering her face. Then the interior door opens and she ups and scarpers quick as you like as the door slams shut.

'Well. This isn't weird at all,' I mutter. 'Did you have to kill all of them?' I ask, looking about the room again. 'Fuck it, let's just go...' again I trail off as a new sound breaks through that groan of infected. The steady beep beep of a Tesco delivery van being reversed. 'Wankers, they're nicking our van...'

I burst out through the door into the street, blanching at the size of the horde now cramming towards us as Dave runs out behind me, both of us threading a wide route just in time to see our van reversing away with kids in the front. Then it stops and I hear the engine being re-started from one of the thieving little shits stalling it.

'OI...GET OUT...' I shout out, running towards it.

Dave stops and my heart misses a beat when he fires at the van, thinking he has shot a child – a thieving little shit, but still a child.

The front driver's side tire blows out and the van drops down a little. He then slams the bolt and shoots again – the passenger side tire deflates. The van then stops and three children get out and start running away.

Dave immediately raises the rifle and takes aim.

'NO!'

He pauses for a second and drops the rifle down, then looks back at me.

'They're just kids ...'

'Okay, Mr Howie,' he says as though nothing just happened.

Fuck, this man is cold; I swear he would have shot them as they ran away. The front tires are blown out and the van is resting lower.

'Grab the stuff, we'll have to run for it.'

Cartridges and ammo are shoved into the rucksacks. Dave goes around to the rear as I pull my rucksack on, fastening the waist and chest straps. The axe is there but I can't carry it and two shotguns. I take the axe and drop the shaft down between my back and the bag. The large metal head catches on the top of the bag and holds steady. I tighten the chest straps, drawing it closer to my body. It might be cumbersome but it's better than leaving it here.

Dave comes back with the other two shotguns and the rifle strapped to his back, over the rucksack.

If we go back, we'll get brained by rocks and missiles from the bridge. I move out, looking down to the building to see the door is now shut again. There's no clear way out. I spin around again and look at the row of shops and stores off to the right. We'll have to go through them and out a back door.

'That way,' I say and head off, giving thanks that the windows and doors are already smashed in.

'I'll go in, Mr Howie,' Dave says as we reach the closest one. 'Wait here...' he rushes on by with the rifle up and aimed as I come to a stop and wonder what I'm meant to do. Like cover him or something? I turn around and aim my shotgun about at different things. A wall. A car. A building. Some zombie. That sort of thing.

'No way through,' he says, running back out. We go down and repeat the same thing, with Dave running in and me aiming at stuff. He comes back and we try the next one. A hair salon but even that has been looted. Someone has even stolen one of the big heavy hairdressing chairs. Unbelievable.

'This way, Mr Howie,' Dave calls out.

'Righto,' I head in and follow through to the back to see Dave battering a back door open and we squeeze through into a back service alley littered with rubbish.

We start off, following the alley into a residential area of small terraced houses – a cheap rental area – already rough and grotty anyway, it is looking even worse now.

There are small streets leading off to the left. They must loop around the back of the barricade and, seeing as Dave has just killed several of them, I think we should try and avoid it.

We keep going until we have passed several of the side streets, then we turn left and head down one of them. We get about halfway down and hear a loud bang from behind us. Dave instantly grabs my arm and drops down, pulling me behind the back of a parked car. I look around to see a group of men holding handguns running towards us as the bullets whizz by into cars and bounce off walls.

'Fuck, they've got guns. Where'd they get them from?'

Dave doesn't reply but pulls the rifle around and lifts the rifle to aim as he stands up.

'Dave! What the fuck you doing? They've got guns...'

Dave fires, dropping the lead man who goes down hard, slamming face first into the ground, not that he'll feel anything, what with half of his head now missing. The others scatter into the road, dodging behind parked cars as Dave slams the bolt back and steps out into the road, aiming this way and that as he scans the area while I listen to the loud panic filled voices of the men shouting at each other.

A head pops up and Dave fires with staggering reactional speed and I see the head explode with blood and matter spraying out as the guy is flung backwards against another car.

Dave rams the bolt and keeps moving. His movements are fast, but controlled; the rifle looks steady in his hands.

'Go down the other side, Mr Howie,' he says, as calm as ever while motioning with his left hand, indicating for me to head down the side we just came up.

My chest is heaving and I can feel my hands shaking as I set off with the shotgun braced in my shoulder. My vision seemingly coming in strobing flashes. Men shouting. Hoarse ragged voices but they sound confused as though they're all trying to tell the others what to do at the same time.

'I'LL KILL YOU ALL ...' Dave bellows out, in that drill sergeant voice again. 'I'LL KILL YOUR FAMILIES. YOUR WIVES AND YOUR CHILDREN.'

'Fuck me,' I mumble, feeling the dread myself of his threats and the brutal, awful way he shouts the words. The effect seems to work though and the men starburst out to start running. Dave fires fast, dropping one. Bolt back and he aims, firing again, killing another that sprawls out on the ground. Bolt back and he turns to aim at the last one.

'Please! Please don't shoot yeah...'

I reach Dave to see a young man cowering on his knees in the gap between two cars. His hands on his head, his eyes wild and full of fear with tears spilling down over his spotty cheeks. 'Please mate, please don't kill me,' he gabbles the words out in that harsh Portsmouth accent as Dave aims the rifle at his head.

'Are you armed?' Dave demands.

'Please don't shoot, please...' the lad stammers the words out as Dave kicks him hard, knocking him over onto the ground.

'ARE YOU ARMED?' Dave roars the words out.

'No, no I'm not. I swear.'

'HANDS ON YOUR HEAD, INTERLOCK YOUR FINGERS.'

'Please, please.'

Dave kicks him again.

'DO IT NOW. HANDS ON YOUR HEAD, INTERLOCK YOUR FINGERS.'

The man responds, quickly putting his hands to the back of his head.

'STAND UP ... SLOWLY.'

'Oh fuck ... please don't. Please don't,' he begs as he gets to his feet. He's just a skinny kid, maybe eighteen years old. Tattoos on his arms and neck, the obligatory earring hanging from his ear. Dave looks at me and nods firmly towards the boy. I shrug my shoulders, not understanding what he wants me to do.

'Would you search him please, Mr Howie.'

'Oh right … of course.'

Dave steps forward and pushes the end of the rifle into the boy's neck, which sets him off whimpering again as I step forward and start patting him down. He's only wearing tracksuit bottoms and a t-shirt and I'm finished in seconds.

'Check the waistband please, Mr Howie.'

I run my fingers around the waistband. 'He's clear,' I try to sound *military*, but just feel silly.

'MOVE.'

Dave pushes the lad over the pavement up against a wall then turns and once more nods at me. 'All yours, Mr Howie.'

All mine? What am I supposed to do with him?

'Er. Right. Um…where are you from?' I ask, still trying to sound like I know what I'm doing.

'What?' the boy stammers, still terrified.

'I said where are you from?'

'Carter Street.'

'Is that where the barricade is?'

'Yeah. Don't kill me yeah … I didn't wanna do nuffin' but he said I had to didn't he…'

'Who said?' I ask.

'My dad did, didn't he…that's his brother innit, my uncle yeah…'

'What the fuck?' I say, struggling to understand the spew of words. 'Who is?'

The boy nods at the body on the ground, the one that Dave shot first.

'That's your uncle?' I ask. He nods again. Fast and shallow, his eyes flicking from me to Dave but I can still see the feral cunning in them. 'Who's your dad?'

'John Jones?'

He says it like it means something.

'Who is he?'

'John Jones innit. Like fuckin' everyone knows him don't they, he runs the area don't he, he's the fucking boss innit...' the boy's tones grow more confident as he speaks.

'What does that mean?'

'Everyone knows him don't they. Like, this is his patch yeah, even the pigs don't touch him.'

'And you're his son?'

'Yeah.'

'So he sent you after us?'

'Yeah,' he says, starting to sneer as he talks, puffing himself up.

'Why?'

'Cos of what you did yeah,' he says, eyeballing me.

'What did we do?'

'You killed his mates, no one does that.'

'His mates? Oh you mean the men in that room? We were trying to help that woman, why was she pushed out?'

'She didn't do as she was told. Dad said we got to keep a firm grip of 'em. Stop 'em thieving and fuckin' about yeah...like...like my dad yeah, he said there's rules and there's gotta be rules and if cunts break 'em then they can fuck right off...'

'What's your name?'

'Jim Jones, ain't it.'

'What wouldn't she do, Jim?'

'Fucking bitch, she thieved didn't she.'

'I'm sorry ... what?'

'The fucking bitch thieved, she stole from my dad, didn't she?'

'What did she steal?'

'Milk.'

'Milk? Why didn't she have her own milk?'

'We got it all stacked in the fuckin' house yeah, Dad said we needs to ration it and stop the greedy cunts eating it all now...'

'So you took everyone's food and put it in your house?'

'Yeah, fucking right we did.'

'Why?'

'Cos the greedy cunts will have the lot.'

'Why did she steal milk? Why not something else?'

I already know why she took milk. I heard what she shouted out, but I want him to say it.

A pause. A second's worth of hesitation. 'Dunno,' he says, instantly sulky and petulant.

'Why did she take the milk?'

'I dunno do I,' he snaps, glaring at me. 'Fuckin askin' me for…'

'Yes, you do, Jim Jones. You do know why … so tell me why she took the milk?'

I can feel anger building in me; the arrogance and cocky attitude is winding me up. I can just imagine this little shit bullying his way through life, knowing his dad is the local big man.

'I don't fucking know, do I?'

'Jim, I will ask you once more,' I say in a voice now very low. 'Why did she take the milk?'

'I fuckin' said that I don't fuckin' know,' he sneers, defiant and angry.

I slap him across the face. Hard and stinging. Then I step in and take a fistful of his hair to yank his head back. 'You listen to me, you little cunt. I don't fucking care who your dad is. Right now, there is me and you and that's it.'

He squirms in my grip, still cocky, still arrogant, still entitled, and that anger inside spikes again so I head butt him square in the face, driving my forehead into his nose. he drops down and puts his hands to his nose, blood pouring out between his fingers, but I wrench his head up again.

My own forehead really stings. I had no idea it hurt that much when you head butt someone. I want to rub it, but don't want to do it in front of him.

'Why did she take the milk?'

'Her kids,' he gasps, spraying blood as he speaks. 'She took it for her kids didn't she…'

'You forced a mother out into that lot, because she took milk for her kids? You tell me now, why? Why did you do that?'

'Dad said to ...'

'Did you help?'

'No, no I swear I didn't.'

'You're fucking lying to me. Your dad is the big man, so you're the big man too. You fucking helped, didn't you?'

'No, no I didn't.'

'Lie again and see what happens.'

'I had to ... Dad told me to.'

'What happened when she went back in? You killed her, didn't you?'

'*They* did, not me. I swear it wasn't me that did it ...'

'You fucking little cunt.' I punch the boy in the face then rain blows into him with fists pounding his head. He drops down and I kick him several times in the stomach and ribs. I step back, breathing hard. The fury is taking over. 'Get up.'

He staggers to his feet; his face is bloodied and bruised. I take the shotgun back from Dave.

'You are going to lead us out of here, do you understand?'

'Yeah.'

'It's yes – not yeah.'

'Okay, yes.'

'Now walk.'

I push him forward, down the street, and he staggers, then gains his composure and starts walking slowly.

'Take your clothes off,' Dave says to the boy.

'What?'

'Take your clothes off.'

I look at Dave, confused at the strange order.

'It's hard to run away when you're naked.'

'Okay, you heard him – strip off.'

'No, please ... please don't do that.'

Dave shoves the rifle into his face, pushing him hard against the wall.

'Now.'

'Okay, okay.'

The boy starts stripping, taking his shirt off first, then his shoes and trousers, stripping down to his filthy once-white boxer shorts.

'Please, I won't run, I swear.'

'Off. Now.'

He slowly bends down and pulls his boxer shorts off, covering his privates with his hands.

'Nice skid marks, Jim Jones. Did your dad tell you to do them too – try wiping your arse next time – you filthy little shit.'

A few days ago this act would have sickened me; if someone explained this situation to me in the staff canteen, I would deny that it was right and say no person should ever be treated like that – that we have law and order and everyone is entitled to respect and dignity.

Not now.

'Hang on, Mr Howie.'

Dave runs back to the body lying on the pavement. I see him pick the gun up and pull the top bit back, then a magazine pops out of the bottom. He checks inside, then takes the gun apart, flinging bits in different directions. He puts one piece in his pocket then runs back.

'It was empty, Mr Howie.'

We start walking down the road with Jim covering his bollocks, but Dave makes him put his hands back on his head. He looks pathetic, just a skinny kid; black tribal tattoos stand out on his pale skin. We reach the end of the road and Jim turns left.

'Where are we going, Jim?'

'You said you wanted to get out, didn't you? Please, I'll tell you the way – just let me go home yeah.'

'You want to go home ... do you, Jim?'

'Yeah.'

'What?'

'I mean yes. Yes, please ... Mr Howie.'

Fuck it, now he's calling me that too.

'Okay, take us to the barricade at this end.'

'Really?'

'Yes, but do as you're told or we'll kill you.'

'Okay, Mr Howie.'

We walk on past houses with doors battered in and broken windows. Like a warzone with blood and gore smeared over walls and cars.

'Did you take all of the food from here too?'

'Dad sent the boys out didn't he, told 'em to bring it all back so's everyone has enough.'

'Regular saint, your dad.'

CHAPTER FIVE

The barricade comes into view. Well-constructed and dense too. Stretching from the end of the last house on one side and right across the junction to the end of the next house, sealing off Carter Street. There's also lots of bodies lying broken and dead and left to rot in the high sun. Grotesque and awful. A few infected too, shuffling and groaning off to one side close to one of the building entry doors.

'Who killed them, Jim?'

'We did,' he says, surly and sulky from being forced to walk naked.

'What with?'

'I dunno, anything we could find.'

'Got any more guns in there?'

He pauses.

'No.'

A look passes between Dave and I.

'So, what are the rules in your street?'

'What rules?'

'There must be rules; can people leave if they want to?'

'Yeah, 'course they fucking can,' he snaps in that nasty goading tone. Dave reacts quickly, yanking the bolt back on the rifle as he prods the end into the back of Jim's head.

'Don't lie, Jim,' I say calmly. 'He *will* kill you, trust me. He won't think twice about it.' That's probably very true, and from what I've seen so far, Dave wouldn't even blink.

'Okay, okay – they can't leave, but Dad said it was for their own benefit cos they would just get eaten by the fuckin' zombie things and then the zombies would get inside.'

'How would they get inside?'

'I dunno ... Dad said they would.'

'So how does your dad stop people getting out?'

'He's got the boys watching both ends ain't he.'

'How do you get in from this end?'

'Through the houses.'

'And I suppose the boys have got the end houses to stay in?'

'Yeah.'

Dave prods him again.

'Sorry, yes ... Mr Howie.'

We stop about a hundred metres down from the end of the barricade. I look at Dave and motion towards a brick wall on the other side of the road.

'Get on your knees,' I tell Jim, pushing him towards the wall. 'Keep your hands on your head.'

The lad does as he is told as I quickly clamber over the waist high wall and prop one of the shotguns down while pressing the other end to the back of his head as Dave gets over and hunkers down.

'John Jones!' I shout out, but my voice cracks and doesn't come out so loud, then I remember Dave shouting earlier. 'Dave, can you shout?'

'JOHN JONES!' The voice is just huge, and I imagine it booming out across a parade square, terrifying new recruits. 'JOHN JONES ... COME OUT OR WE'LL KILL THE BOY.'

Within seconds we spot faces in the windows of the houses overlooking us. Men seen snatching views as they try and stay hidden. Then one of the ground floor doors opens and a burly man walks out looking supremely confident. Swinging his thick arms as he swaggers almost casually and glances at the infected staggering across the road towards young Jim Jones on his knees with his hands on his head.

'Dad,' Jim whimpers, he cuts off when I prod the shotgun a bit harder and watch the closest infected. An adult male that looks the same type as John Jones with thick arms and torso and tattoos on his arms. Half of his face is missing though, bitten off and the skin is shredded down to the bone exposing teeth through the ragged holes in his cheek. Drool hanging from his lips but also coming from the holes too and his red, bloodshot eyes stay fixed on Jim as he staggers on, jerky and slow but still closing the distance.

'Fuck … Oh fuck …' Jim squirms as John Jones stops in the middle of the road with arms hanging down at his sides. Tension in the air. Thick and palpable. Dave standing silently. The infected groaning and the scuff of their feet as they shuffle forever on. Two of them veer off towards John Jones who just watches them without expression before exploding with violent motion, lashing out to slam a fist into the closest infected, sending it reeling backwards. He grabs the next one by the throat, seemingly fearless of the risk of infection and throws it down like a ragdoll before stamping on the head with a sickening display of utter brutality. Like a message is being sent.

Then he looks up, his face flushed and his eyes set and hard as he moves towards us while lifting an arm to point. 'IF YOU TOUCH MY FACKIN' BOY…'

I raise the shotgun and fire over Jim's head at another infected, blowing it away. Jim drops to the ground, screaming in fear at the noise. If John Jones wants to show force, we can both play at that game. I drop the gun back down to aim at the sorry sight of a naked Jim sobbing on the ground. 'Don't fucking move,' I say, looking from the lad to his father.

'Dad, do something!' Jim cries out.

'Shut up, Jimmy,' John snaps, his voice hard and rasping. 'Easy now boys ... what's the problem eh?' he asks, switching instantly to a charm offensive, smiling as he speaks.

'You killed that woman.'

'Yes. I did,' he says firmly. 'Is that your problem? Yeah, I killed her and I'll kill others if I have to. There's plenty of people in there you see, they need protection and the food won't last forever will it. I've got kids and families haven't I. Who's gonna feed 'em and look out for 'em ... you?'

'She only took some milk.'

'Is that what Jimmy told you?' he asks with a roll of his eyes. 'The lad's a fuckwit, he ain't all there. Kids these days, they're different in the head,' he adds, tapping the side of his head as though to demonstrate the point. His tone stays calm and natural, easy going – like he's talking to his best mate; the charm oozes off him. 'Now listen, gents, fair enough, you thought we done wrong, fair play. I appreciate you keeping to yer principles, I admire that in a man, but that woman was a smack head, and she kept thieving from us. We told her to stop but she wouldn't listen. I gotta whole street to take care off, and well ... it might look hard to you boys but there's gotta be order. Now, do me a favour, boys, and let the lad go eh.'

He sounds so reasonable, so calm and genuine.

'Between me and you, gents,' he says, lowering his tone as though imparting a secret. 'I don't much care for the little shit, but hiss mum yeah, you know what women are like, he can't do no wrong in her eyes, and she'll give me hell if anything happens to 'im.'

'I'll tell you what John, I'll let him go, but only if you tell everyone in there that they are free to leave if they want to.'

'Sure, sure I'll do that. They can go anytime they want. But where to? Have you seen what's going on? They won't last five minutes out here. They ain't like us; they ain't survivors. Those things will tear 'em apart ... you must have seen what they're like at night – they change don't they...get all fast and angry eh?'

'Yeah ... we've seen.'

'Well ... there you go, I'm only protecting 'em till help arrives, just for now until the law gets a grip of it – you boys can see, that can't you?'

Fuck me, he sounds so normal. I imagined some tyrant with a harem and armed bandits surrounding him. Fair enough, he was shouting when he came out, but I *am* holding a gun to his son's head.

'So, let me take the boy in. I'll give him a good hiding for the trouble he's caused you gents, then you can be on your way. Or, here's an idea, tell you what, why don't you join us? We got food and plenty of booze...' He takes a step closer, nodding earnestly. 'And we got some nice looking birds in there too, if you know what I mean, gents, couple of young lads like you – well, they'll be all over you,' he adds with a wink and a sneer and a flash of his true colours.

'No, you tell those people they can leave if they want to.'

'Or what?' he asks, staring straight at me, unblinking, unflinching.

'Or we'll kill Jimmy.'

'You'll kill him will you? What, just shoot him dead right here? Go on then, one less mouth to feed – if I'm honest.'

'Jimmy, you tell your dad what we did to his brother and his mates.'

'They shot him Dad, they shot Uncle Jamie.'

John, Jimmy, Jamie – talk about inbred families.

John Jones' face flushes red, his fists start clenching and he breathes hard. Then he stares straight at me, and although I'm the one holding the gun, I can see the power in the man and why his son said he was the boss.

'You killed my bruvver? You fucking cunts.'

He takes a step forward and Dave shoots him in the leg.

'Fuck,' I gasp as John drops to roll on the ground, writhing and clutching his leg.

'DAD!' Jimmy screams out.

'Jimmy,' I shout. 'You run in there and you tell those people they can leave if they want to, you do that now or we'll finish your old man off, you got it?'

'You shot my dad ...' Jimmy whimpers, scuttling over to his father, his bare arse poking up into the sky as he bends down to him.

'Jimmy, you listen to me. We'll kill him if you don't get in there now and tell them.'

'Go on,' John grunts, pushing his son roughly with blood smeared hands before going back to grunting in agony as I notice Dave appears to have shot him through the kneecap. Just the sight makes me wince and I catch sight of Jim legging it across the road towards the door, just as another man comes out, grabs Jimmy and disappears inside.

'FACK OFF,' I snap back to see John Jones trying to crawl away from an infected woman staggering towards him

I take aim and shoot her down, watching again as the pellets tear chunks from her body and send her flying back. A few seconds to reload and I glance to the blood pouring from John's knee leaving a slick across the road as he tries crawling away, sobbing and crying as he goes.

The sound of breaking glass comes a split second before a deep crack and a chunk of the wall in front of us peppers with pellets, making me and Dave drop quickly from someone firing a shotgun. A second shot comes, hitting the wall but with a few pellets going overhead where we were standing but a second ago.

Everything happening so quickly, and once more I think I should have watched where we were bloody going and avoided the city. Motion to my side and Dave surges up to his feet, aiming quickly and sending a shot back at the window used by the shotgun man who falls away out of view. Another shot from somewhere near the top of the barricade; this one strikes the wall with a loud ricochet, not a shotgun this time.

'Any ideas?' I ask Dave.

'Shoot back, Mr Howie,' he says in a way that would sound sarcastic coming from anyone else. It does, however, seem like sound advice, so I jump up and fire both barrels of the shotgun in the rough direction of the barricade as someone screams out in pain.

'Good shot, Mr Howie.'

'Trust me, that was more luck than judgment.'

A loud crack and splinters of brick chip off near my head; whoever is firing from the window is using the rifle now and is getting better with their aiming. Another shot comes, closer again with more brick chunks flying off.

'Bloody hell … he's getting closer.'

Dave lays down on the ground and starts wriggling along the base of the wall, towards the entrance.

A groan above me and I twist over with a yelp to see an infected man leaning over the wall, his mouth already opening to bite with bloodied saliva hanging down. 'Shit!' I gasp out and push the end of the shotgun barrel into the face and pull the trigger. 'Holy fuck,' I say when his whole head disappears, flinging his body backwards.

'Mr Howie … can you draw him out please?' Dave asks.

'Eh?' I ask, still wide eyed from shooting someone's head off.

'Can you draw him out please?'

'Who?' I ask as the rifle from the building line fires again, tearing another chunk out of the wall. 'Ah right, you mean him…er…what do I do?

'Give him something to shoot at.'

'Are you taking the piss?' I don't know Dave that well but I really don't think he's taking the piss. 'Fucking hell…okay, hang on.'

I take the other shotgun that Dave was using – the one with the barrels on top of each other – and start to raise it up to the wall until the barrel is poking out of the top. Two shots ring out, one of them from the window, which hits the barrel and sends it flying out of my hands; the other shot is a split second after the first and comes from Dave.

'Got him, Mr Howie,' Dave says calmly,

'Thank fuck for that,' I say, not so calmly, peering at the dented barrel of the shotgun. 'He broke your shotgun.'

'You used my shotgun?' Dave asks, looking back at me.

'Err … yeah – he broke it.'

'Right.'

He almost sounds annoyed as he shuffles back and takes it from me, inspecting the damaged barrels.

'Sorry, Dave.'

'It was a good gun.'

'We still have two more, you can have one of these, if you want.'

'No, it's okay.'

'Honestly mate, I really don't mind. I shouldn't have used it.'

'It's okay, Mr Howie.'

'I feel bad now … shit, I'm sorry, mate.'

He looks genuinely upset, his face is impassive as ever, but just the slightest change in his manner portrays his feelings.

'Honestly, Dave, have one of these. I can't carry both of them anyway, just take it for now, until we get you another one.'

He slowly raises his head and looks at me, then at the shotgun lying by the wall.

'Really mate, go on, take it.'

'Are you sure, Mr Howie?'

I pass the shotgun along so that the wooden end is just in front of him.

'Honestly, please have it – I want you to.'

He takes the gun and pulls it towards him.

'Thanks, Mr Howie. I'll look after it.'

'It's all yours.'

He busies himself for the next couple of minutes, reloading the rifle first, and then he looks at me before starting on the shotgun.

'Where now, Mr Howie?'

'I don't know, we should get going, I guess. Mind you, I feel awful if the people in there are being trapped by that wanker…talking of which…' I pop my head up and look over the wall, then straight back down again. 'Or rather until you shot him in the leg and he got eaten by a zombie …'

We both raise up and look over the wall.

John Jones is dead. He had crawled most of the way back to the door but the infected got him; two of them are bent over him now, one gnawing on his already injured leg, the other on his face.

'He's almost at the door, why didn't they come out and rescue him? They could have got him in while we were pinned down.'

'I guess they didn't want to, Mr Howie.'

'Hmmm ... I guess you are right.'

The door opens, and a still naked Jimmy gets launched out. He looks even more battered and bruised now with blood pouring from his face and there are clear, distinct welt marks on his back. Behind Jimmy, another boy of roughly the same age also gets pushed out.

Several men come out behind them holding long sticks; one of them has a samurai sword.

They start pushing the two boys away, beating them with hard strikes across the legs and back, making the lads scream out, begging them to stop as another man steps out of the doorway, holding a rifle in one hand.

He looks at the boys being beaten and says something to the men. They stop and all step away from the boys. The man with the rifle looks over and starts walking towards us.

Dave is over the wall instantly, rifle up and aimed. The man stops and raises his hands up to his sides, then looks at his rifle and seems to realise what he's doing. He turns back and hands the rifle to one of the other men, then starts walking towards us again, arms up and palms facing us, a clear gesture to show that he isn't threatening.

He veers around John Jones and the infected munching on him. Several of the other men are on them instantly, beating them with the sticks.

'It's all right, I'm not armed,' the guy says, pausing to spit on the corpse of John Jones before walking on towards us.

I start to climb over the wall but the axe handle hanging from my back gets caught and I fall backwards with a gargled yell then spring back up and try and smooth it out by walking through the entrance a few feet up. The guy pretends not to have noticed, but then Dave is aiming a rifle at him.

'Easy, Dave,' I say.

'Okay, Mr Howie.'

Dave lowers the rifle but keeps his hands in the same position, and I have no doubt that it would take him less than a second to shoot the man, who keeps glancing at the weapon, clearly thinking the same thing.

'So you are Mr Howie? I'm John.'

Another John? Carter Street clearly has no imagination when it comes to names.

'Don't worry, I'm not related to that prick,' he motions towards John Jones, then looks to the group of males gazing down at him.

'Derek, you'd better finish him off before he turns into one of them.'

The man with the sword nods and thrusts the blade into the throat of John Jones, then hacks away, ripping the flesh open. More of the men start beating the corpse; they are clearly angry and are whacking the shit out of him.

'As you can see, he wasn't well liked around here,' new John says.

'What happened?' I ask.

'He was a nasty bastard,' he says with a shrug. 'Loved throwing his weight around, but got this barricaded quickly and his mates all tooled up and took over...'

'His boys must still be in there, what about them?'

'I think your man here did most of them in that room on the other side. Jones went nuts and sent more after you, but only a couple of those came back. I've never seen him so angry. It was bloody great. We took care of the other couple when you lot were shooting each other, and them two there of course ...' He nods towards Jimmy and the other boy. 'That Jimmy is an evil little shit, untouchable 'cos of his dad.'

'Who's the other one? Don't tell me, James? John? Jamie?'

He smiles. 'Close ... it's Jack.'

Another commotion at the door as a group of women come steaming out, dragging another woman with bleached blond hair and orange-looking skin with them and I watch her fighting back and screaming out. Thrashing and kicking as the woman grab her hair and pull her on.

A large, well-built woman breaks away and marches up to the men standing over John Jones' corpse. 'Give me that stick, Terry,' she snaps at one of the guys who hesitates and looks about for help. 'TERRY, GIVE ME THAT BLOODY STICK.'

She snatches it from his hand and marches back to the thrashing woman, pulling the stick back and striking at the back of her legs; she goes down to the ground. The other women start kicking at her, blows hitting her stomach and back. The woman starts trying to fight her way back up but is beaten back down and eventually curls up into a little ball.

The women are screaming at her, spitting down. One of them grabs her hair and yanks her head back, then starts slapping her in the face. Jimmy and Jack start running up, but the men move closer, brandishing the sticks and they stop still – both of them crying and putting their hands over their faces, taking steps forward, then backing off again.

'That's John's wife – she was the worst one. Trust me, she had this coming for a long time.'

I look at the man and he grimaces at the beating the woman is taking. The large lady drops the stick and grabs at the woman's feet, then starts pulling her shoes off. The other women grasp the idea and, within seconds, the woman is stripped bare. Scrawny, sinewy and near on bright orange from fake tan.

'That's enough, leave her be now,' new John shouts.

The well-built woman spins around and screams back at John. 'You stay out of this, John. You saw what she did...fucking bitch...'

John raises his hands and takes a step back. The large woman is furious; spittle shooting from her mouth as she screams and goes back to pulls the woman onto her feet by her hair. 'YOU CAN FUCKING BEG, GET DOWN AND BEG NOW.'

The woman drops to her knees and crawls around, sobbing and begging at the women's feet.

'Look at those saggy tits, no wonder he kept trying to shag us,' one of other woman says. The rest start cackling, joining in with the humiliation while the fake-tanned woman clutches at their feet, but they kick her away, laughing at her plight and I look away, unable to watch it.

'TAKE YOUR FUCKIN' MOTHER AND FUCK OFF.'

The boys gather the woman up and start walking her away, hobbling and limping from the beating they've all had.

John turns back to me as the women start heading back inside. A strained silence. Awkward and heavy.

'Er, so Jimmy said people can go if they want,' new John says.

I nod, not sure what to say.

'Great,' he says, nodding. 'Er, so…I think a few might stay, now John's dead and his mates are…you know…'

'Also dead,' I say.

'Yeah,' he replies. 'Where are you from?' he asks with a sudden change of topic.

'Boroughfare.'

'I know it. Is it the same as here?'

'Everywhere is. I heard a radio broadcast saying that London has gone.'

'Yeah, we heard about that. John Jones said someone told him.'

He doesn't mention the other part of the radio message.

'What about the Forts?' I ask.

'What Forts?'

'The radio message said for survivors to head for the Forts on the coast.'

'That fucking shit! He told us the message said that the cities had gone and we had to wait for help. The fucking wanker … is that where you're going?'

'Eventually. I'm going for my sister first.'

'Where is she?'

'London. She got a message out saying she's locked in her flat.'

'Well, I was going to ask you to stay with us – we could do with the extra protection – and we've got plenty of food, John saw to that.'

'Thanks mate, but I can't.'

'Well lads, if you change your mind? I guess we'll stick here for today and see about them forts tomorrow. Did they say which ones?'

'No, but I guess any of them will do the job.'

'I might see if we can send someone out to check first.'

'Good idea.'

'Right ... well, I'll let you boys get on then.'

'One more thing mate, sorry ... but how do we get out of here?'

'To London? Well, that's easy enough ...'

'No, er, we've got to run another errand first, something else we got to take care off. We're heading towards Salisbury.'

He raises both his eyebrows and nods knowingly.

'Ah, Salisbury – yeah, I understand. Don't worry – I won't say anything. You need to head for Southampton.'

'Is there another way, without going through the towns?'

'Yeah, head north on the London road, then work your way over – but it'll take much longer.'

He gives directions to a junction, then explains that we have to decide: north through the countryside or west to Southampton, which will be much quicker – but will keep us in the towns.

Dave shoulders the rifle and takes the shotgun in his hands. My shotgun is loaded and ready and I can feel the weight of the axe hanging from my back.

We turn from the barricade and walk away.

CHAPTER SIX

'It will be dark soon, Mr Howie.'

I glance over at him as we walk on through the deserted suburban streets. A heavy silence hangs in the air that's filled with the stench of death and fire. Bodies everywhere. Lying in the road or across doorways. We saw a crawler a few streets back too. An old woman with red bloodshot eyes dragging her legless torso along the road. We just stopped, stared and carried on walking. Flies too. Not too many but enough to start the spread of disease and these corpses will soon be writhing with maggots.

A few more days and this will be a very dangerous place, not just with the infected but also from the risk of decaying bodies festering in the baking summer sun. I swallow in the heat, feeling oppressed and hemmed in.

Coming here has sucked the spirit out of me. Up until now I had a purpose, a plan and somewhere to go. We still have that plan, but the last few hours have taken their toll. Seeing real people being killed, not infected, but real, normal people has left me feeling empty. The world is crumbling at such an alarming rate. Everything we know has been taken away and men still want to hurt each other.

I'm not some naïve dreamer, and I know what people are capable off, but seeing it happen and the speed it's taking place has left me appalled with a pervading sense of shame inside me. Shame that we had to do what we did. Shame that I beat Jimmy and made him walk naked back to the barricade; I was no better than them.

The clear lines of distinction between right and wrong have merged. John Jones was an evil psychopath – of that there is no doubt – but in his mind, he was providing protection – maybe he felt that he was doing the right thing.

He wasn't a James Bond baddie stroking a cat and laughing evilly. He was violent and nasty, but he had the sense to build that barricade and gather food, and he offered protection to people who couldn't defend themselves.

I guess this was how the world was in times gone by, the strong protecting the weak, but at a cost. The end result was that we took John Jones out, but the people that replaced him could be worse, far worse. Maybe they'll get a taste of power and grow corrupt too. Power corrupts, after all.

At the supermarket, it was common for shop workers to be promoted and enter into the management team. Some of them were hungry for it and people could see that they were different; most of the lads always said they wouldn't change, that they would represent the floor workers and do what they could to make it better for them: better hours, better pay, more breaks. For the first few days they would keep to their word and keep the banter going and sit with the floor workers at break times, but, within a short time, they changed.

Just wearing a shirt and tie marked them out and, before long, the gap was there – evident and clear for all to see.

I know because I did it. I tried to keep in with the lads, stay as one of them, and I swore to myself I wouldn't change – but I did. I made myself get out on the floor with them. When I didn't have my own duties, I would be working alongside them, but then familiarity breeds contempt and some would try to take advantage, which was uncomfortable at times. I remember the general manager taking me to one side, just after I was promoted, and telling me to keep a healthy distance from them.

I blink the sweat from my eyes and bring my mind back to the now and this harsh reality of feeling like the buildings are pressing in. It's too quiet. Too hot and I glance around at the dark windows that look like they're watching us. This city was active, rough, and violent, but it had life; a vibrant life, full of people of all colours and backgrounds, now it's empty and sullen. It's only been a couple of days ... what will it be like in a week, a month, or a year?

Stick to the plan, Howie – get your sister and get to the Forts. The Forts are strong and safe and will be full of good people: soldiers, policemen, doctors and nurses – there will be structure and order.

'I said it will be dark soon, Mr Howie.'

I look at Dave, assessing his quiet demeanour and manner, no chitchat or witty banter, but then he doesn't show any sign that what we are seeing or doing is affecting him either, then I think of the giant mound of bodies in Tesco and come to a stop while staring at him. He stops too and stares back. Silent. Expressionless.

'Dave, why are you here?'

He looks about. 'We walked here, Mr Howie.'

'No! I mean, I mean why are you here with me.'

'To get your sister, Mr Howie.'

'No, I mean why did you come? Why go through all of this with me, just because of my sister. You didn't have to come, you could walk away any time you want. You worked for Tesco and that's gone, it doesn't exist anymore, you can do whatever you want now.'

He doesn't say anything but just looks at me.

'So why come with me? Why do this? What about back there? You killed loads of people, Dave. You slit their throats and shot them, you shot them as they ran away. Doesn't that bother you?'

'No, Mr Howie.'

'Why? How can it not bother you?'

'They would have killed us.'

'But it's only because you were with me that it happened in the first place. If you hadn't come with me, you wouldn't have had to kill those people.'

He just stares.

'It's not okay, Dave. None of this is okay, and it'll never be okay. Never again. We stripped a man naked and beat him. We killed people. We took their lives away...why are you here? Why are you with me? What for? You don't owe me anything. Tesco is gone. It's all gone, Dave. You're free to...to...to do what you want...I'm not your manager now...' I stop from suddenly becoming acutely aware that I'm ranting in the street. Even my heart is going like the clappers. I rub the stress from my face and groan softly. 'Sorry. I didn't mean it like that. Those things didn't happen because of you...I shouldn't have come through the city...' I stop again to sigh heavily, glancing around then back at him and although he looks exactly the same there is a change in the energy about him. Like he's a bit crestfallen.

'I'm not like other people, Mr Howie.'

'No, mate. You are decidedly not like other people...' I say quietly, rubbing my face again. 'How the hell you can do what you do is something else. You're an amazing person, Dave, and I'm glad you're with me. I don't know who trained you or what they trained you for, but it's incredible.' I open my eyes to see him staring unblinking at me as though studying every word I say. 'Okay, look mate, I'm sorry for sounding off. I shouldn't have. It's just ... it's fucking mental. Just know you can go whenever you want. You don't owe me anything. Okay?'

He nods, then goes back to scanning around, eventually looking up at the sky. 'It will be dark soon, we should find shelter,' he says as though that entire conversation just didn't happen.

'We'll look for a car,' I say, heading off back along the filthy oppressive street.

We keep going, moving away from the epicentre of the mass civil unrest. There are still signs of devastation here, but less so. Another few streets over and we find some houses that look quite normal, with just the front doors open.

'There's a lot of undamaged cars here. What do you fancy? Sports car? Van? Something executive perhaps? Or shall we go for a four-wheel drive?'

'I don't mind, Mr Howie.'

'Oh, but sir must have a choice, sir must choose from one of our exciting range.'

Silence.

'How about the colour, sir? What colour would you like your vehicle to be? Metallic paint and alloys may incur an additional fee ...'

'How about that one?' Dave asks, pointing to a very old, beaten up Skoda Fabia.

'You really can't drive, can you?' I say, moving on quickly towards a Range Rover parked up ahead. 'Now that is more like it, what do you reckon?'

Dave looks back at the Skoda, then at the Range Rover and shrugs. 'I don't mind.'

'You really have no taste Dave, no taste at all.'

I try to keep the tone light, to make up for my outburst a short while ago. There's something about Dave that makes me want to keep my head and wits about me and I feel a bit embarrassed about having a go at him. 'Let's try in here.'

We move up to the front door of the house next to the parked *Range Rover*. The door is shut and locked. I knock several times. 'Hello, anyone there? We're not zombies ... we promise.'

A terraced house with no obvious way of getting to the rear. I step back and aim a kick at the central panel of the UPVC door that rattles but remains undamaged. 'Like that is it,' I mutter propping my shotgun down to start kicking hard, whacking the flat of my foot into the door that bounces and flexes but stays shut.

'Mr, Howie.'

'Hang on, mate,' I gasp, kicking away merrily but the flexible material absorbs most of the energy from my kicks, rendering me pretty much useless until I give up and bend forward to suck air into my lungs. 'It's no good mate, we'll have to use the axe or find another house.'

'What about this?' he asks, standing nearby holding a key in his hand.

'Where did you get that?'

'Under that gnome.'

'Right. You could have told me though.'

'I tried to.'

Again, I swear there is a glimmer in his eye.

'Shall we then?'

He steps up and unlocks the door, pushes it open and waits with the shotgun raised at waist height. He stands still and listens for several minutes. I know what's coming ... yep, here he goes, waving his hands around, twirling and pointing.

'Dave, if there are zombies, just say so.'

He turns to face me. 'Stay here and I'll check, Mr Howie.'

'Okay mate, we really have to practise these hand signals though. I'll wait here then.'

He enters and starts checking each room, which takes seconds as the house is tiny: just two rooms downstairs, a lounge and a kitchen – dining room at the back. He comes back to the front door.

'Would you like me to check upstairs, old chap?'

He looks at me then at the stairs, then back to me.

'Tell you what, why don't I stay at the door and you check it.'

He's up the stairs within seconds and I'm not surprised after my bumbling performance at the farm house. I hear him banging about and then he's back down.

'All clear.'

'I wonder where they went to then?'

'Who?'

'The people that lived here.'

'They're upstairs.'

'You said that it was clear.'

'It is.'

'Then who is upstairs?'
'The people that live here.'
'Are they zombies?'
'No.'
'Then why haven't they said anything or come down?'
'They can't.'
'Why?'
'They're dead.'
'Shit ...'

I run up the stairs into the bedroom and see an old couple in the front bedroom covered in the blankets. The woman snuggled into the man with her head resting on his chest. Both with dried vomit around their mouths and I spot the empty pill containers next to the bed.

I stare at them for a few minutes. At how they look so peaceful and serene and it breaks my heart to see this: an old couple who made the choice to see the end in peace. Together in death, as in life.

I go to turn away and pause on seeing a photograph of young children clutched in the woman's hand, and something about it chokes me up with tears stinging my eyes, and suddenly I feel like an intruder. I rush out, closing the door quietly while murmuring an apology.

Downstairs I find the coats on the rack in the hallway and search the pockets until I find the keys to the Range Rover.

We lock the door and put the key back under the gnome, then I think better of it and put the key back into the door lock and leave it there. The house is secure and it might just save someone else's life. I feel bad for the old couple, but the living will need it more than them now.

We backtrack through the side streets until we are back in town; it wastes a few minutes but at least this way we can stick to the directions that John gave us. A heavy sigh and maybe we can get on and make progress, or at least get out of the city before nightfall. Then I glance down at the display. 'Shit! No fucking fuel. Trust us to pick the only car with no petrol. Cock it, we've got less than hour before it's dark. Keep an eye out for a fuel station.' Then I smack myself in the forehead. 'There's no power,' I add with a groan. 'The bloody pumps won't work without power ...'

'We can siphon it.'

'Do you know how to do that?'

'Yes, Mr Howie.'

'Dave ... you're a bloody genius.'

I check the fuel gauge. It's on the right, so the filling cap will be on the right too. I pull the Range Rover up alongside a row of parked vehicles and cruise along until we see one with a cap on my side.

'We need a tube and a jerry can, Mr Howie.'

'Oh my fucking days this just gets better and better. Where can we get a tube from?'

'I don't know.'

'It'll take too long, we need to find another vehicle we can take,' I say with a look at the sky. 'And we need to be quick, keep your eyes open.'

We drive on with panic starting to rise in me. I remember the howling from the infected as night fell and then seeing them switch to fast moving, evil fuckers. I really don't want to be here when that happens. Although having said that, we haven't seen any of them about for a while now.

'Stop. Go back, Mr Howie.'

'What? What did you see?' I select reverse and pull the car back, adjacent to a junction on the left. 'What am I looking at?'

'Down there.' He points down the road to a recovery truck with an orange light bar on the top. The back of the truck is lowered down to the ground like a ramp.

'Dave, you beauty, well done, mate.'

The recovery truck has a double cab and the words 'POLICE RECOVERY' written on the side. I look to the row of vehicles and see a police car parked, the recovery truck positioned ready to start winching it onto the back.

The police car is an old Ford Focus and has seen better days. It must have broken down on Friday night and they'd called for it to be recovered, just as the world went nuts.

I park alongside and get out as Dave moves up to check the cab of the recovery vehicle.

'Mr Howie,' he calls. I follow his voice to see him looking intently at an infected uniformed police officer a few feet away, shuffling towards us with his hands ravaged down to the bone, and blood all over his face. He must have been on the ground, on his back and punching up at them; his knuckles have taken most of the damage and I imagine him laid out, with infected leaning down into him, punching up repeatedly until they bit into his fists. Poor bastard.

'Dave ... you get what we need and I'll take care of him.'

I wait for him to get a little closer, then move away a few steps, keeping him busy while Dave hunts around for whatever we need.

'Got it ...'

He comes out of the cab of the truck, holding a length of pipe and a green, plastic fuel can and sets to work syphoning fuel from the police car into the Range Rover.

I keep dancing around the undead copper, leading him a few steps one way, then back in another direction, figuring just to keep him busy until we can go. Then I realise that if we leave him here he could infect someone else. I rush back to the Range Rover, grab my axe and run back while Dave starts pouring the newly filled fuel can into the Range Rover.

'Sorry about this,' I say with an apologetic wince and rush forward to chop down into the infected coppers head. Bursting apart with bone and flesh spewing out as he falls to the floor. I wipe the axe on his trousers and walk back to the Range Rover. Which is when I glance at the green fuel can on the ground then at the open fuel cap on the police car and the one word that stops me in my tracks: DIESEL.

I run around the back of the Range Rover, hoping and praying that it has a letter D somewhere in the model type: *TDCi, TDC* or anything that will indicate it's a diesel engine. Nothing on the back. I open the fuel cap and my heart sinks: PETROL ONLY.

'Dave, Quick. Check the recovery truck … are the keys in the ignition?'

Dave runs off and sticks his head into the driver's side. 'No, Mr Howie.'

'Bollocks …fuck it, we'll have to run. Get the stuff quick – we'll have to go on foot.'

'Why?'

'You've put diesel in the car and it only takes petrol. It's fucked.'

'I'm so sorry, Mr Howie.'

He looks distraught with the same fleeting look of panic and confusion that he had in the supermarket when I told him he should go home.

'Dave, honestly, it's okay – it's really okay. Christ, look how many times I've fucked up.'

I put my bag on and drop the axe down before tightening the straps. Next, I break the shotgun and check that it's loaded and ready.

Within seconds, Dave is kitted up, the rifle on his back and the shotgun in his hands. We start off back the way we came, but within a few steps, we stop.

There are several infected shuffling down the road towards us. They must have come out of the buildings on the side. I look over and see more of them slowly emerging.

'Fuck it … back this way, come on.'

We start running down the road and around the recovery truck with the light fading fast. We need to find somewhere quickly but the houses here are all smashed in, plus the infected behind will see where we've gone.

'We can't hide here, they'll see where we've gone and surround us.' I'm gasping for breath from speaking while running.

'Okay, Mr Howie,' he says, the fit bastard not showing even breathing hard yet.

We run down a straight road towards a T-junction; the buildings on both sides prevent us from seeing any further than a few metres in either direction. The running causes the axe to slip down and catch between my legs, tripping me over. I fall with a yelp, inadvertently clenching my grip on the shotgun and pulling the trigger with a deafening bang as I shoot the side of a parked car with loud metallic ricochets pinging off.

A second for me to gawp at the shotgun then up to Dave staring at me. 'Sorry mate, I shot that car.'

'Keep your hand away from the trigger until you need it, Mr Howie.'

'Righto. Yep. Will do mate.'

I wince as I get up with both of my knees hurting from the impact of falling. I take the axe in one hand and the shotgun in the other and set off running again, albeit a bit slower and a bit more carefully now.

We reach the end of the road to the T junction with one long, grey building ahead of us running in both directions.

'Shit,' I gasp at seeing the left side entirely blocked by a huge crowd of infected a few hundred metres up the road. All of them facing in towards the big grey building, but the crowd is too dense for me to see what they are looking for.

We look right and my stomach sinks again. A set of very high blue metal gates topped with rolls of razor wire blocking that side off. We can't go back as there are too many infected. We can't go left or right either. 'Fuck...fuck...' I grunt the words out at our misfortune, clenching my jaw while trying to think what to do as some of the closest infected start turning towards us, groaning and moaning as more seem to notice us.

And then, as if that wasn't bad enough, the last tendrils of light fade and the shadows drop as daylight sods off and lets the night come down upon us and the air charges. Everything charges.

The crowd of infected all stop moving. All of them growing still. The sight sends a creep running down my spine and I spin to see more behind us doing the same. Just standing still blocking our way out. as one.

I run over to the gates, hammering and tugging to see if they'll budge but they're solid and strong. The only way out is to climb up, but the razor wire at the top will cut us to pieces.

Dave drops down onto one knee and shrugs his bag off, then opens the main compartment and takes out a plastic bag full of rifle ammunition and lays it on the ground. Next, he fills his pockets with shotgun shells, then puts the bag back on.

That's it then. No way back and no way forward. I take my cartridge shell bag and fill it up, then tie it off on my belt the way Dave did, the hole ready for my hand to dip into. Neither Dave or I say a word, and strangely, I don't feel that scared either. More annoyed. Irritated even. Pissed off and frustrated at not being able to get where I want.

Then, as one, every single infected looks up to the sky at the same time with a silence that holds forever. And the darkness grows deeper, the night coming proper. The land growing dark.

They howl as one, and that noise, that awful, terrible, inhuman noise makes the hairs on the back of my neck stand up.

That long, continuous, drawn out, blood-chilling roar. An immense sound and my throat goes dry as the fear ramps. Pushing into my mind and gut. Or maybe it's adrenalin. I don't know, only that my hands and legs are shaking and I'm bloody glad that I'm not using that rifle; I'd probably miss all of them.

I can feel my knees weakening. I heard this first last night, but I only had one infected in front of me then, now there are hundreds all uttering the same deep, guttural bellow.

I look to Dave but he doesn't flinch or do anything other than stare ahead. Even his hands holding the rifle are rock steady, and in this second, in this place, I take comfort from his courage.

'Dave, I just want to say ... what the fuck is that?'

He looks at me in puzzlement, but I'm looking over his shoulder at the light on in the window behind him. There is a light on ... in a building with power.

Then the light goes out and the window goes black like the rest.

'That light went on and off – there's someone in there.'

I look deeper into the shadows and see a door secreted in the corner, recessed in a small porch area.

'Fuck me ... There's a door.'

I race over and start banging on the solid metal door, using the flat of my fists to rain blows down on it while shouting out. 'HEY! LET US IN...PLEASE...' I scream out while the infected howl and the world fills with noise.

Then the silence comes as the roaring ceases as the hundreds of infected all stop at the same time and lower their heads to stare directly at me and Dave. The lolling, shuffling slow things are gone. This is night. These are different. Fixed. Murderous and driven with hunger. The fast, evil undead once more.

Dave stands stock still, the rifle braced in his shoulder. The entire horde now silent and staring as though all waiting. Everything poised, holding on a knife edge.

An infected male out front. A twitch in his head. A growl coming from his throat and as he lifts a foot to start running so Dave shoots him in the face and the whole fucking lot of them start charging at us. Screeching wildly and once more the air fills with noise.

'HEY! LET US IN...PLEASE...' I hammer on the door while Dave aims, fires, yanks the bolt back and repeats with the pauses in between becoming less as he speeds up. His accuracy is awesome with every bullet striking a head, but still they charge, closing that distance fast.

Dave pauses with the rifle to lift the shotgun that was resting against his leg and blasts both barrels at the front of the crowd. The pellets spread with a ripple effect as bodies are slammed backwards into the dense crowd, causing more to trip and fall;. The effect is marginal; for every one he drops, more are coming, filling the gaps.

I give up hammering at the door and start back towards him, firing my shotgun at them then breaking the thing open to reload and do it again.

A buzzing sounds behind me, on and off, urgent and loud. I

glance back and the buzzer keeps sounding with a clicking noise coming from the door that signifies the lock being activated on and off.

'Dave! we're in ... come on...'

I rush over and push the door, finding it opens easily with bright light flooding out. Dave grabs his shotgun and runs for it, rushing through as I spot my axe propped against the metal gates. A reaction born only from instinct and I dart out to run for it, ducking to grab the handle before running back as Dave holds the door open and fires the rifle over my shoulder as I run back with snarls and screeches sounding but feet behind me.

'GET IN,' he roars out, grabbing my arm and wrenching me in before slamming the door shut as the infected reach the recessed area and slam into it from the other side. I bounce off a wall from running in so hard and slam back into the door, heaving with Dave to get it closed, both of us bracing to push as we fight to get it closed, then finally, with an audible click, the door seals shut.

CHAPTER SEVEN

A brightly lit, small room with a wooden bench on one side fixed to the ground with big bolts. Concrete walls painted institutional beige all covered in frayed and peeling posters telling people to take their *offences into consideration*, and that they are *entitled to legal advice*. A police station. We're in a police station. The big gates topped with razor wire make sense now. So does the solid metal door. This looks like a waiting area where arrested people are held, and I spot another poster pinned to an internal door.

'OFFICERS SHOULD WAIT UNTIL THE CHARGE ROOM IS CLEAR BEFORE TAKING THE DETAINED PERSON THROUGH.'

A hatch opens above the poster as I finish reading with a small female face peering out, twisting side to side to get a good look at Dave and I. 'Are you infected?' she asks in a bossy, high pitched a squeaky voice.

'No, no of course not.'

'You're bleeding.'

'Eh?'

'I said you are bleeding,' she repeats.

'I fell over,' I say quickly, turning to look at the metal door behind us and the wild screeches and loud bangs coming from the other side. 'I promise we're not infected. We haven't been bit or scratched ... nothing.'

The hatch closes and we hear muffled voices. It reopens after a few seconds.

'We need to make sure you are not infected. Strip off.'

'Strip off? Now just hang on a minute...'

'I'm not arguing with you. Strip off or get out.'

Dave and I look at each other. 'But, no... this is a police station, right? You are meant to protect us.'

'Listen to me. You are bleeding, and you are both armed – you won't get through this door and I can easily unlock the outer door and let them in.'

I nod grimly and cast another look back at the outer door before dropping my bag and tugging my top off. We undress in silence, using the bench to unlace and pull our boots off until we're both just in our boxer shorts, and without trying to look I notice that although Dave appears to be a small built man his body is rock hard with lean muscle without an ounce of fat. He looks like someone from a movie and his thigh muscles look solid as anything.

I look down at my wobbly stomach and un-toned body in embarrassed comparison. Actually, maybe my tummy has gone down a bit. Probably through lack of food. I wasn't like fat or anything, just not lean or defined. I tuck my gut in then push it out and twist a little to the side, examining my own form while thinking I'm really sure I've lost a bit of weight. Then I look up to see Dave watching me silently then glance over to the woman peering through the hatch with my face flushing red.

'Lost a bit of weight,' I say, trying to sound casual and nonchalant. 'Running and...you know...er...'

'Pants off then,' the woman says.

'Do what now?' I ask.

'We have to be sure you are not bitten.'

'Right. Look, I'm pretty sure I haven't been bitten on my willy...' I say, only realising how stupid the word willy sounds while standing mostly naked in a police detention room.

'Off or out, your choice,' she says primly.

Quietly seething, but with no choice, I take my boxer shorts off and step out of them, covering my privates with my hands. Dave does the same but stands with his arms at his sides without any concern at all.

'Drop your hands and turn around.'

I take my hands away and copy Dave by staring at a spot on the wall for a second before we both do an about turn and face the other way. Another second goes by and I turn to catch her taking a lingering look at Dave's backside and lift an eyebrow at her.

'Yep, that's fine,' she snaps. 'Get dressed,' she adds, slamming the hatch shut.

'They won't let us in with the weapons, Mr Howie,' Dave says as we get dressed.

'Yeah, you're probably right. Let's see what happens.'

'Well done,' the woman says after opening the hatch a few minutes later. 'Now, if you want to come in, you will have to leave those weapons there.'

'Do we get them back later?' I ask

She pauses for a minute before answering. 'We'll see about that ... right ... put the guns over by that far wall and stand in front of the door. And the bags too ...'

We do as told, stacking our kit and guns before moving back to the door.

'Hands on your heads please gentlemen and we'll open the door. Got it?'

'Yep,' I say.

We both put our hands up on the top of our heads and hear the buzz of a lock being turned off and the door swings in to show a long narrow room with a high desk to the right side with a larger space behind it.

Painted concrete walls and floor with two feet marks set at the base of a long wall-ruler measuring up to seven feet. I glance behind the desk to see monitors fixed high showing CCTV images, one of which shows the outside door and the infected throwing themselves at it. Black and white, soundless too, and somehow more sinister. Another monitor shows a man lying on a bench within a cell, apparently fast asleep. Either that or he's dead.

Then I look back to the front at the young policeman aiming a bright yellow tazer at us with trembling hands.

'Don't move or you'll be tazered!' he says, trying to sound manly and in charge with a quavering voice.

'Okay mate, no problem,' I say calmly as he twitches aim from Dave to me.

The woman that spoke to us through the hatch has retreated behind the desk. She looks to be in her late thirties with a pinched face and lines in her pursed mouth and at the corners of her eyes. Sergeants stripes on her shoulders. She looks different. Then I realise she isn't wearing any make-up, which stands out in this day and age and makes her look harsh and mean.

'Right,' she snaps, all high-pitched and bossy again. 'If you're coming into my police station then you will be searched while PC Jenkins covers you with the tazer.'

'Okay, miss,' I say, trying to stay polite and calm.

'It's not miss, it's Sergeant,' she snaps.

'Okay, sorry ... err ... Sergeant.'

A silence descends while PC Jenkins and the sergeant stare at us, then at each other, then back to us.

'Um ... who is searching us?' I ask politely.

'PC Jenkins will be searching you.'

'I can't, Sarge ... I've got the tazer.'

'Right. Where's Ted?'

'He went to the toilet, Sarge.'

'What about Steven? STEVEN!' she yells out and a very thin man with large, thick glasses appears at the doorway dressed in the blue shirt of a community officer as I notice the sergeant and PC Jenkins have black shirts on.

'Yes, Sergeant?' Steven asks.

'Search the prisoners ... I mean these men, while PC Jenkins covers you with the tazer.'

'Me? I'm just a PCSO – I can't search people ...' he says, looking scared witless.

'It's not a request, Steven, and you can search persons under the supervision of a uniformed police officer.'

'Why don't I take the tazer and let Tom search them?'

'He can't take the tazer – he's not had the training.' PC Jenkins says, looking very alarmed at the prospect of his tazer being taken away.

'Oh, but I can search people though, can I?'

'Well yeah, it's completely different, it takes training and skill to use a tazer, it's not a toy.'

'Enough ... Thank you. Tom will cover with the tazer and Steven will search them,' the Sergeant barks out and they both fall quiet.

Steven moves forward and stops in front of me. I smile at him, feeling sorry for the position he is in and the fact he's clearly terrified.

'Steven, you're in the way,' PC Jenkins says with a huff.

'Eh?' Steven asks, turning to see he's in the way. 'Oh, sorry...er... can you move over a bit, mate,' he says to Dave. 'Then you go back a bit,' he adds, looking at me. I go to move as Dave steps into me then turns to go back where he was.

'No, that way,' Steven says.

'Er, I've got no aim?' Tom says, moving over as Dave turns and bumps into me again then goes back the wrong way and does it again as Steven starts getting stressed and I glance over to see the sergeant rolling her eyes and PC Jenkins shaking his head while telling Steven to tell Dave to move.

'I'm trying!' Steven says, tutting as Dave steps towards him. 'No! That way...'

'Can you just search them please!' the sergeant snaps.

'Steven's in the way,' PC Jenkins says.

'I'm not! He is,' Steven says, pointing at Dave.

'Sorry, sir, I'll move.' Dave gets it wrong again, seemingly confused at the orders and moving into me as I move to block the copper with the tazer while Steven grows red in the face.

'Steven. Get a grip and search these men!' the Sergeant yells at him.

'I'm sorry, I'll go this way,' Dave says, stepping around Steven so he's between him and PC Jenkins. 'Is that right?' he asks.

'Oh my god, this is just stupid.' PC Jenkins says, squeezing his eyes closed in frustration. Which is the precise second Dave spins and snatches the tazer while driving the flat of his hand into the coppers chest, sending him staggering back. Dave moves past him and aims the tazer at the sergeant then at Steven, then back to PC Jenkins still righting himself as the room falls silent with shock at the speed of the man.

'Now just you wait ...' the sergeant starts to yell at Dave in her squeaky voice.

'SIT DOWN,' Dave roars. She drops instantly onto her high chair and I imagine her feet dangling down, not touching the floor. Then I smile as I stare at Dave in admiration.

'Bloody hell mate, well done.'

'Thanks, Mr Howie,' he replies, moving his aim from one to the other to show he has a clear shot as Steven and PC Jenkins stand slack jawed and wide eyed, somewhat frozen to the spot.

'Ello ello, what's going on here then?' An older man walks in: late fifties, thick set and bald, with weathered features. A folded newspaper under his arm as he carries two disposable cups of hot liquid and pauses with a brief look about the room. 'Oh dear ... tut tut – well, this seems a bit of a pickle, don't it? Excuse me mate, these cups are scalding hot, it's these cheap cardboard things, they burn your bloody fingers off.' He moves past Dave behind the desk and puts the cups down before blowing on his fingers. 'Tea's there, Debbie,' he says without a glance at the silent sergeant and I notice he's also wearing a black shirt but has the initials D.O on the shoulders. He sits heavily in the other chair, groaning as though with pleasure at taking the weight from his feet and finally looks at Dave then at me.

'So? What's it like out there? Still hot 'n' horrible, is it?'

'Er, yeah, you could say that,' I say.

'Well, it had to happen, didn't it. So, which one of you has the Army voice? I heard it all the way down the block and I thought to myself there's a voice from the services if ever I heard one. It took me back a few years, I can tell you.'

'It was him.' I point at Dave, almost feeling like a schoolboy, dropping my mate in it.

'It was you, was it? What were you in?'

'I can't say.'

I bloody knew he would say that.

'Ah, I get it,' the older guy taps his nose and winks knowingly at Dave, then looks at the tazer with distaste. 'You got that off young Jenkins, didn't you? I kept telling him not to keep waving it about. Did he listen though? No, he didn't. They never do, these young 'uns. Mind you, we never needed 'em in my day.'

'Oh, you're a policeman, too?' I ask him.

'No, no, not anymore. I did my time and got out.' He points to the initials on the sleeve of his shirt. 'Detention Officer now. Five years Army, then twenty-five in the job and I thought to myself, Ted, it's time to get out, but I keep coming back, like an old fool.'

He speaks calm and easy, but I can see that he is appraising Dave and I constantly. Years of hard situations and having to rely on his wits have left him sharp and the experience is oozing off of him.

'Ted? I'm Howie and this is Dave – it's very nice to meet you.' I step up to the desk and extend my hand; it's awkward, but Ted stands up and leans over, dwarfing my hand in his.

'Nice to see someone still has manners,' he says, offering his hand to Dave who just aims the tazer at him.

'Dave ... I think we can put it down now,' I say.

'Yes, Mr Howie,' Dave says, lowering the tazer and putting his hand out to Ted; they shake hands very briefly and then Dave pulls back and wipes his hand on his trousers.

'I did wash them, you know,' Ted says.

Dave looks at his hand, then back at Ted.

'I'm only joking,' Ted says, deadpan. 'I didn't wash them really.'

Dave goes back to wiping and Ted laughs out loud: a nice, deep, hearty laugh.

'Ah ... you Special Forces boys are all the same, trained killers, I'll grant you, but funny buggers though.'

PC Jenkins' mouth drops open at the mention of Special Forces as his eyes start shining with love hearts. 'Bloody hell, are you SF? I knew you were SF the way you took that tazer off me. Wow! Two SF in here. Are you on operations then? I knew they would send the SF in.'

'We aren't Special Forces,' I say. 'We're just trying to get somewhere and got caught out, that's all.'

'Where are you going?' Ted asks.

'Salisbury.'

I knew it was a mistake the second it came out of my mouth.

'Salisbury?' Tom asks, his eyes now even wider. 'The army base? Wow, that's so cool! Is that where your HQ is?'

'What? No ... Look, we aren't Special Forces.'

'Are you like planning a counter attack yeah? Did they send you to rescue us? Can I have gun? I'd be good with a gun...'

'That's enough,' Ted says heavily, nodding at the young copper. 'You leave it alone with all the questions.'

'Dave ... I think we can give the officer his tazer back.'

Dave looks at me, then at PC Jenkins; he checks again to make sure I'm not going to change my mind then slowly hands it over, turning it so that the handle is facing PC Jenkins, who takes it and looks at Dave like a puppy.

'You can keep it – if you want.'

'PC Jenkins, that is the property of the constabulary and not yours to give away,' the sergeant says, clearly feeling confident again now that Ted is here, and Dave has handed the weapon over.

'Sorry, Sarge.' He looks crestfallen, chastised in front of his new hero.

'Can we get our weapons back now?' Dave looks to Ted, not at the sergeant.

'I don't think that will be a problem, will it ... Sergeant?'

Ted defers to the sergeant, but has made it clear what he thinks – she looks trapped and scared.

'Look, Sergeant. I promise you that we are not psychos or anything – we just got caught out, you've seen what's happening out there. The weapons can stay there if you're sure we're safe in here ...'

'Oh, this nick is safe enough,' Ted says. 'It's built to handle terror suspects, so the security is very enhanced. The only way in to this part of the building is through the big gates or that outer door. The interior door is solid and can only be opened from this side.'

'Okay, then we'll leave them there, for now.'

'Tell you what gents, why don't I take you to the canteen for a brew – that all right with you, Debbie?'

'Well, it's time for the emergency strategy meeting anyway, and you two can come.'

She gets up and walks out from behind the desk. Stepping down from the raised area, she looks tiny – shorter than Dave by inches, but with the same, wiry frame. She walks out of the room and down the corridor.

'I'll show you the way, after me.' Ted goes out next, followed by Steven and PC Jenkins.

Finally Dave and I leave the room and start down the corridor.

The corridor is long and we pass cell doors on both sides and every few metres we have to turn sharp left or right. 'It's designed that like on purpose,' Ted explains. 'Stops anyone being able to shoot all the way down the corridor, and it disorientates anyone trying to escape.'

'Are we leaving this area?' I ask as we reach another fortified door being opened by the sergeant.

'It's okay, the whole building is safe,' Ted says.

The sergeant opens the door with a key and steps out; Steven follows her, then PC Jenkins.

'Tom, where are you going?' she asks.

'To the meeting, Sarge.'

'Tom, you know you have to stay here.'

'But, Sarge ...'

'No buts, stay here to let us back in and watch the prisoner.'

'But that's not fair, why can't *he* do it?' PC Jenkins points to Steven.

'Don't drag me into this, I'm not trained to look after a prisoner.'

PC Jenkins then stares at Ted, clearly thinking the detention officer should do itm but Ted just lifts and eyebrow and stares down at the young officer. 'Something on your mind, lad?'

'No, I'll stay ...' Tom sighs and steps back in, holding the door open for Dave and I to step through.

Ted chuckles as the door closes. 'Keen as mustard and just about as bright too.'

'Did he say *prisoner*?'

'One of our locals,' Ted replies.

'You've got a prisoner with all this going on? Can't you just let him go?'

'Old Harry?' ted chuckles. 'He don't want to go anywhere – he's homeless. He spends more time in here than at the shelters. Every time it gets too cold or too hot he breaks something and waits to be arrested, bless him.'

'Bloody hell, does he know what's going on out there?'

'What, him? He's madder than a bucket of frogs. We tried telling him but he just gibbers on ... nah, he's alright – wouldn't hurt a fly.'

'So ... why is he in a cell then?'

'He always has the same cell and gets very strange if someone else is in there. Besides, the door's wide open and he can help himself to a drink or food. Not that he will. He'll just press the buzzer and wait to be served the cheeky sod.'

We go up a flight of stairs and Dave is keenly looking about, taking in all of the exits and windows, checking and re-checking constantly. We head along a carpeted corridor, passing several dark and empty offices on the way, full of blank monitor screens and office swivel chairs.

'Where do you get the power from? The grid went out everywhere else,' I ask.

'There's a generator in the basement; we have to be able to run the cell block in the event of a terrorist attack – we turned everything else off, so we don't use too much juice,' Ted says as the sergeant opens a door into a large conference room and switches the lights on, flooding it with bright, fluorescent light.

I walk in after her feeling better now that we are with the organised authorities. They must have contingency plans and regular updates from the government, and they might be able to help find my sister.

The sergeant is odd, but I guess she is just the Desk Sergeant, or whatever they call them. We enter the room and the sergeant indicates for us to be seated at the large, oval desk. Then she goes to one end and sits down in front of a bunch of hardback files and manuals resting on the table top.

'Steven, make everyone a drink please,' she orders in that curt tone.

'Yes, Sergeant,' he replies, toddling off to the end of the room to busy himself with a kettle plugged into the wall.

Within minutes, we both have a steaming mug of tea in front of us as we hear voices coming down the corridor. I look to the door in expectation of seeing senior officers, but only two people enter, both young women. One with a blue shirt on and one with a black. I realise now that the blue shirts are for the Police Community Support Officers and the black shirts for the proper officers. They sit down and I realise that Steven has made them a drink, and that he hasn't made any more, which suggests there is no on else coming.

'Where's everyone else?' I ask.

'Err ... thank you. We'll come to you in a minute, there is an order to these meetings you know,' The sergeant says, giving me a withering look.

Ted just sits back and drinks his tea.

'Right, everyone's here,' she says crisply, looking about the room. 'Then let us begin. The time is now 22:07 hours and I am opening the emergency strategy meeting. As the senior officer, I will chair the meeting and PC Trixey will take the minutes.'

I look to the new female officer, blonde hair pulled back into a bun; she looks very young but very serious and is studiously holding a pen over some writing paper.

'PC Trixey, please record that we have two members of the Armed Forces with us.'

'We're not in the army,' I say.

'Yes, okay, I understand. PC Trixey will note that we have two members of the public as observers – just note down, separately, that they are Armed Forces, obviously they can't officially be here in this meeting,' the sergeant says, making air quotes as she speaks.

'For God's sake. We're not in the bloody Army!'

'Er ... thank you ... Mr?'

'It's Howie,' I say tightly, rubbing my temples.

'Thank you, Mr Howie, but please stop interrupting the proceedings.'

Bloody hell, why is everyone calling me Mr Howie?

'Now, for the record, also present is PCSO Steven Taylor, PCSO Jane Downton, Detention Officer Ted Harding, PC Terri Trixey and ...' she looks at Dave.

'Dave ...' he says.

'Dave what?'

'Just Dave.'

'Oh, of course. Terri, mark that down will you? Obviously, they can't give their full names for security reasons. Now, on to proceedings. PC Trixey will just go over the minutes from the last meeting.'

PC Trixey flicks to some previous notes made on the same writing paper, then clears her throat. 'The last emergency strategy meeting was held today at twenty-hundred hours.' She looks up and glances round at everyone. 'Er … the same people were present at the previous meeting, with the exception of our two 'members of the public' here.' She does the quote things with her fingers too. 'At the last meeting it was required for a full inventory of supplies to be done. There was also an issue with PC Jenkins walking into the female officers' shower room, and consideration to be given to the fuel supply for the generator.'

'Thank you, PC Trixey,' the sergeant says. 'First I would like to say that, in relation to agenda item two, I have spoken with PC Jenkins, who assures me it was an accident and promises that it won't happen again.'

'Fucking pervert.'

'Yes … thank you PCSO Downton. I have dealt with the matter and made it clear that disciplinary procedures will be instigated if it happens again. Now … in relation to item number one, who undertook the assessment of the supplies?'

'You said that you would ask Tom,' says PC Trixey.

'Ah yes, of course I did … well he isn't here, so we can find out later. What about the fuel for the generator? Who did we task with that one?'

'It was Tom, again.'

'Right, well we can find that out later too … on to new items. We need to establish a cleaning rota, any volunteers to draft one for approval?'

'I can do that.'

'Thank you, Steven. Please draft the cleaning rota and submit to me for approval – once it has been approved it will be posted in the canteen. Now we also need a sleeping rota so that we make sure we don't all sleep at the same time – like we did last night.'

'I can do that, too.'

'Thank you, Steven. Please draft the schedule and submit it to me for approval – once it has been approved it will be posted in the canteen.'

'Tom should go first. He slept all bloody night.'

'Yes, thank you, PCSO Downton, good point. Steven, make sure that Tom goes down for the first night.'

'Yes, Sergeant.'

'Right, well, that just about covers everything. Questions from the floor? Steven, do you have anything?'

'Er ... just one thing, Sergeant ... Tom keeps eating all of the lasagnes from the prisoners' food cupboard. He knows I can't eat the curry and I don't like the all-day breakfast.'

'Thank you, Steven. I will speak to Tom and request that he does not eat all of the lasagnes. PCSO Downton?'

'Nothing from me, just keep that pervert out of the showers.'

'Yes, I've already covered that. Listen, Jane, if this is really bothering you, then you can take out a grievance against PC Jenkins, just submit a report to me for approval and I will deal with it.'

'Okay, thanks Sarge.'

'PC Trixey?'

'Yes I have a point to raise. At a previous meeting a decision was taken to limit each person to a five-minute shower each. Now, while I accept that the water supply and power are important, I feel this is victimisation and prejudice. Female officers have longer hair and it takes more time to wash and rinse out, therefore I request that the showering time for female officers be extended to ten minutes.'

'Good point, PC Trixey. I am in favour of this. It is true that female officers generally have longer hair and need more time for adequate cleaning. I pass the notion and this will be effective immediately. Please note that down PC Trixey.'

'Noted, Sarge.'

'I hope that isn't just female police officers. I have longer hair too, and I don't wish to be discriminated against just because I am a community support officer.'

'Very true, PCSO Downton – and a good point raised. Please amend the notes to show that all female *employees* are entitled to the extended shower period. DO Harding?'

'No, nothing to raise, thank you.'

'Thank you DO Harding. And now the observers ... Dave, do you have any points?'

'When can we get our weapons back?'

'Ah, right ... a good point for discussion. Mr Howie? Do you have anything?'

'Yes! I bloody do. What kind of shit is this? What the fuck are you lot going on about? Showers, cleaning rota? What the ...'

'Stop right there, Mr Howie. I will not allow the use of profane or abusive language within this building.'

'I DON'T GIVE A FUCK,' I say, slamming my hand down hard on the table, making them all jump, with the exception of Dave and Ted, who both just carry on drinking tea. 'Where's the senior officers? Where's the inspectors and superintendents? Where's the bloody policemen?'

'Er ... excuse me – the term is police officer actually – not policemen,' PC Trixey says, glaring at me.

'I don't fucking fuck what the term is, and forgive me for not being politically fucking correct, Miss or whoever the hell you are ... but what are you all going to do about that lot out there? The...the... the fucking thousands of zombie things running about eating people. Other people are killing each other too. Where's the riot squad and the armed officers? Why aren't they here? What about the government? What have they said to you? Have you had updates or been told anything?' I glare at the sergeant.

'No, we haven't been told anything,' she says softly.

'Nothing? No updates?'

'No, nothing.'

'What about your radios? You must be able to speak to each other?'

'They went down with the phones. They work off mobile phone networks,' she says. Dropping her eyes.

'Fuck me. What about the old radios that use radio frequencies?'

'They were destroyed when we got the new ones.'

'Jesus Christ,' I rub my temples again.

'You must have secure phone networks, some hot line to your headquarters?'

'This isn't the movies, Mr Howie, we don't have anything like that.'

'Email? You have power ... what about emails? Oh ... they won't work without phone lines. Policemen, or officers, people in fucking uniforms. Where are they all, and the senior officers?'

'They've gone ...'

'Gone where? Be specific.'

'It was a Friday night. We had a duty inspector, but he left when the troubles started; some of the officers were out patrolling and just never came back, and those that did, left to be with their families.'

'What about your armed officers?'

'We didn't have any on, we don't have enough as it is, the next division was covering our sector.'

'So, this is it? The glorious British police reduced to a couple of community support officers, two infant coppers and you?'

I don't mention Ted, out of respect; he doesn't seem to notice, but carries on drinking the tea. That cup must be bloody deep.

'Yes, this is it.'

'So why are you here? Why didn't you leave to be with your families?'

'We don't have anyone. Steven and Jane are both single. Terri and Tom are new and got posted away from where they grew up. I'm not married and ... I have no family.'

'Ted?' I ask, softening my tone.

'Me? Oh no, I'm quite happy here. The wife took my kids to Australia years ago. The job's been my family ever since.'

I lean forward and rest my head in my hands, looking down at the desk as the realisation hits me that this is it. The end of the world.

'We lost the plot a few years ago, I'd say,' Ted says with a long sigh. 'We used to be good at this sort of thing. Oh ... we were shit at the community policing and yeah, we did isolate people – but we nicked more then than we do now, and we were good at major incidents. We always trained and undertook exercises to prepare, but now it's all done from a desk. Us old dinosaurs tried telling them about the new radios but they didn't listen. These young 'uns get more training in *diversity* than they do in crime or major incidents now.'

I sit back, rubbing at my chin, which is fast becoming stubbly. 'I guess you couldn't have done much anyway,' I say quietly. 'It spread so fast. I don't know, I was just hoping that there'd be some plan or something, you know? *Hold on ... help is coming* – that sort of thing.'

He shakes his head. 'Nope.'

'So what will you do? Just wait here?' Silence – no one wants to answer me. I look at Dave, but he is devoid of expression, as usual. 'Armoury? You must have one ... with weapons ... firearms?'

The sergeant shakes her head.

'No, we used to, but they centralised it and all the firearms officers have to go to the divisional HQ to arm up.'

I shake my head slowly, dumbfounded at the turn of events and looking at the desperate people around me clinging on to a world that has already disappeared, trying to use grievance procedures and making cleaning rotas. Maybe it's better than John Jones and his way, but it's sad, very sad.

'So you have no weapons, no communication, no direction – what will you do?'

'We do have weapons,' PC Trixey butts in.

Dave looks at her.

'In the evidence room,' she continues. 'We seized a load of stuff a few days ago.'

'What are they?' I ask her.

'There's quite a few air rifles.'

Dave carries on drinking his tea.

'And some bullets,' she adds.

'What kind?' I ask.

'I don't know? They all look the same to me.'

'Can we see?' I ask the sergeant.

'Terri will show you.'

'Dave, do you want to go?'

'Okay, Mr Howie.'

He gets up and follows PC Trixey out of the room. The sergeant then asks Steven and Jane to leave us in private for a few minutes, and, as soon as the door closes, she turns to me.

'I'm not stupid, Howie. I know how this looks, but they have nowhere to go, none of us do,' she pauses, looking at me. 'But we're safe here, the building is strong and we can wait it out. We have plenty of food and water.'

I look to Ted who just nods. What else can he say?

'It must seem strange to you,' she continues. 'But they won't last five minutes out there so we keep on. It gives them hope. Anyway, what have you seen out there, what do you know?'

I recount to them what we had seen so far, but I leave out the bit about Giselle the stripper and Marcus, I guess they wouldn't be that interested.

I also tell them about John Jones and the Carter Street barricade, then about the radio message and the forts. They both lean forward and listen intently, asking probing questions. I answer all of the questions as best I can, which doesn't take long, seeing as I don't know much.

Finally, I tell them of my plan to head to London for my sister then trail off into silence.

'Well, we can't do anything tonight, Debbie.' Ted says, looking at her. 'But those forts sound good, and they'll need a good sergeant.'

'And an experienced officer, Ted,' she replies.

'How will you get there?' I ask. 'You've got a few hundred infected outside your gates.'

'There's an old riot van in the yard outside, we can put the grille down to cover the windscreen and plough through,' Ted answers.

'Sounds good. Mind you, you said you're safe here. Maybe you could just wait it out and hope help comes.'

'No, I er, I don't think any help will be coming,' Debbie says. 'And I think we need to be with other people.'

'What about you?' Ted asks.

'We have to push on. We'll join you later when I've found my sister,' I sit back and rub my face again, feeling weary to the bone. 'Do you mind if we bed down here for the night and get going in the morning. When they're slow again.'

They look at each other and nod.

Twenty minutes later we sit in the canteen eating microwaved ready-made prisoner food with the others, and even Tom has been let out of the custody section.

'What about Harry?' I ask.

'He's alright, fast asleep on his bed, besides he can't go anywhere,' Tom replies, but looks to the sergeant for confirmation.

'He'll be fine for a few minutes, Tom.'

'Thanks, Sarge.'

A change to the atmosphere. A softening perhaps. I know Ted and the sergeant told them about the forts and the plan to leave and I guess that has eased the tensions a little.

We've even got our weapons back, which Dave is clearly happy about. And when I say happy I mean he shows no reaction whatsoever, other than stripping them down to clean while Tom stays glued to his side, watching every move and asking questions about Special Forces.

'I can't tell you,' Dave replies each and every time, which just seems to excite Tom even more.

It's only been two days since this began. Three if you count today, but it feels like weeks, and if these past few days have been anything to go by then getting into London will be a bloody nightmare. I eat my fill, drink tea and grow sleepy until Dave and I are left alone with thick blankets to use as mattresses and start settling down, ready to sleep.

The lights go out as the lights are killed to preserve power coming from the generator and I sit still for long minutes, looking about the room bathed in moonlight coming through the windows.

Tomorrow we go to Salisbury, find an armoured vehicle, and head for London. Not the best plan in the world, but it's a start.

I look over at Dave, thinking maybe we'll chat and talk it through but spot him lying flat on his back with his hands folded across his front, seemingly fast asleep.

Fair play. It's been a hell of a day, and we've been lucky so far.

How long will it last?

FEED AN AUTHOR
with your love ♥
LEAVE A REVIEW

ALSO BY RR HAYWOOD

EXTRACTED SERIES

EXTRACTED
EXECUTED
EXTINCT

Block-buster Time-Travel

#1 Amazon US

#1 Amazon UK

#1 Audible US & UK

Top 3 Amazon Australia

Washington Post Best-seller

In 2061, a young scientist invents a time machine to fix a tragedy in his past. But his good intentions turn catastrophic when an early test reveals something unexpected: the end of the world.

A desperate plan is formed. Recruit three heroes, ordinary humans capable of extraordinary things, and change the future.

Safa Patel is an elite police officer, on duty when Downing Street comes under terrorist attack. As armed men storm through the breach, she dispatches them all.

'Mad' Harry Madden is a legend of the Second World War. Not only did he complete an impossible mission—to plant charges on a heavily defended submarine base—but he also escaped with his life.

Ben Ryder is just an insurance investigator. But as a young man he witnessed a gang assaulting a woman and her child. He went to their rescue, and killed all five.

Can these three heroes, extracted from their timelines at the point of death, save the world?

Printed in Great Britain
by Amazon